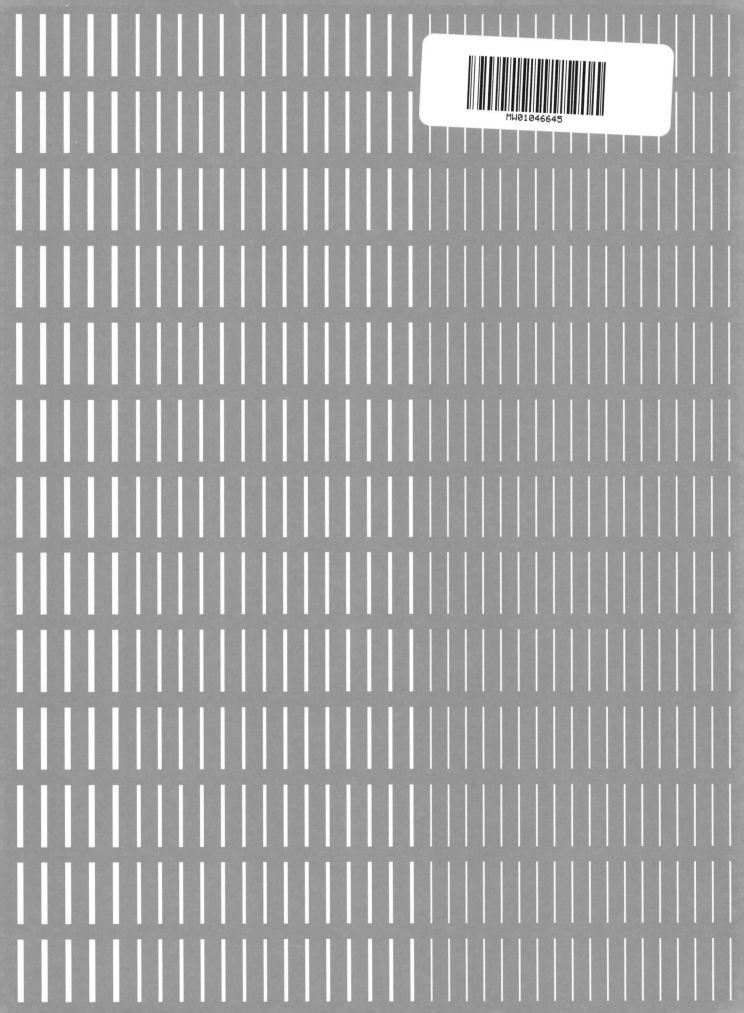

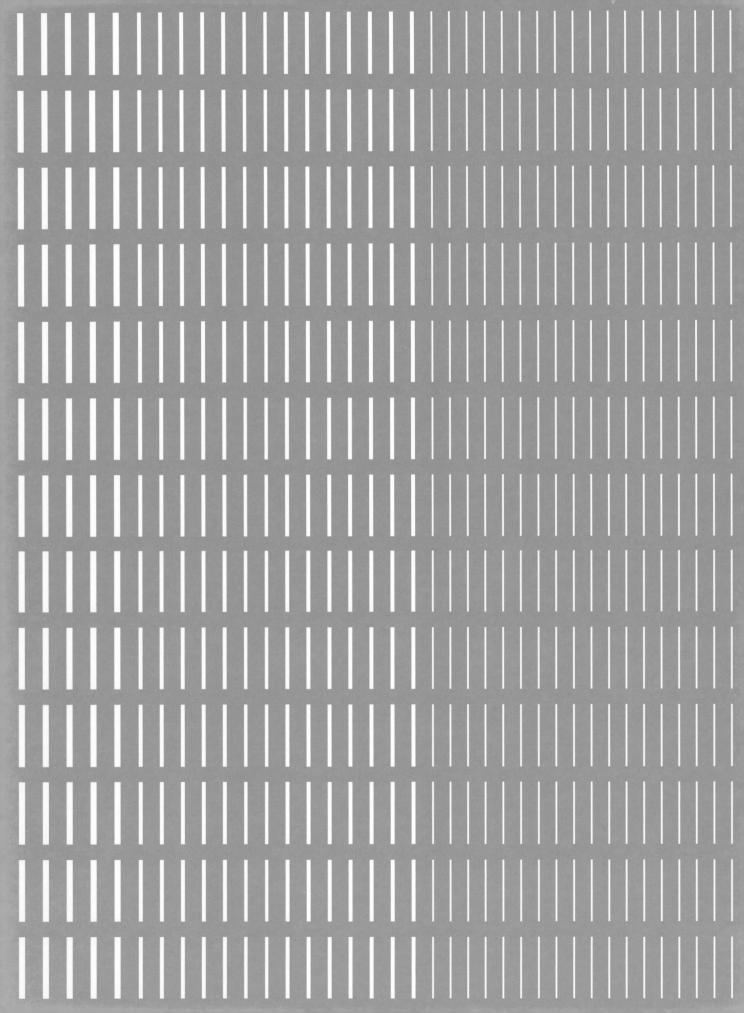

MID-CENTURY TYPE

Chisel Robert Harling 1939	**Sabon** Jan Tschichold 1964–67	**Impact** Geoffrey Lee 1965	**Franklin Gothic** Morris Fuller Benton 1902
Brush Script Robert E. Smith 1942	**Nord** Roger Excoffon 1962–66	**Helvetica (originally Neue Haas Grotesk)** Max Miedinger and Eduard Hoffmann 1957	**Albertus** Berthold Wolpe 1935–42
Univers Adrian Frutiger 1957	**Avant Garde** Herb Lubalin 1970	**Countdown** Colin Brignall 1965	
Sistina Hermann Zapf 1950	**Banco** Roger Excoffon 1951	**Peignot** A.M. Cassandre 1937	**Profil** Max and Eugen Lenz 1947

David Jury

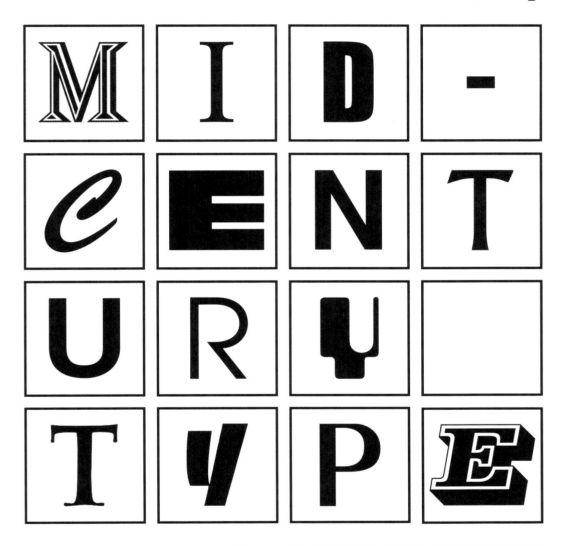

MID-CENTURY TYPE

TYPOGRAPHY ∙ GRAPHICS ∙ DESIGNERS

MERRELL

LONDON ∙ NEW YORK

Monotype
Series. No. 302

Brush

Lanston Monotype Machine Company

Twenty-fourth and Locust Streets, Philadelphia 3, Penna.

CONTENTS

INTRODUCTION

The years immediately after 1945 were a cathartic time as Europe set about rebuilding its war-shattered economies and infrastructure. After six years of conflict, curfews and blackouts, there was optimism not only for physical rejuvenation but also for genuine cultural change. Across the continent, almost every country faced an unprecedented challenge of economic remobilization, and for the first time, designers were recognized as having an essential role to play.

In Britain, confirmation of this official policy was a major exhibition, *Britain Can*

Ashley Havinden
Britain Can Make It
1946

Poster.

OPPOSITE
Abram Games
Festival of Britain
1951

Poster. Games designed the Festival of Britain symbol and the ochre background. The London Press Agency added Phillip Boydell's Festival titling and other information.

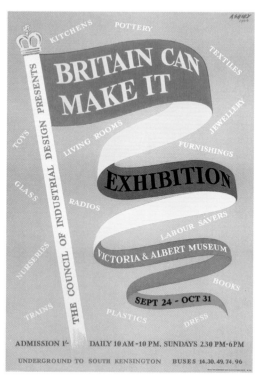

Make It, which occupied half the total area of the Victoria and Albert Museum in the autumn of 1946. More than 3000 items were displayed across thirty-two sections, among which were 'Furniture', 'Heat, Light, Power' and 'Books and Printing'. Most of the last-named section reflected the pre-war New Traditionalism of the 1920s and '30s, with the presswork of the Curwen, Kynoch and Cambridge University presses and the design work of Edward Bawden, Barnett Freedman and Reynolds Stone being much in evidence. Work reflecting trends towards modernism was rare, although recent distinctive book covers by, for example, Berthold Wolpe for Faber & Faber (Wolpe designed six of the eight jackets on display) and a number of posters designed by Abram Games, F.H.K. Henrion, Tom Eckersley and others were included. It was intended that the exhibition demonstrate a determined allegiance to modern manufacturing and design, but in truth this would take several more years to become reality.

Ashley Havinden's exhibition poster shows the hallmarks of having been created by committee, and reflects the internal conflicts that impeded Britain's progress in the years immediately after the war. His bright, clean colours provide a veneer of modernism, but the imagery – a medieval banner on a heavy pole topped by a royal crown – does not encourage a sense of progressive thinking. Five years later, the Festival of Britain was a

FESTIVAL OF BRITAIN

MAY 3 – SEPTEMBER 30

MAIN INFORMATION CENTRE · SWAN & EDGAR BUILDING · PICCADILLY CIRCUS · LONDON

Frederic Ehrlich
*The New Typography
& Modern Layouts*
Frederick A. Stokes
(New York); Chapman
& Hall (London)
1934

*Spread showing
examples of poor
advertising that
use arbitrary forms
and arrangements
unrelated to the
message. Ehrlich
was an advocate of
Jan Tschichold's New
Typography.*

far more ambitious exhibition, featuring truly futuristic architecture and inventive exhibition design, with an iconic poster by Abram Games that manages to contain pomp and pageantry within a distinctly modern setting. A corner had been turned.

The years 1948 to 1952, during which the Marshall Plan – a $13 billion economic aid package – was in operation, saw the fastest period of growth in European history. With their manufacturing capability still in disarray, European markets – having once been vehemently resistant to American goods – were now more pliable. The successes of American exports, and the resultant post-war economic boom that many Americans experienced, were fuelled to a large extent by a vibrant print and publishing industry, which, together with film and television, became a dominant presence across Britain and Europe and a major force in the promulgation of American culture and goods.

BEING A TYPOGRAPHER IN 1945

The paucity of professional typographers before the war was due to the printing industry's firm physical control of type and typography. Requiring an understanding of apparently unfathomable, rule-bound processes, complex machinery and specialist tools, expertise in typography was restricted to those undertaking the lengthy – usually six-year – print apprenticeship. Independent typographers working outside the print industry were, therefore, a rare breed because they required a knowledge not only of the terminology and processes but also of the technical constraints and working methodology of the printer's composing room. Most independent typographers working before the Second World War had gained their knowledge of typography within the printing industry before going on to establish themselves as 'typographers'. This meant that virtually all

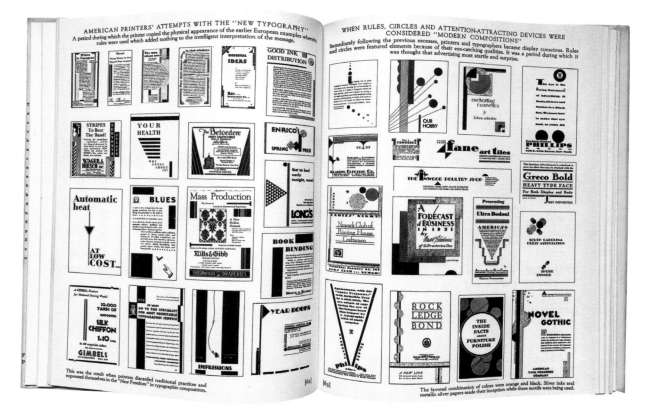

independent typographers in the immediate post-war years, and throughout most of the 1950s, were men because women were denied entry to the printing industry by its unions.

It is not surprising, then, that pre-war typography generally reflected the values of the printer. Modesty and restraint were the aims, and the typographer's role was to enable the author's words to be read free from distraction. The idea of the typographer imposing himself between author and reader was abhorrent. For this reason, typographic design was essentially a rule-governed and predictable process, described persuasively as one of discipline and humility by Beatrice Warde, publicity manager for the British Monotype Corporation, in her famous essay 'The Crystal Goblet' (published in book form in 1955 but first delivered as a lecture, titled 'Printing Should Be Invisible', in 1930).[1] This idea had already been set out by Stanley Morison, typographic adviser to the Monotype Corporation and Cambridge

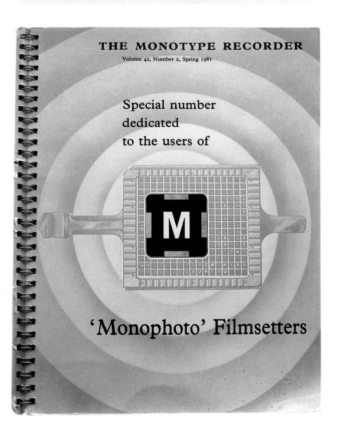

RIGHT, TOP
Beatrice Warde
'This Is a Printing Office'
1932

Broadside written by Warde, in her role as publicity manager at Monotype, to help promote Eric Gill's Perpetua typeface.

RIGHT
The Monotype Recorder
Vol. 42, no. 2
Spring 1961

Front cover of special issue published to coincide with 'an exhibition of books, periodicals and general printing composed by "Monophoto" filmsetters in many countries'; includes bound-in samples.

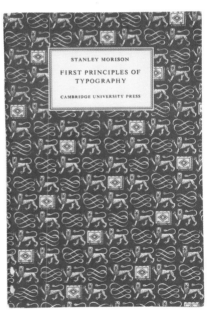

Stanley Morison
First Principles of Typography
Cambridge University Press
Second edition, 1967

Front cover.

W. A. DWIGGINS

Layout

in Advertising

A new revised edition

of this standard work on all phases of advertising layout
and design, by a modern master of the graphic arts

University Press, in his short but influential essay 'First Principles of Typography', written in 1929 for *Encyclopedia Britannica* and then published in a revised form in the final issue of *The Fleuron* (1930). Over twenty years later, Morison's view remained resolute: the book typographer's acceptance of 'universal consensus … the result of a twenty-five-century process of evolution' was unequivocally 'the best guarantee against experiment or innovation or irresponsibility'.[2]

However, independent typographers were already freeing themselves from the restraint of 'universal consensus' and, to Warde's consternation, were 'beginning to elbow-in between printer and customer'.[3]

A half-page advertisement by the American graphic designer Paul Rand to promote his book *Thoughts on Design* appeared in the British typographic journal *Signature* in March 1947. Oliver Simon, *Signature*'s designer and editor, mischievously placed Rand's notice opposite the opening page of a warm homage to Stanley Morison, Simon's long-time colleague. The announcement, though modest in content, was startling in its design, reflecting Rand's fascination with (and Morison's abhorrence of) the work of such European designers as Jan Tschichold, Herbert Bayer and László Moholy-Nagy.

The huge success of *Thoughts on Design* and its consequent influence were the likely reasons for the re-issuing in 1948 of *Layout in Advertising*, a book by another, arguably even more remarkable American designer, William A. Dwiggins. Originally published in 1928, the 'revised' version was almost unchanged and yet remained vibrant and eminently current in its thinking. Dwiggins's description of 'modernism' in the postscript to the book is striking for its tolerant and pragmatic tone at a time when the 'modern spirit' was still far from acceptable as a standard, even in the United States: 'Actual modernism is a state of mind that says: "Let's forget (for the sake of the experiment) about Aldus, and Baskerville, and William Morris … and take these types and machines and see what we can do with them on our own. Now." The graphic results of this state of mind are extraordinary, often highly stimulating, sometimes deplorable. The game is worth the risk …'[4]

Young typographic designers increasingly enjoyed the freedom and took on the risks of freelance work, either as individuals or in group practice, to forge a new profession built on the pioneering work of Tschichold, Dwiggins and Morison (it is surely impossible to imagine three more contrary typographers). Herbert Spencer, doubtless with Morison's aversion to 'experiment or innovation or irresponsibility' in mind, wrote on the opening page of the first issue of his important journal *Typographica* in 1949, 'We cannot equal the great typography of the past by imitation', but 'by having a definite objective in all our experiments … we shall make our own real contribution to the development of the Art of Typography.'[5]

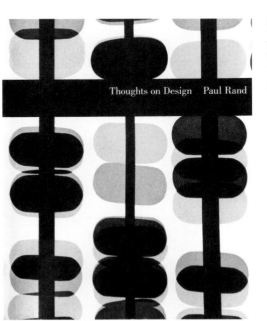

TYPOGRAPHIC TECHNOLOGY AND WORKING PROCESSES

A typographer working in the design studio of a publishing or advertising agency in the 1940s and early '50s was often known as a 'layout artist'. The term 'typographer' was generally used only by those working independently.

A publishing house supplied the layout artist with its own 'composition instructions' or 'composition rules'. (The work that the printer's compositor did when setting a page of type was called 'composition'.) Tschichold's concise four-page 'Composition Rules', written in about 1947 for the printers of Penguin Books (see pp. 154–55), is a perfect example. An independent typographer also had to provide the compositor with typesetting instructions, but these would almost always be drawn up on a project-by-project basis and called a 'type specification'. Before this, the typographer would have made preliminary sketches and then drawn a detailed layout to demonstrate clearly the intended outcome. This might be for the benefit of the client or a senior colleague, but it would also serve to establish exactly what the typographer was going to need from the compositor. A copy of the layout, marked up with notes specifying typefaces, style, sizes, leading, etc., would be passed to the compositor, who would set the type, usually using a Monotype or Linotype composing machine. The type would then be locked up in a metal frame (a chase) and a proof print would be pulled. This would be sent to the typographer to be proofread and returned to the compositor with corrections; then (it was hoped) a final proof would be pulled. During this process the typographer never came into physical contact with the type.

By 1950 it was increasingly common for letterpress printing to give way to lithographic printing. Nevertheless, all type material was still produced using letterpress, the difference being that the printed proof

Rudolf Hostettler
The Printer's Terms
SGM
1949

Front of jacket and spread from an illustrated dictionary of typography and printing specifications used by designers of the time.

OPPOSITE
Berthold Wolpe
Service Slang
Faber & Faber
1943

Marked-up artwork.

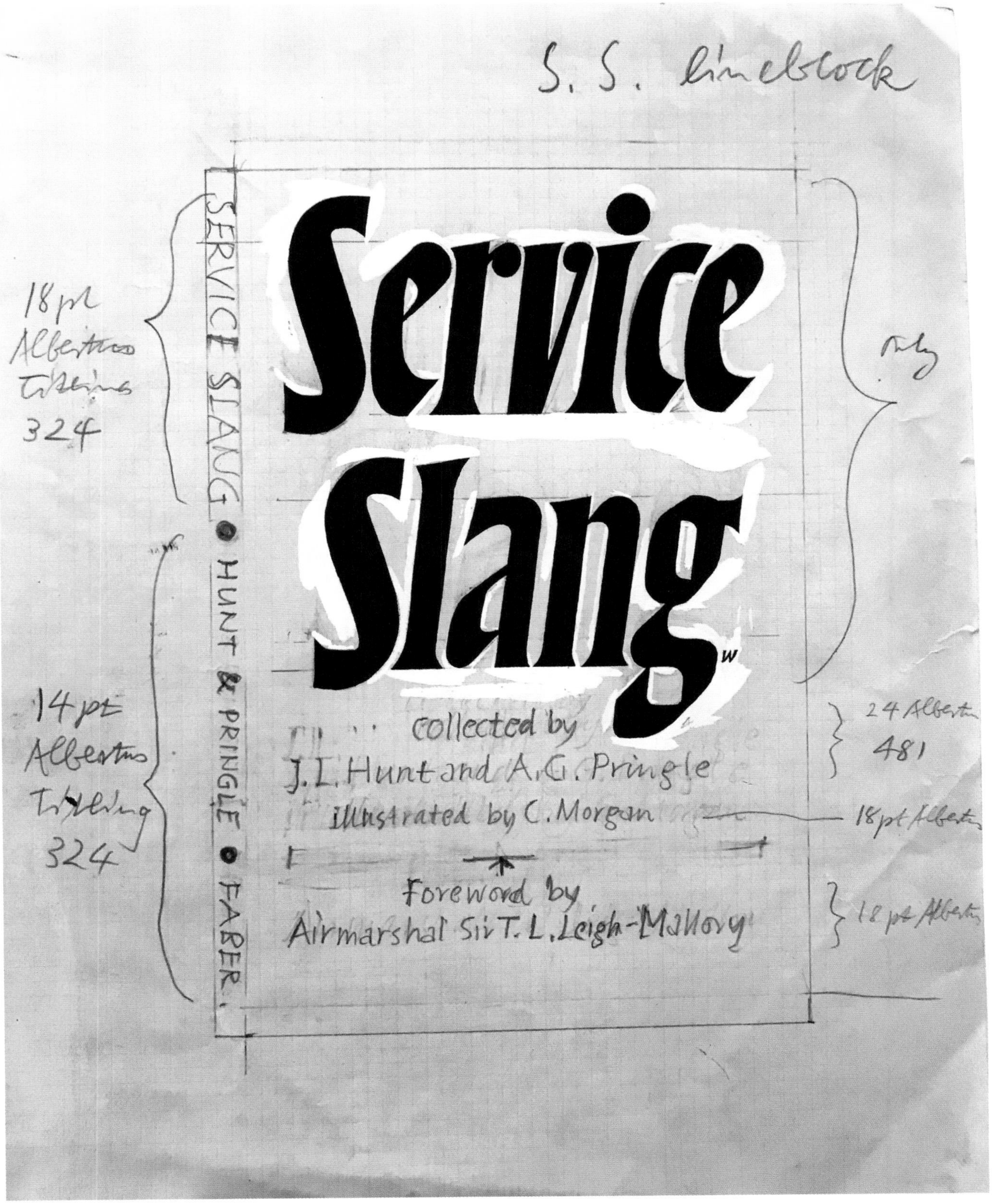

S. S. lineblock

Service Slang

SERVICE SLANG • HUNT & PRINGLE • FABER.

collected by
J. L. Hunt and A. G. Pringle
illustrated by C. Morgan

Foreword by
Airmarshal Sir T. L. Leigh-Mallory

18 pt
Albertus
Titling
324

14 pt
Albertus
Titling
324

only

24 Albertus
481

18 pt Albertus

18 pt Albertus

LETRASET *instant lettering*

Simply put the Letraset sheet in place, press lightly over
the letter you want, lift the sheet off. And there is perfect
lettering, of reproduction quality. For Letraset is the
high-speed, type transfer system now in use all over
the world. It is perfect on literally any smooth surface: the
quick, economical answer to the need for highest quality
lettering on display panels, roughs, signs, labels, graphs, charts, TV cells.
Standard sheets cost 7/6 each.

LETRASET LIMITED. VALENTINE PLACE. WEBBER STREET. LONDON SE1. WATERLOO 1401

was now 'composed' by the typographer;
the compositor set the metal type, then
the typographer would cut and paste
the printed proofs on to art board using
adhesive. By the end of the 1950s, textual
material was increasingly in the form of
bromides – the photographic printed output
of a phototypesetting machine. When the
individual pages were complete, a translucent
paper cover sheet would be attached, on
which instructions to the printer were added.[6]

Pasting small cut-out pieces of paper on
to a board was always a precarious process,
despite the use of T-squares, set squares
and desks with parallel motion. Ensuring
everything remained straight and in alignment
was especially difficult when work had to be
done quickly and glue had not had sufficient
time to harden. Communication was generally
by telephone (desk-bound in those days) and
by post. If something had to arrive the same
day, a courier might be hired, or more likely,

if the client was local, someone would carry
it – by bus, taxi or on foot.

Computers were already newsworthy
items in the late 1950s. When the treasury
department of Norwich City Council in the
UK installed its Elliot electronic computer
in 1957, the streets around its main building
were closed to traffic for a day while the huge
machine was lifted by pulley and the physical
strength of a dozen men. It was, the local
paper reported, the most powerful computer
available and considered to be little less than
a miracle machine. By the 1960s, predicted
changes wrought by computer technology
were already much discussed in typographic
circles, and in 1968 the creative potential
of computer technology was acknowledged
in the celebrated exhibition *Cybernetic
Serendipity* at the Institute of Contemporary
Arts in London. Another sixteen years, and
the predicted digital revolution became a
reality with the arrival of the Apple Mac.

Franciszka Themerson
Studio International
1968

*Front cover of special
issue published
to coincide with
the* Cybernetic
Serendipity *exhibition
at the Institute of
Contemporary Arts,
London.*

TYPE DESIGN

Monotype and Linotype, with their type-design programmes and skilful adaptation of historical typefaces, dominated the fields of typography and printing during the first half of the twentieth century. However, by the middle of the century their authority was beginning to falter. No one disputed that letterpress printing from metal type provided superb results, but phototypesetting – the new technology on the horizon – apparently not only offered a cheaper alternative but also provided the typographer with far greater control. With typographers in sole command of the technology surely, it was argued, creative benefits would follow.

Charles Peignot (1897–1983), director of the Paris-based Deberny & Peignot type foundry, had concentrated his company's typeface development on display types for hand composition. Jobbing work – which was undertaken by hundreds of small-scale printers – was plentiful, much of it coming from designers within advertising agencies. But by the 1950s Peignot was anticipating the challenge of photocomposition, and he was determined that his foundry should not fall behind in such developments.

In 1952 Peignot took the opportunity to partner with the American-based company Photon, Inc. This firm had patented the Lumitype, the first photographic type-composition system, which had been developed in 1944 by two French engineers, Louis Moyroud and René Higonnet.[1] The transfer of letters on a spinning glass disc via a beam of light on to light-sensitive paper caused predictable distortions to the letters, most notably the softening of outer corners and the filling-in of inner corners. Realizing that he needed a range of typefaces designed to correct these distortions, Peignot required a young designer who had a sound knowledge of typographic form and was also open-minded and enthusiastic about new technology. He met the young Swiss typographer Adrian Frutiger (1928–2015) and with remarkable foresight, or good fortune, invited him to Paris.

Frutiger found himself redrawing classic typefaces such as Garamond, Baskerville and

OPPOSITE
Choc
Roger Excoffon
1955

Specimen book.

Brochure for the Intertype Fotosetter Photographic Line Composing Machine, 1950.

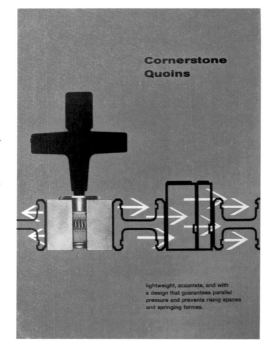

Bodoni for the Lumitype phototypesetter. It was an unhappy experience.[2] However, when Peignot decided that he needed a sans serif to add to the Lumitype range, Frutiger saw an opportunity and persuaded Peignot to allow him to develop a typeface he had begun as a student in Zurich, rather than to adapt Europe, as Peignot had suggested. (Deberny & Peignot had acquired the rights to distribute Paul Renner's Futura in France under the name Europe.) Trials of Frutiger's efforts were made and approved, and production went ahead. Univers appeared in 1957 both in film and in foundry metal for hand-setting.

Univers comprised a family of twenty-one variants. This was planned from the outset and demonstrated by a grid-like presentation, with each variant bearing an index number. This gave Univers an air of cool, systematic objectivity, but its visual sophistication was based on Swiss craft and tradition.

Although Univers was designed to take advantage of the cost- and space-saving potential of phototypesetting (Deberny & Peignot advertised each of its Lumitype glass master discs as replacing three tons of brass matrices), Peignot also arranged licensing deals with other type foundries, most notably Monotype, which produced it for its letterpress typecasting and Monophoto machines. Univers became one of Monotype's bestselling typefaces.

Folio, designed by Walter Baum and Konrad Bauer for the Bauer foundry in Germany, and Neue Haas Grotesk, designed by Max Miedinger and Eduard Hoffmann for the Haas foundry in Switzerland, were released in the same year as Univers. (Neue Haas Grotesk was later renamed Helvetica.) These three iconic typefaces represented a sans serif whose style was 'no style', capable of being used for any purpose, anywhere. This 'modern' new typography (generally referred to as the Swiss International Style or International Style) was cultivated by the second generation

The developing Univers

Univers-Typographie
Bruno Pfäffli
(Atelier Adrian Frutiger)
Paris

American Type Founders
Elizabeth
New Jersey

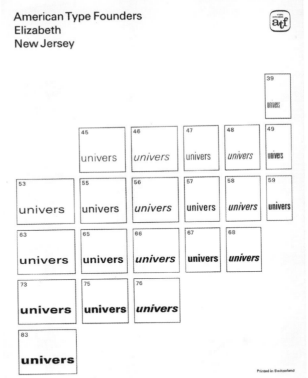

Printed in Switzerland

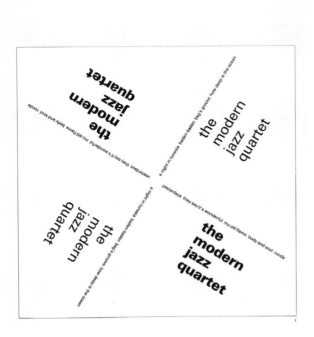

TOP AND LEFT
Univers
Adrian Frutiger
1957

*American Type
Founders specimen
book, mid-1960s.
The back cover (left)
features a design by
Bruno Pfäffli.*

ABOVE
Frutiger
Adrian Frutiger
Mid-1970s

*Signage at Charles
de Gaulle Airport,
Paris. The airport
opened in 1974,
and the typeface
was released
commercially in 1977.*

Folio
breit halbfett

of Bauhaus-influenced designers, among them Max Bill, designer, artist and teacher; and Ernst Keller, designer and influential teacher at the Kunstgewerbeschule in Zurich, where the young Frutiger, eight years earlier, had sketched his first ideas for Univers.

Emil Ruder, influential writer, teacher and graphic designer and a leading disseminator of International Style ideology, also actively supported Univers, first in *Neue Grafik* journal and then in a special issue of *Typographische Monatsblätter* (*TM*; with German, French and limited English texts), in which the Monotype cutting made its first appearance.[3] The international showcase provided by *TM* was pivotal in establishing Univers as a truly 'universal' typeface. It did, of course, also attract some criticism, albeit limited. Karl Gerstner, a prominent graphic designer and writer who would later help to guide International Style typography out of the ultra-cool impasse it had created, complained

Folio
Walter Baum and
Konrad Bauer
1957

Specimen book (top); specimen pages from Printing Types, *produced by the London College of Printing, c. 1970s (left).*

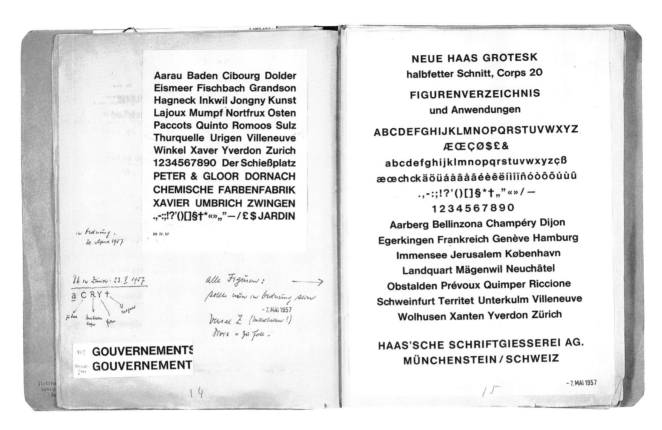

Helvetica (originally Neue Haas Grotesk)
Max Miedinger and Eduard Hoffmann
1957

Hoffmann's notebook from 1957 documents the early development of the type (above); brochure designed by Hans Neuburg and Nelly Rudin, 1963 (left).

Ludlow specimen pages (Ludlow Tempo Light):

LUDLOW TYPOGRAPH COMPANY · CHICAGO · BOSTON · NEW YORK · ATLANTA · SAN FRANCISCO

60 and 72 Point
Ludlow 28-L Tempo Light

COSTS ARE CUT
By Ludlow method
states the manager

72 Point Ludlow 28-L Tempo Light

MODERN TYPES ARE
Pleasing to advertiser
in national periodicals

60 Point Ludlow 28-L Tempo Light

The two sizes of Ludlow Tempo Light shown above are one and one-quarter inch matrices.

LUDLOW TEMPO LIGHT

LUDLOW TYPOGRAPH COMPANY · CHICAGO · BOSTON · NEW YORK · ATLANTA · SAN FRANCISCO

PRINTERS LIKE THE
New typefaces that
Ludlow is designing

48 Point Ludlow 28-L Tempo Light   Length of lower-case alphabet: 521 points

OLD MANUSCRIPT IS
Discovered by worker
in ruins of razed abbey

42 Point Ludlow 28-L Tempo Light   Length of lower-case alphabet: 448 points

MODERN MODE IS MET
With approval by the large
advertisers of the country
to put punch into their ads

36 Point Ludlow 28-L Tempo Light   Length of lower-case alphabet: 391 points

COMMITTEE OF PRINTERS TO
Meet and hold discussion as to
what effect the new postal bills
will have on the printing industry

30 Point Ludlow 28-L Tempo Light   Length of lower-case alphabet: 323 points

BOOK IS GIVEN
By Cicero dealer
24 Point Ludlow 28-L Tempo Light
Length of lower-case alphabet: 264 points

EASE OF OPERATION
Greatest of its features
18 Point Ludlow 28-L Tempo Light
Length of lower-case alphabet: 193 points

PRINTING PERIODICALS ARE
Helpful to graphic arts student
14 Point Ludlow 28-L Tempo Light
Length of lower-case alphabet: 146 points

SMALL ILLUSTRATED WORK WITH
Large circulation gains in popularity
12 Point Ludlow 28-L Tempo Light
Length of lower-case alphabet: 124 points

SYMBOL ON THE BOAT APPEARED TO
Be a black swastika within a large red circle
10 Point Ludlow 28-L Tempo Light
Length of lower-case alphabet: 104 points

REPUBLICAN NATIONAL CONVENTION WILL
Meet in the country's second largest city next year
8 Point Ludlow 28-L Tempo Light
Length of lower-case alphabet: 90 points

Characters in Complete Font
A B C D E F G H I
J K L M N O P Q R
S T U V W X Y Z &
$ 1 2 3 4 5 6 7 8 9 0
a b c d e f g h i j k l m n
o p q r s t u v w x y z
. , ; : ' " ! ? – ( ) [ ] +
Characters listed below sold separately.
a   &
Variants from 8 to 72 point inclusive.
%
The per cent mark is made for all sizes.

LUDLOW TEMPO LIGHT

---

57   Gothic, Franklin No. 107

Printing has performed a role of achievement unparalleled in the revela $1234567890   6 pt. Monotype
PRINTING HAS PERFORMED A ROLE OF ACHIEVEMENT UNPARALLELED IN

Printing has performed a role of achievement unparalleled in $1234567890   7 pt. Monotype
PRINTING HAS PERFORMED A ROLE OF ACHIEVEMENT UNPARAL

Printing has performed a role of achievement unparallele $1234567890   8 pt. Monotype
PRINTING HAS PERFORMED A ROLE OF ACHIEVEMENT UNPAR

Printing has performed a role of achievement $1234567890   10 pt. Monotype
PRINTING HAS PERFORMED A ROLE OF ACHIEVEME

Printing has performed a role of achie $1234567890   12 pt. Monotype
PRINTING HAS PERFORMED A ROLE OF AC

Printing has performed a role of a 123   14 pt. Hand Composition
PRINTING HAS PERFORMED A ROL

Printing has performed a 456   18 pt. Hand Composition
PRINTING HAS PERFORMED

Printing has perfor 789   24 pt. Hand Composition
PRINTING HAS PERFO

Printing has p 246   30 pt. Hand Composition
PRINTING HAS PE

Printing has 357   36 pt. Hand Composition
PRINTING HAS

ABCDEFGHIJKLMNOPQRSTUVWXYZ
abcdefghijklmnopqrstuvwxyz $1234567890

Printing has performed a role of achievement unparallel

SOUTHERN NEW ENGLAND TYPOGRAPHIC SERVICE, INC.

Franklin Gothic Condensed
(Foundry sizes for reproduction only)

A CONDENSED MEMBER
A condensed member oft

36 Point
(Foundry)

A CONDENSED MEM
A condensed membe

42 Point
(Monotype)

A CONDENSED M
A condensed mem

48 Point
(Monotype)

ABCDEFGHIJKLMNOPQRSTUVWXYZ
1234567890.,-:;'!?&$
abcdefghijklmnopqrstuvwxyz

25

that Univers (as well as Helvetica and Folio) was too smooth, too regular in tone, and that regardless of any aesthetic or ideological qualities to which it aspired, it was certainly not a 'functional' typeface: 'What has ocular clarity may appear monotonous when read.'[4] Surprisingly, Frutiger agreed.

Around 1980, when Frutiger was asked why he resisted pressure to adopt Univers when commissioned to design the signage for the new Paris airport, Charles de Gaulle, his explanation was similar to Gerstner's comment: 'Univers would not suit either the general aesthetic or the principles of optimum legibility ... The characters of Univers are a little too "smooth" for sufficiently rapid and accurate reading on indicator panels.'[5] The resulting new typeface – originally called Roissy, the name of the airport when commissioned in 1968, and renamed Frutiger by Linotype on its release in 1977 – was groundbreaking: a highly

efficient sans serif, but one that also had personality and bonhomie.

The popularity of European geometric sans serifs had also been all-consuming in the United States and did not decline until 1945. At this point, post-war euphoria created a renewed interest in America's own long-standing sans serifs, in particular Franklin Gothic, designed by Morris Fuller Benton for the American Type Founders Company (ATF) in 1902. Revolutionary when first released, Franklin Gothic had been almost entirely subsumed by the clever marketing of Kabel and especially Futura (both 1927). The response of American type founders was to try to create a geometric typeface that incorporated an American spirit. Robert Hunter Middleton's Tempo (1930) for the Ludlow Typograph Company was one of the best among several interesting options. Even Benton at ATF did the much the same, creating

OPPOSITE, TOP
Tempo
Robert Hunter
Middleton
1930

*Specimen pages
from Ludlow
Typograph Company
supplement, 1933.*

OPPOSITE, BOTTOM
Franklin Gothic
Morris Fuller Benton
1902

**Franklin Gothic
Condensed**
Morris Fuller Benton
1906

Specimen cards.

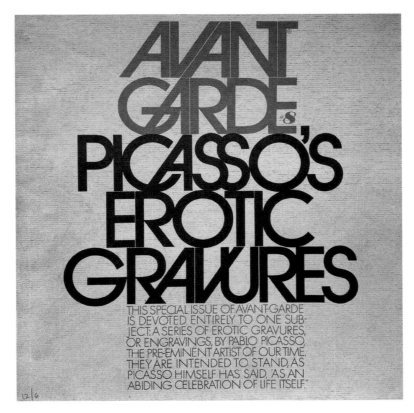

Avant Garde
Herb Lubalin
1970

Special issue of Avant
Garde *magazine
(no. 8, September
1969), published
before commercial
release of the
typeface by the
International Typeface
Corporation.*

Albertus
Berthold Wolpe
1935–42

*Monotype specimen
book, c. 1940 (right);
Westerham Press
specimen book, 1969
(below).*

Series 481

THE MONOTYPE CORPORATION LIMITED

Monotype–Registered Trade Mark

Albertus Wood Letter

ABCDEFGM
HIKLMNOR

Spartan (1939). None succeeded in dislodging Futura. A triumphant post-war America, however, rediscovered its own Franklin Gothic sans serif, and Benton's monumental letters were suddenly lauded as being the embodiment of the American spirit – strong and resilient. By the 1960s, Franklin Gothic (and its two sister typefaces, Light Gothic and the medium-weight News Gothic) had been recut for photocomposition. Nevertheless, when Ivan Chermayeff chose to use Franklin Gothic for the logo of the Museum of Modern Art in New York in 1964, he went back to Benton's original evocative metal version. It would be several years before the arrival of an entirely new kind of all-American sans serif: Avant Garde was initially devised by Herb Lubalin (and realized by Tom Carnase, one of Lubalin's partners) for the masthead of a magazine of the same name (see pp. 146–47), and was quickly extended to a complete typeface. Although essentially a geometric sans serif, it marked a distinct detour from its European counterparts, its expressive potential demonstrated by the large number of uncommon ligatures on offer. The International Typeface Corporation (ITC), of which Lubalin was a founder, released a full version in 1970.

In Britain, the geometric sans serif had been resisted in favour of the softer, more humanistic Gill Sans, which was recut for photocomposition by Monotype in 1961. In part as a reaction to the new technology of photocomposition (which caused a flood of working letterpress machinery and equipment to suddenly be available at almost giveaway prices), there was a second revival of private printing. Presses of various degrees of accomplishment emerged, but the best was one that had remained in operation since the height of the first revival: Will Carter's Rampant Lions Press, established in Cambridge in 1924. Carter was both printer and letter cutter (he had learnt letter cutting from David Kindersley), and these skills naturally led to his designing his own

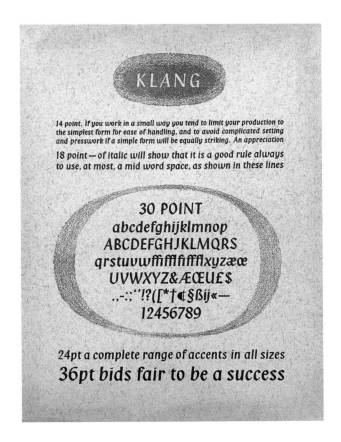

Klang
Will Carter
1955

Sample.

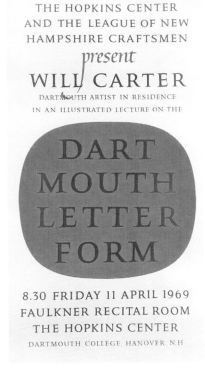

Dartmouth Titling
Will Carter
1961

Poster to promote a talk by Carter in 1969, the year the typeface was released by Letraset.

Impact
Geoffrey Lee
1965

*Front cover of
promotional brochure.*

Compacta
Fred Lambert
1963

*Front of jacket of
Graphic Design
Britain, edited
by Lambert and
published by Peter
Owen in 1967, with
title set in Compacta.*

Countdown
Colin Brignall
1965

Sample.

typefaces. His typeface Klang (the German word for 'sound') was released by Monotype in 1955. It was influenced by the work of another letter cutter, Rudolf Koch, in whose studio in Offenbach Carter had spent several months before the war. (Koch also mentored Berthold Wolpe, whose typeface Albertus, designed between 1935 and 1942, would have a major impact in Britain.) In 1960 Carter and Kindersley collaborated on the design of a very different typeface, Octavian, the aim being optimal clarity and transparency. In 1961 Carter was commissioned to design a commanding set of roman capitals for the signage at Dartmouth College, New Hampshire, which he adapted for Letraset in 1969 as Dartmouth Titling.

Letraset was launched in London in 1959. It manufactured plastic sheets on which were printed letters that could be rubbed down on to artwork. The key advantage of Letraset was that the designer was no longer reliant on the services of a typesetting bureau. It had a huge impact on studio practice, although its lack of precision meant that its use was generally confined to jobbing work. For Letraset, the process of bringing a font to production was relatively straightforward, certainly far simpler than that required by type foundries. The first of these – Compacta, a bold condensed sans serif – was commissioned from Fred Lambert in 1963. Countless others, including Countdown by Colin Brignall and Impact by Geoffrey Lee (both 1965), followed, all becoming synonymous with British printed ephemera during the 1960s.

Fonderie Olive was a small, family-run type foundry based in Marseilles, directed by the ambitious Marcel Olive, who had taken over from his father in 1940. In 1945 Olive offered his brother-in-law Roger Excoffon (1910–1983), then a failing artist with no design education, the job of running the Paris-based design studio.[6] It was an

Peignot
A.M. Cassandre
1937

From a Deberny & Peignot specimen book for poster type.

Chambord
Roger Excoffon
1946/47

Specimen card.

Nord
Roger Excoffon
1962–66

Specimen book. Nord is the name of the 'Ultra Bold' version of Antique Olive, initially designed by Excoffon to compete with Neue Haas Grotesk and Univers. Nord was used for the Air France logo.

Vendôme
François Ganeau
1952

Banco
Roger Excoffon
1951

Specimen books.

unlikely success story, but Excoffon's rapport with Olive proved remarkably productive. Excoffon took responsibility for the design of all advertising and general promotion of the foundry's typefaces, including specimen booklets, exhibition stands and advertising in trade magazines. However, he also found himself 'supervising' the design of typefaces and learnt quickly from the expertise of José Mendoza and others working around him. When Marcel Olive suggested that the studio look again at a typeface it had developed a few years previously, Excoffon decided to do it himself.

The typeface would be Chambord. An advertising campaign was launched that ran throughout 1948, and Chambord became the foundry's first major national success. However, its triumph was marred by accusations that Excoffon had seen proofs of a typeface named Touraine in development at Deberny & Peignot and that Chambord was a

blatant copy. In fact, Touraine was essentially A.M. Cassandre's Peignot (1937) but with several alternative and more traditional cuts (entrusted to Guillermo Mendoza, father of José) of some of the lower-case characters begun around 1942. For reasons unknown, the release of Touraine was delayed until late 1948, after the release of Excoffon's Chambord. It has been suggested that Charles Peignot moved to sue Olive, although no official documents have been found to support this claim. It is also not known whether Excoffon had a copy of Touraine, but in a conversation with Peignot he suggested, perhaps mischievously, that he had. This conversation was relayed to John Dreyfus (who took over from Stanley Morison as typographic adviser to Monotype): 'Charles Peignot once told me with a chuckle that when he suggested to Excoffon that the similarity between Chambord and Touraine was a little too close for comfort, Excoffon tried to set

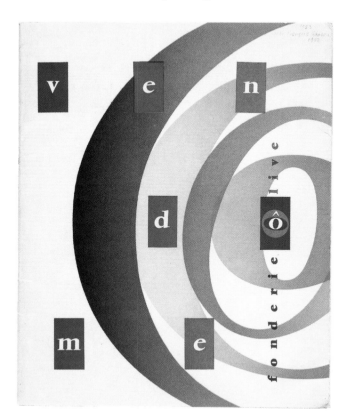

aaaaaaaaaaaaaaaaaabbbbbbbbb
bbbbbbbbbccccccccccccccccc
ddddddddddddddddeeeeee
ffffffffgggg
hhhhhiiiiiii
jjjjjjjjjjjkkkk
iiiiiiiiiiiiiiii

NORD

mmmmmmmnnnnnnnnnnnn
ooooooooooooooooopppppp
ppppppppppppppqqqqqqqqqqq
rrrrrrrrrrrrssssttttttttttt
uuuuuuuuuuuuvvvvvvwwww
xxxxxxxxxxxxyyyyyyyzzzz

ABCDEFGHI
JKLMNOPQRS
TUVWXYZ
abcdef
ghijklmnop
qrstuvxyz
1234567890

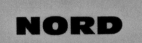

A
TU MÉCANIQUE

ATELIERS DE THÉODORE URBAIN

Motel

RELAIS

sur la route de Paris
en lisière de la forêt de Fontainebleau

BARBIZON - TÉLÉPHONE 188

VORNEY
ÉDITEUR

ABCDEFGHIJKL
MNOPQRSTUVWXYZ
1234567890
abcdefghijklmnop
qrstuvwxyz

C 24 16 H 5 A 9 k 100

Peignot's mind at rest by assuring him that he had kept Cassandre's design in front of him all the time he was working on Chambord – "just to make sure that he didn't copy a single letter".[7]

Whether it came to litigation or not, Peignot and Excoffon apparently remained good friends despite their fierce commercial and creative rivalry. Nevertheless, the difficulty of establishing the legitimacy of authorship and ownership of a typeface had never been better demonstrated. After Peignot became involved in the development of the Lumitype-Photon in 1952, he and others, including Excoffon, founded the Association Typographique Internationale (ATypI) with the purpose of combating illegal copying of type designs.

Fonderie Olive, helped by the success of Excoffon's Chambord and a reinvigorated post-war advertising industry, persuaded Marcel Olive to concentrate on the development of display typefaces. For a

smaller type foundry, such faces had the advantage of not having to be cut in multiple sizes, each in roman and italic, and in three or four weights. Instead, a display face could be effective in just four sizes, making its manufacture efficient and profitable. Excoffon's Banco was such a typeface.

Banco is a sans serif yet also a cursive type, but without any direct reference to historical scripts. As such, its appearance in 1951 came to represent, for good or bad, the rest of the decade in its expression of France's post-war exuberance, or alternatively, the abnegation of everything for which the country had once been admired – elegance, sophistication and passionate intellect. Chosen by jobbing printers, signwriters and neon-sign manufacturers alike, it was applied to every kind of business in which speed, expediency and inexpense were primary concerns.

Banco was the first of a distinctive series of typefaces by Excoffon characterized by

Banco
Roger Excoffon
1951

Specimen card.

Ritmo
Aldo Novarese
1955

Specimen page for a typeface similar to Banco.

3 scriptes

AUGUSTEA

A NEBIOLO SERIES

AUGUSTEA

SOLE DISTRIBUTORS

AMSTERDAM CONTINENTAL TYPES
AND GRAPHIC EQUIPMENT, INC.

268-276 FOURTH AVENUE · NEW YORK 10, N.Y. · SPRING 7-4980

their energy, boldness and gestural lines.
Mistral (1953) and Choc (1955) were based on
Excoffon's own handwriting; the former was
reminiscent of a soft-grade pencil on textured
paper, with lower-case letters ingeniously
designed to connect and flow into one another
– a considerable technical achievement.
However, the impact of these typefaces was
most striking on the streets of every French
town and city, and documented in the tracking
shots of Paris in the 1960s by such New Wave
film directors as Jean-Luc Godard, François
Truffaut and Agnès Varda.

Aldo Novarese (1920–1995) had been
recruited at age sixteen by Alessandro
Butti, art director of Nebiolo's Studio
Artistico. Nebiolo thrived in the first half
of the twentieth century not only as a type
foundry but also as a major manufacturer
of printing presses and allied tools and
equipment. Before the establishment of
the Studio Artistico in 1933, Nebiolo's
contribution to type design had been
minimal; the company preferred simply to
follow the successes of its rivals until Butti
took charge of design. Butti (1893–1959)
was determinedly scrupulous and refused to
approve anything that was not absolutely
right, both technically and morally. One such
example was Augustea. Butti took the young
Novarese with him to Rome in 1938, and
together they photographed the inscription
on Trajan's Column and many other Imperial
Roman inscriptions – all of which, of course,
were in capital letters. Butti studied the
variant examples they had recorded, made
numerous drawings and, some thirteen years
later, allowed Augustea titling (capitals) to be
released. Before its release and throughout
the following year, Butti worked on a lower-
case Augustea. Pressure was put on him to
allow the lower-case version to be put into
production, but Butti refused, not because
he was dissatisfied with his drawings but for

OPPOSITE
Augustea
Alessandro Butti and
Aldo Novarese
1951

Specimen book.

RIGHT
*Catalogue of recently
released typefaces
from the Nebiolo type
foundry, 1950s.*

BELOW
Microgramma
Alessandro Butti,
extended by Aldo
Novarese
1952

Specimen book.

Eurostile

sintesi espressiva del nostro tempo

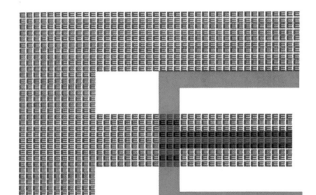

AABBCCDDEEF
FGGHHIIJJKKLL
MMNNOOPPQQ
RRSSTTUUVVX
XYYZZWWaabb
ccddeeffgghhiijjkk
llmmnnooppqqrrs
sttuuvvxxyyzzww
112233445566

SEGNI GRECI →

ΓΔΘΛΞ ΓΔΘΛΞ
ΠΣΦΨΩ ΠΣΦΨΩ

CARATTERI ORIGINALI DI CREAZIONE NEBIOLO TORINO

movimento funzionale nell'architettura grafica

La ricerca di forme nuove è compito degli artisti; la perfezione dei mezzi per realizzare tali forme è compito dei tecnici. Artisti e tecnici sono al servizio dell'arte tipografica per il rinnovamento continuo della forma del carattere. La nuova serie **EUROSTILE**, che si ispira alla serie Microgramma ormai diffusa in tutto il mondo, ha una sua fisionomia inconfondibile e ben si adatta al dinamismo che ci circonda. Questa serie può considerarsi un simbolo schematico della civiltà attuale, allo stesso modo in cui altri caratteri hanno schematizzato civiltà passate. Oggi, più che mai, il lavoro e lo studio del grafico si basano sull'equilibrio della pagina. Gli spazi, le linee, i fondi, il tono del colore sono elementi strettamente collegati, interdipendenti, che si influenzano reciprocamente. Essi debbono perciò equilibrarsi in una perfetta composizione architettonica. Tra questi elementi il carattere ha evidentemente un'importanza particolare. L'**EUROSTILE** costituisce un mezzo altamente efficace per esprimere la modernità, attraverso la sua linea quadrata e compatta; esso sintetizza lo spirito evolutivo verso un movimento funzionale che risolve i diversi problemi estetici e conferisce un'impronta attuale e caratteristica allo stampato.

fear that adding a lower case would offend the 'majesty of Roman lapidary'.[8] It was not until 1964, five years after Butti's death, that Augustea was 'reprised' as Nova Augustea, this time with lower-case letterforms.

When Butti, modest and undemonstrative to a fault, was made redundant in 1952, credit for the design of many of the typefaces he had created – admittedly sometimes with significant additional work by Novarese – was given wholly to the younger man; Nova Augustea, relaunched with Butti's lower case amended by Novarese, being a typical example. Nebiolo deftly presented the dashing Novarese as the new and sophisticated 'face' of its company. Excoffon fulfilled a similar role at Fonderie Olive.

Of the many typefaces on which Novarese worked closely with Butti, the most successful were Microgramma in 1952 and Recta in 1958. Microgramma

is a distinctive squarish titling sans serif designed by Butti. Ten years later, Novarese designed a set of lower-case characters to accompany Butti's capitals and added a condensed version; the typeface was then re-released as Eurostile. Recta, designed by Butti shortly before his dismissal, is a neutral sans serif predating Frutiger's Univers and Miedinger and Hoffmann's Neue Haas Grotesk. It was ignored by Nebiolo's managers until they saw the success of these typefaces. Belatedly recognizing its potential, they quickly produced and released Recta in 1958. Novarese expanded the typeface into various widths and weights in the years that followed.

With its new director of type design having revived Nebiolo's financial stability, the studio continued to concentrate primarily on display typefaces such as Veltro, Neon and Razionale, all created during the 1930s by another in-house designer, Giulio Da Milano.

OPPOSITE
Eurostile
Aldo Novarese
1962

Specimen book. Novarese developed Eurostile to succeed Microgramma. The two typefaces are essentially the same, but when Novarese designed the lower case the name was changed to Eurostile.

FAR LEFT
Recta
Alessandro Butti, extended by Aldo Novarese
1958

Specimen book.

LEFT
Neon
Giulio Da Milano with Alessandro Butti
1933–35

Specimen book. Da Milano was director of typography at Nebiolo before Butti and was instrumental in the establishment of the Studio Artistico in 1933.

By the late 1940s, German type foundries realized that they needed new roman types. The debate concerning the merits or otherwise of Germany retaining the use of black letter had been raging for generations. Aware that black letter was apparently indecipherable in non-German-speaking countries, many now demanded that post-war Germany become more inclusive by radically reducing its use. In addition, the international popularity of German geometric typefaces of the 1920s such as Futura and Erbar had waned, and many in Germany thought a more humanistic, old-style serif typeface was the answer.

On his arrival at the Stempel foundry in 1946, Hermann Zapf (1918–2015) was immediately tasked with the design of a roman type, but his work was cancelled late in production. Following this disappointment, in 1948 Zapf began work on Palatino, based on fifteenth-century Venetian types. The large x-height and open counters that make Palatino such a legible typeface were designed primarily to overcome the disadvantages of poor-quality paper, while its weight was made slightly heavier than that of other types in order to adapt to the growing popularity of lithographic and gravure printing processes.

Zapf's intention was that Palatino would be used for display work, and for this reason he included its distinct calligraphic characteristics.[9] Nevertheless, this did not discourage some book typographers, especially in the United States, from wanting to use it, and they pressed Stempel to provide alternative characters to replace certain 'problem' – that is, overtly calligraphic – characters (the *t* with its unusual ascender, for example).[10] When Zapf later designed a lighter-weight Palatino, he took the opportunity to reduce its calligraphic character to give it a more 'bookish' look. He wanted to call it Palatino Book, but the Stempel marketing department

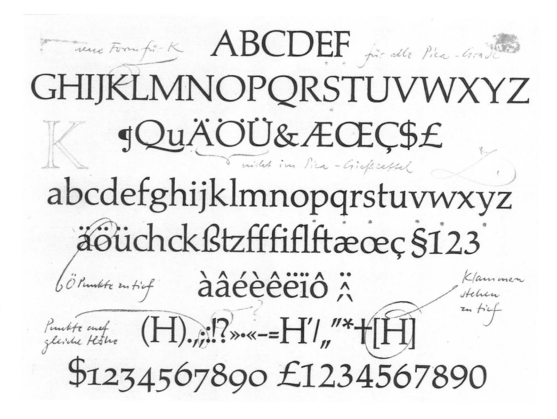

decided it should be marketed as a separate typeface and called it Aldus, despite Zapf's protest that it had little in common with the types of the fifteenth-century Italian printer Aldus Manutius. Aldus was released in 1952–53. (The name Palatino had also been decided by Stempel, after Giovanni Battista Palatino, a sixteenth-century calligrapher. Zapf had wanted to call the typeface Medici.)

With the design of Palatino complete and in production, in 1950 Zapf went to Italy, where he visited Rome, Florence and Pisa to study at first-hand Roman inscriptional letters. On his return, he designed Sistina, a strong titling typeface, based on the Italian sketches he had made.

This period, from 1948 to 1954, was hugely productive for Zapf. As well as undertaking the more humdrum task of drawing characters and additional sizes for typefaces already in Stempel's library, he designed Saphir, decorative capitals, in 1952; Janson, for Linotype, also in 1952; Virtuosa, a script, in 1952–53; several Greek alphabets; and, most significantly, a newspaper typeface, Melior.

During a visit in 1951 to New York, where an exhibition of his work had been mounted, Zapf visited Linotype's headquarters in Brooklyn to study the effects of various newspaper printing processes, chiefly rotary letterpress and web-fed lithography. Melior was the result of these deliberations and appeared in 1952. It is distinctive: sophisticated but also robust on account of its strong, squared serifs.

In the midst of this burst of activity, Zapf also created his most original and recognizable typeface, Optima. It was designed in 1952 and released in 1958. Although classified as a sans serif, Optima has a subtle swelling at its terminals that suggests bud-like serifs. (Zapf called it a 'serifless roman'.) The original intention was that it should be a display face, but when Zapf showed proofs to Monroe Wheeler of the Museum of Modern Art in

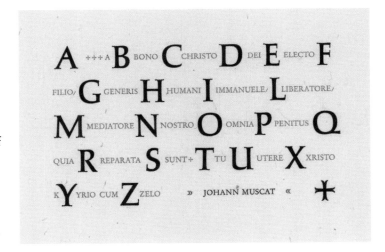

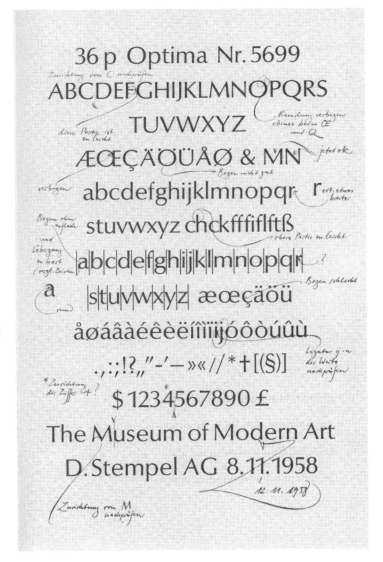

Sabon
Jan Tschichold
1964–67

*Sample, marked-up
proof and matrices.*

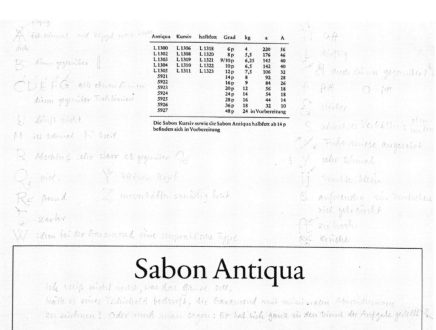

Antiqua	Kursiv	halbfett	Grad	kg	a	A
L 1300	L 1306	L 1318	6p	4	220	56
L 1302	L 1308	L 1320	8p	5,5	176	46
L 1303	L 1309	L 1321	9/10p	6,25	142	40
L 1304	L 1310	L 1322	10p	6,5	142	40
L 1305	L 1311	L 1323	12p	7,5	106	32
5921			14p	8	92	28
5922			16p	9	84	26
5923			20p	12	56	18
5924			24p	14	54	18
5925			28p	16	44	14
5926			36p	18	32	10
5927			48p	24	in Vorbereitung	

Die Sabon Kursiv sowie die Sabon Antiqua halbfett ab 14 p
befinden sich in Vorbereitung

Sabon Antiqua

ABCDEFGHIJKLMNOPQ
RSTUVWXYZÄÖÜ
abcdefghijklmnopqrstuvwxyz
ßchckfffiflft&äöü
1234567890 1234567890
.,:;-!?.'()[]*†‹›»«„"/£$

In Vorbereitung:

Sabon Kursiv

New York in 1954, Wheeler explained that there was a need for an elegant sans serif that could also be used for extended texts in art books and magazines. With this in mind, adjustments were made to enable Optima to function as a text type. Zapf followed the convention of a sans serif, providing a sloped, not italic, companion.

The resilience of letterpress technology, even by the 1960s, was demonstrated when Walter Cunz from the Stempel foundry commissioned Jan Tschichold (1902–1974) on behalf of the German Master Printers' Association to design a typeface that would appear identical whether produced from hand-composed foundry type or from Monotype or Linotype composing machines. A further stipulation was that the appearance of the typeface, its weight and x-height, should be based on Monotype's Garamond, but be 5 per cent narrower to add efficiency. Tschichold appears to have relished these limitations and technical difficulties.

As a lecturer, writer and typographer, Tschichold had played a major role in the dissemination of 'New Typography' ideology inaugurated in Germany at the Bauhaus during the 1920s. His elemental Universal Alphabet, designed 1926–29, and particularly his book *Die neue Typographie* (1928) meant that his work was deemed 'un-German' when the Nazi Party came to power in 1933, and he had to flee to Switzerland.

In response to Cunz, Tschichold based his typeface on a type specimen sheet printed by Konrad Berner, who in 1580 had taken over a successful printing and type foundry business in Frankfurt from Jakob Sabon. Unusually, Berner included the name of the punch-cutter alongside each typeface on the specimen sheet, and so 'Claude Garamond' appears several times. Tschichold's drawings for the roman version were based on one of

these types, while the italic was based on a type cut by the Frenchman Robert Granjon.

Tschichold's typeface Sabon (a name suggested by Stanley Morison) was designed between 1964 and 1967. Because Linotype technology required that the italic was the same width as the roman, Tschichold's italic had to be considerably wider than Granjon's. Another major consideration for Tschichold, but one necessary for all twentieth-century revivals of fifteenth- and sixteenth-century types, was that Garamond had cut his type to be printed on rough-textured, dampened, hand-made paper of uneven thickness. To mitigate these problems, it had been necessary for early printers to apply considerable pressure to ensure full contact between type and paper, causing the ink to be squeezed beyond the edges of the type. However, twentieth-century power-driven, precision-built presses and the use of smooth, machine-made paper meant that the contact between type and paper required little more than a 'kiss' to transfer a clean image of the type on to the paper surface. Therefore, to obtain a printed letter similar to that intended by Garamond, Tschichold added a little extra weight to Sabon.

Tschichold's drawings were passed to Stempel, which made any fine adjustments necessary on behalf of the three joint manufacturers. Considering the enormous technical demands, the design-to-manufacturing process went remarkably smoothly, reflecting the characteristics Tschichold sought in Sabon – a typeface rooted in tradition, with a strong and principled sense of restraint and propriety.

ITS

Cool

insidE

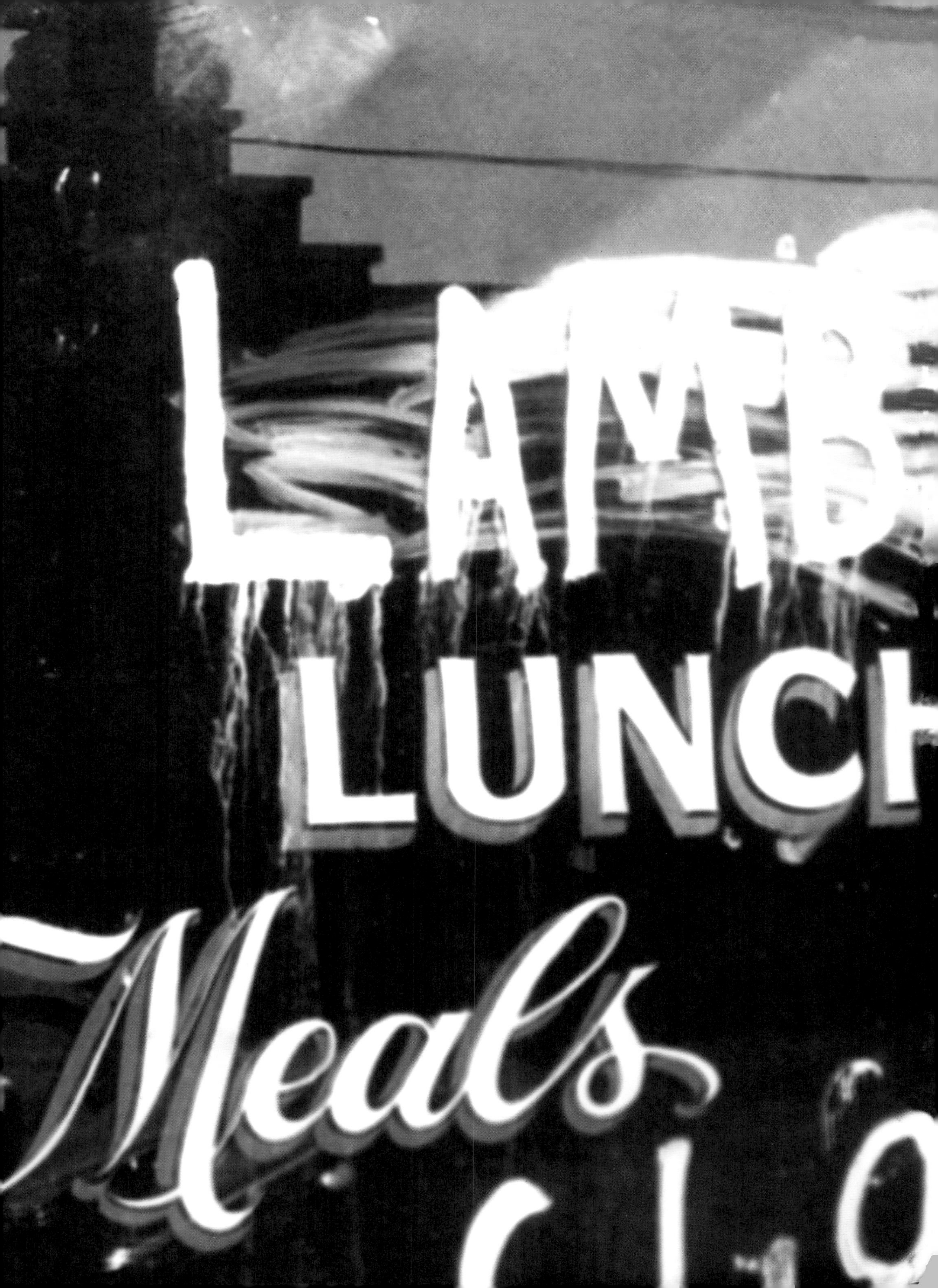
LUNCH
Meals

TYPOGRAPHICA 1

CONTEMPORARY TYPOGRAPHY AND GRAPHIC ART   1949

TYPOGRAPHIC JOURNALS

In 1945 there were several excellent typographic journals to provide an aspiring typographer with reading matter. Monotype's journal, *The Monotype Recorder*, edited on an ad hoc basis by Stanley Morison and more often by Beatrice Warde, was dispatched free to all companies that had bought Monotype equipment. (Linotype published its own journal, *The Linotype Bulletin*.) Oliver Simon's *Signature*, originally launched in 1935 and relaunched in 1946, was equally important and was broader in its scope. (His book *Introduction to Typography* had been published in 1945 by Faber & Faber.) Simon, who was working as art director for the Curwen Press, shared his central London office with Morison, who since 1923 had been typographic adviser to the Monotype Corporation. Together they had designed and edited the groundbreaking typographic journal *The Fleuron*, publishing seven book-size issues between 1923 and 1930.

The design of Simon's *Signature* remained true to the romantic Arcadia of pre-war publishing's New Traditionalism as heralded in the pages of *The Fleuron*. A far broader, more playful and distinctly less reverential context for typography was provided by Robert Harling in 1946 with *Alphabet and Image*. Modernism was slow to become established in Britain; indeed, it could be argued that it never really bloomed at all, and Harling, together with his pioneering publisher, James Shand, owner of the Shenval Press, certainly showed

Signature 3
New Series
Oliver Simon,
designer and editor
March 1947

Front cover.

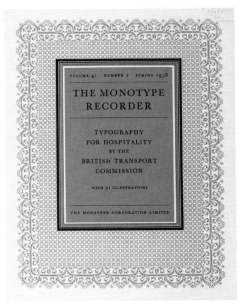

The Monotype Recorder
Stanley Morison
with Beatrice Warde,
editors
Vol. 41, no. 2
Spring 1958

Front cover.

OPPOSITE
Typographica 1
Series 1
Herbert Spencer,
designer and editor
1949

Front cover.

45

Typography 6
Robert Harling,
designer and
editor
Summer 1938

Front cover.

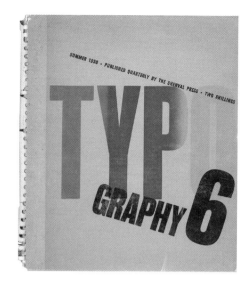

Image 1
Robert Harling,
designer and
editor
Summer 1949

Front cover.

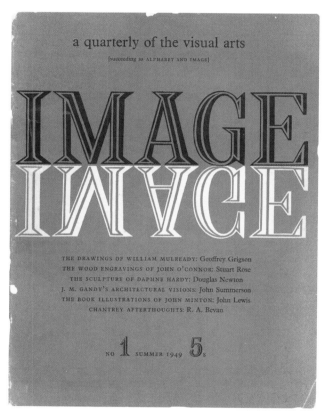

OPPOSITE
Alphabet and Image 5
Robert Harling,
designer and editor
September 1947

Front cover and spread.

Alphabet and Image 7
Robert Harling,
designer and editor
May 1948

Front cover.

little interest in its more severe continental manifestation. Shand was shy and reserved, 'a bohemian in a business suit',[1] much happier in the company of artists and writers than he was running the family business. Publishing a magazine gave him a creative outlet, in addition to being a showpiece for his company's excellent printing skills.

Alphabet and Image, a quarterly magazine, was Shand and Harling's second journal, the first having been *Typography*, published between 1936 and 1939. *Alphabet and Image* was initially bound by plastic comb – a distinctively 'progressive' statement at the time, one that gave it the 'everyday' feel of a manual or exercise book, which was ideally suited to Harling's egalitarian outlook and the inquisitive nature of the journal's content. 'A work in progress' might have been the reaction of the reader. As the title suggests, *Alphabet and Image* was devoted to typography and the graphic arts, presenting type and typography less as something to be revered than as something to be shaped and formed by the task in hand. Harling, who served as both designer and editor, was particularly interested in the broader, often transient function of letterforms. Unlike Simon and Morison, he had no allegiance to the print industry, and had no hesitation in lambasting printers and print unions for their wilful lack of interest in, even boastful ignorance of, design.

It may be that Shand regarded the natural lifespan of a journal as around three years, because *Alphabet and Image* was published between 1946 and 1948, and then *Image*, again with Harling, was published between 1949 and 1952. *Motif*, the fourth and final journal to be published by Shand, broke with this tradition: it was published over the course of almost a decade, between 1958 and 1967, although in only thirteen issues. This time Ruari McLean, first and foremost a typographer, was designer and editor.

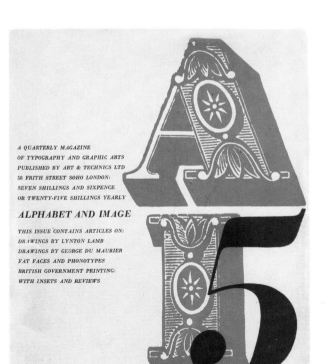

A QUARTERLY MAGAZINE
OF TYPOGRAPHY AND GRAPHIC ARTS
PUBLISHED BY ART & TECHNICS LTD
58 FRITH STREET SOHO LONDON:
SEVEN SHILLINGS AND SIXPENCE
OR TWENTY-FIVE SHILLINGS YEARLY

ALPHABET AND IMAGE

THIS ISSUE CONTAINS ARTICLES ON:
DRAWINGS BY LYNTON LAMB
DRAWINGS BY GEORGE DU MAURIER
FAT FACES AND PHONOTYPES
BRITISH GOVERNMENT PRINTING:
WITH INSETS AND REVIEWS

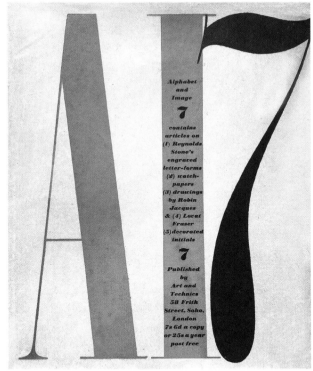

Alphabet and Image 7 contains articles on (1) Reynolds Stone's engraved letter-forms (2) watch-papers (3) drawings by Robin Jacques & (4) Lovat Fraser (5) decorated initials 7

Published by Art and Technics 58 Frith Street, Soho, London 7s 6d a copy or 25s a year post free

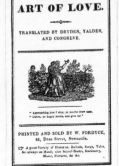

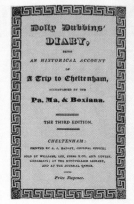

1839 shows a full range down to *Nonpareil*. The smaller sizes would hardly be legible on posters. This range of Thorowgood's had no particular name—each specimen is known by the size only—nor did any of the other founders invent a name for the family. We have to remember that 'Fat Face' is a twentieth-century title and that fat types, as already said, included various families. It was not until the 'fifties that we find the Caslon foundry using the name *Albion* for a Fat Face and the Figgins calling their variety *Elephant*, a very apt descriptive title and one revived in recent years.

In the later years of the nineteenth century Fat Faces ceased to be shown in the specimen books, crowded out perhaps by the new German and American importations. But they never altogether ceased to be used, for example by the Queen's Printers, Eyre & Spottiswoode, on Proclamations. The official printers were naturally conservative in their typography and were slow to adopt any innovating letters.

52

On the OPPOSITE PAGE are shown Fat Faces in two typical title-pages from popular pamphlets issued during the reign of George IV. ABOVE: a selection of headings from broadsides of the same era. Display lines were usually set in variants of Fat Face types and two verses were printed side-by-side on each broadside.

53

ABCDEFG
HIJKLM
NOPQRST
UVWXYZ

98

ABCDEF
GHIJKLMN
OPQRS

99

ABCDEFG
HIJKLMN
OPQRSTU
abcdefghi
jklmnopq

100

This is a failure in both patron and craftsman, one which would sadden both Johnston and Gill, for the Ministry's dull alphabet is drawn with a complete lack of sensitivity ('love', I suppose, would be the Ruskinian word) and the writer is incapable of transforming them by his own skill.

The self-conscious preoccupation of the arts and crafts with the morality of tools and materials, while it has led to a sane philosophy of industrial design, has tended to stultify the work of the less original craftsmen. At the same time, there has developed an increasing appreciation of 'the unsophisticated arts'. Most of these, such as the cut and sand-blown decoration on pub windows (and we might include the old signwriter's work), are valued for their triumphantly vulgar vitality, and an extravagant expenditure of talent which it would today be prohibitive to attempt. Their death-blow was dealt by what was perfectly expressed in John Betjeman's phrase 'ghastly good taste'.

Betjeman was one of those — James Shand, Harry Carter and Robert Harling have been others — who rediscovered the qualities of the early display types, the fat-faces, egyptians, tuscans and grotesques, that were so evidently lacking in contemporary types from the designer's drawing board. In most cases the original matrices had been kept by the typefoundries who first cast them, and it was possible to produce a revival in every way identical with the original.

These revivals were the last major typographical event before the outbreak of war suspended the production of new designs and concentrated attention on this new source of material. The effect of these revivals on architectural lettering in this country was considerable. Trehearne's Finsbury Health Centre (1938), which bears a version of the letter known as Thorne Shaded, must be one of the first to put one of these three-dimensional types back into its original form. The revival of early 19th-century egyptian types for architectural use at the Festival of Britain in 1951 encouraged their tentative use even for buildings of a semi-official nature. Here, at least, was a letter conceived in terms of solid structure, and often more suitable for the purpose and for this country than the classical incised roman letter. The committee, headed by Charles Hasler, which selected the Festival lettering, explicitly sought a form which was 'British in feeling'. The result was as massively British as any locomotive.

The revival of the Clarendon type during the 1950s made another traditional form familiar. It was started in this case by Swiss and American designers (Robert Eidenbenz and Freeman Craw), each of whom redrew a type which had been allowed to lapse from the repertoire of English founders. The result was the eventual revival of the original and best Clarendon types of the 1840s and 1850s under the name of 'Consort' and the re-cutting of the design by the Monotype Corporation. Through the Clarendon types the form of the robust 19th-century architectural roman was brought back into current use, not only in printed matter, but also in sign...

ABCDEFGHIJKLMNO
PQRSTUVWXYZabcd
efghijklmnopqrstuvwxy
z&1234567890

MANNS THE BUILDERS ARMS MANNS

97 Thorne Shaded. An early shaded letter based on modern face capitals. Probably cut by Robert Thorne, c. 1810. Stephenson Blake.

98 Figgins Shaded. A bold roman letter, with heavy, bracketed serifs (compare 84, 88) first shown in 1815. Stevens Shanks Ltd.

99 Thorowgood Italic. The most brilliantly audacious handling of the heavy modern face. No twentieth-century version has succeeded in recapturing its vitality. Stephenson Blake.

100 The Fann Street Foundry's Clarendon. Extended (c. 1850) under its present guise of 'Consort'. Stephenson Blake.

101 Fascia lettering for a Watney-Mann public-house, a length of fascia 28 ft. 6 in., incidentally adapted from a Monotype titling type by Design Research Unit. A successful evocation of the early nineteenth-century bold roman letter.

102 Flats in Mill Road, Cambridge. Span Developments Ltd (Eric Lyons, architect). Square section Clarendon, incised in slate.

Powder Myrrh
Gargle
BEST ÆTHER
Linitive Electuary
VOLATILE SALTS
SP. OF WINE
ÆTHER.
SYR.CORT.AUR.

60
61

C.DIBDIN Jun.
SONG SMITH
Rigmarole Repository

62 GAZETTEER.

59 Chemists' labels from the same collection as 59, enlarged × 2.

61 Wood-engraved device by Richard Austin, c. 1805. The lettering shows affinities with the roman he 'Bell' type, 13.

62 A wood-engraved heading by Richard Austin.

ABCDEFGH
IJKLMNOP
O.RSTUVWX
YZ ·, Æ &
23456789

No single Charm,
Of hers can warm,
Like years my whole devoted Heart;
Nor can't, I chide,
My soul I hide you,
Nor such Celestial Joy impart.

GEORGE FREDERICK HANDEL Esq.
born February XXIII. MDCLXXXIV.
died April XIV. MDCCLIX. *L.F.Roubiliac inv. et sc.*

63 Brass bookbinders' letters, now in the Royal Library, Windsor Castle, c. 1780.

64 Lettering printed from a punched pewter plate, from J. Walsh, The Merry Musician, vol. 4 (1733).

65 Pleasant and wayward seventeenth-century lettering. Monument to George Sprat, Chapel of St. Benedict, Westminster Abbey.

66 L. F. Roubiliac, monument to G. F. Handel, Westminster Abbey, 1761. Incised in marble.

Motif ran articles concerned with painting, sculpture, photography and architecture as well as graphic design and printing. However, for McLean, typography remained fundamental, as subject matter and, of course, in the design of the journal. A notable article was James Mosley's 'English Vernacular: A Study in Traditional Letter Forms' in *Motif* 11 (Winter 1963/64). This essay was the result of two years' research and ran to about 14,000 words, supported by 106 illustrations over fifty-three pages. McLean took this, and every other article, as an opportunity to use a different typeface and a new arrangement; 'simplicity and consistency' – hallmarks of modernity (by this time de rigueur in typographic circles) – played no part in *Motif*. McLean was criticized for this approach,[2] yet one could argue that the variety suited the range of material and provided a warmth of tone, while the 'typographic disunity' brought to mind the

'gentlemanly world of the 1950s bibliophile'. But by the 1960s, as the gaps between issues lengthened, *Motif* had the distinct air of a publication left behind.

Typographica, which appeared contemporaneously with Shand's journals, was designed and edited by Herbert Spencer (1924–2002) and published by Lund Humphries from 1949 until 1967. Its content was more diverse than its title might suggest – from the eighteenth-century engravings of Thomas Bewick to Robert Brownjohn's experiments with projected images of type for a new James Bond movie – all while surveying ephemeral lettering on, for example, tram and bus tickets, temporary hand-scrawled road signs and cast-iron grid covers. The attention given by Spencer to the peculiarities of letterforms, unavoidable yet rarely acknowledged in everyday life, reflected a particularly English kind of modernism, one combining a romantic sensibility for the

OPPOSITE AND ABOVE, LEFT
Motif 11
Ruari McLean, designer and editor
Winter 1963/64

Front cover by Eduardo Paolozzi (above, left) and spreads from James Mosley's article 'English Vernacular' (opposite).

ABOVE
Motif 12
Ruari McLean, designer and editor
Winter 1964

Front cover by Ceri Richards.

Uppercase 2
Theo Crosby, editor
1959

*Front cover and
spread showing
exhibition
collaboration
between Edward
Wright and Theo
Crosby. Five issues
were published by
Whitefriars Press,
1958–62.*

amusing and often quirky humanity of urban communication with the need to isolate, clarify and study. Spencer's call for recognition of vernacular (or 'invisible') typography was presented with a renewed sense of objectivity that was often captured by photography. What particularly fascinated him was the diversity of typographic communication and its inevitability in a fast-moving, ever-changing urban environment.

In this way, *Typographica* was never shackled to an ideology, as were, for instance, its Swiss counterparts *TM* and *Neue Grafik*. Nevertheless, Spencer introduced readers to such trailblazing modernists as Kurt Schwitters, Alexander Rodchenko, El Lissitzky, Piet Zwart, Herbert Bayer and Max Bill. Yet, alongside these doyens of objectivity he included the artist Richard Hamilton's typographic reinvention of Marcel Duchamp's *Green Box*, the sculpted concrete poetry of Ian Hamilton Finlay and the riotous book projects of artist Dieter Roth.

exhibition stand for Standard Catalogue Company and Architectural
Design at the Building Exhibition, London, 1955, designed by Theo Crosby
and Edward Wright

Typographica 16
Series 1
Herbert Spencer,
designer and editor
1959

*Front cover by Franco
Grignani.*

Typographica 13
Series 1
Herbert Spencer,
designer and editor
1957

*Spread from
Germano Facetti's
article on the
book design of
contemporary French
book-club publishing.*

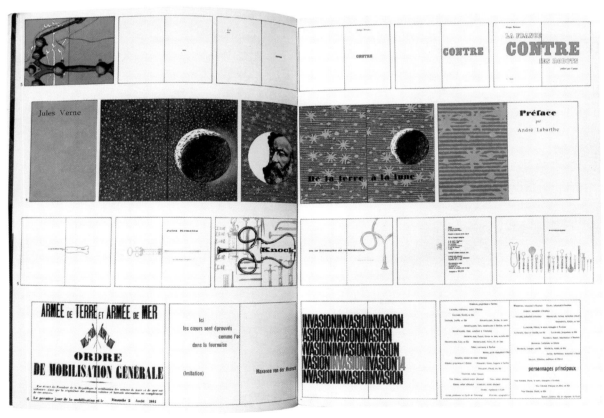

Reprinted from *Typographica*,
review of typography and the graphic arts,
edited by Herbert Spencer
and published twice a year by
Lund Humphries
12 Bedford Square, London WC1
price 12s 6d a copy
by post, 14s (or $2.25 U.S.A., $2.50 Canada)

Dear Dennis:
when in Paris
lay off the

Street Level   by Robert Brownjohn

A visitor to New York taking his first morning's walk down Fifth Avenue stopped to inspect a bit of architectural detail that appealed to him, stepped back, looked up, and was pole-axed with the full force of one hundred and two floors of Empire State Building. The bit of detail that got his eyes above his head was a big, fat, curly letter F.

The fact is that we begin to see our cityscape not so much as architecture as three-dimensional typography. Fifth Avenue has its own unique colour – gold, bronze, aluminium, stainless steel, marble, all the loud, aggressive, dollar-type materials in [Go]d's Own Country. Sixth Avenue is different. So is Coney Island, Times Square, [Ba]ngkok, and London. But, nine storeys or ninety, it doesn't really matter to the [pe]destrian. Until he is knocked down and stares up from the stretcher, his streetscape [is] road, pavement, and the first two floors. He remembers buildings by name, [nu]mber, and any other graphic statement within his vision.

[Our] city areas are a mess of architectorialism, engineering, planning, and tycoonery. [Do]wn around street level designers, typographers, scribblers, shopkeepers, and [eve]n advertising men are welcome if they can keep the citizen's eye well away from discovering how much worse everything gets above his head, up there with the Builders of Our Time.

Until now, however, everything of any interest in this wide-open area of social uplift has been done by dead men or by amateurs or vandals or politicians or accident or neglect or dirty old men or the makers of big, busy neon signs. Architects and their clients spend their bit of culture-money on bad sculpture or crazy screens. They should be spending it on some happy way of showing how to get out again after you have managed to get in.

Altogether, the more we can read our buildings, the less we will twitch at the sight of them. The photographs on the following thirty-one pages were harvested on one trip round London. The things they show have very little to do with Design, apart from achieving its object. They show what weather, wit, accident, lack of judgement, bad taste, bad spelling, necessity, and good loud repetition can do to put a sort of music into the streets where we walk.

Bj
9/2/62

29

Repetition: the hardest, simplest way to sell. Just say it again and again and again and again and again.

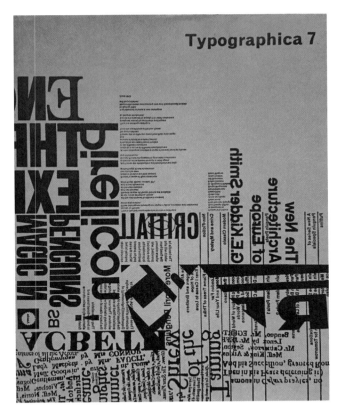

Typographica comprised two series, and the second, 1960–67, became more elaborate, incorporating wrap-around covers and different papers inside. The topics became more eclectic and their delivery more intuitive, one such example being a series of spreads showing manhole covers, not as photographs but rubbings, printed in black only on a softly textured earthen-coloured paper. This elemental treatment allowed the metal covers and their lettering to become isolated from the detritus that normally surrounds them, enabling the reader to appreciate the design of these robust but surprisingly exquisite and decorative objects. A reassessment of late Victorian design – everything modernists generally regarded with contempt or disgust – naturally followed. Nevertheless, through editorial juxtaposition, Spencer seemed to relish demonstrating that modernism, when stripped of its accompanying rhetoric (articles became

increasingly visual in the second series), was not as far removed from softer, more pliable and even unpredictable values of post-war romanticism as many liked to think.

While Spencer's *Typographica* remained quirky and unpredictable, the monthly journal *Design*, published from 1949 to 1999 by the Council of Industrial Design (CoID, renamed the Design Council in 1972), was on a mission. Its remit was to report on the design of consumer products, but from time to time this would include an aspect of typographic design – corporate signage on buildings, the design and display of packaging, or Royal Mail stamps, for example. *Design* frequently used the generic term 'good design', by which it meant 'modernist design'. The CoID was supported by funding from the government, and Britain was seeking entry to the European Common Market. The CoID's *raison d'être* was to improve the design standards of manufacturers and, at the same

Typographica 7
Series 2
Herbert Spencer,
designer and editor
May 1963

*Front cover and
page from Anthony
Robinson's article on
manhole covers.*

OPPOSITE
Typographica 4
Series 2
Herbert Spencer,
designer and editor
December 1961

*Front cover and
pages from Robert
Brownjohn's article
'Street Level'; this
copy with note on
tracing-paper overlay
from Brownjohn to
Dennis Bailey: 'Dear
Dennis, when in
Paris lay off the T
BJ 9/2/62'.*

The Council of Industrial Design

December 1959 No 132 Price 3s

time, inspire an 'improved level of taste' in consumers.

Design reported on new materials and manufacturing systems, and encouraged a less complex, more efficient use of traditional materials. The role of the designer was presented as akin to that of the engineer – the *éminence grise* of modernism, whose modest, analytical approach to problem-solving designers were persuaded to follow. The typography employed in the design of the journal's pages followed a similar path: modest, functional, transparent and rational (quite the opposite of, for example, *Typographica*'s presentation of the distinctly odd, emotive and ephemeral). Consequently, when *Design* reported on typography, it favoured quasi-scientific and civic-minded projects typified by the systematic approach of successful corporate-design manuals, road-signage systems and public information campaigns.

GRAPHIC DESIGN 4

HERBERT SPENCER

Of the many booklets, folders and leaflets which appear on the office desk or are pushed through the letter box each day, few are read thoroughly. The graphic designer has great opportunities for stimulating the reader's interest by lively and imaginative design

A substantial slice of the printing industry's annual turnover is represented by booklets, folders and leaflets, yet only a small part of this enormous output is read or even scanned. Unlike the poster, which today has usually an assured site and a fixed life-span, or the Press advertisement, which the buyer of a magazine or newspaper at least knowingly embraces, the booklet or leaflet often arrives unsolicited and indeed unwanted. Its fleeting life is a battle for survival. If its purpose is to persuade, then the design of the cover or front page must at once arrest attention and intrigue the reader. If its primary function is to provide information, then it must quickly and clearly announce its identity. In both cases the inside matter must be presented in a manner which is clear and efficient but not dull.

Few booklets or leaflets fall neatly into one category or the other; most occupy a position midway between the two extremes. Persuasive sales talk jostles with solid facts. And this provides the graphic designer with opportunities to evolve designs which are lively and imaginative in conception yet disciplined and sound in detail. Relatively few designs, it must be admitted, succeed on both scores. Those that do are invariably simple and dramatic in conception, bright (but not harsh) and emphatic, with typography which is clean, clear and unfussy.

Until quite recently the sales literature, catalogues, and instruction manuals put out by British manufacturers lagged sadly behind those of many of their foreign rivals. But, perhaps stimulated by increasingly keen Continental competition, Britain is today producing a rising flood of printed matter which is both well designed and editorially well conceived. British manufacturers and merchants seem at last to have grasped that cold facts and concise arguments, intelligently presented, serve their ends more effectively than frozen platitudes garnished with an indigestible sauce of visual gimmickry, indifferent photography, irrelevant illustration, and vulgar typography.

Visual and catalogue of service and repair kits. Clean, clear typography, simple and efficient diagrams and rational use of colour make this catalogue a first-rate example of what technical literature ought to look like. DESIGNERS *Richard Dupuis* (typography) and *François de Mauny* (symbols) of H. Hacker Design Group. PRINTER *H. Hacker Ltd.* PUBLISHER *Parts Division of Ford Motor Co Ltd.*

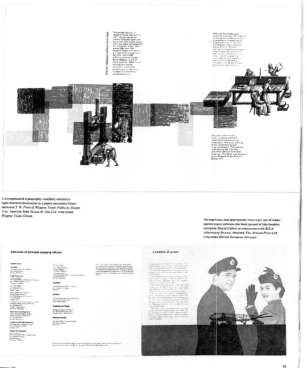

Uncomplicated typography carefully related to light-hearted decoration in a paper specimen folder. DESIGNER *J. R. Prost of Wiggins Teape Publicity Design Unit.* PRINTER *John Swain & Son Ltd.* PUBLISHER *Wiggins Teape Group.*

An ingenious and appropriate "two-way" use of transparent paper enlivens the final spread of this booklet. DESIGNERS *David Collins in conjunction with B.E.A Advertising Branch.* PRINTER *The Artisan Press Ltd.* PUBLISHER *British European Airways.*

Design no. 102
Council of Industrial
Design
Ken Garland,
art director
June 1957

Front cover.

Design no. 116
Council of Industrial
Design
Ken Garland,
art director
August 1958

Front cover.

OPPOSITE
Design no. 132
Council of Industrial
Design
Ken Garland,
art director
December 1959

*Front cover by Ernest
Hoch and spread
showing use of
colour, from an article
by Herbert Spencer.*

Design no. 171
Council of Industrial
Design
Ken Garland,
art director
March 1963

Front cover.

Typographische Monatsblätter
Cover designer unknown
No. 5/6
1938

TM RSI
Cover designer unknown
No. 11/12
1951

TM
Rudolf Hostettler, editor; Robert Büchler, designer; Emil Ruder, contributor and adviser
No. 4
April 1953

TM
Rudolf Hostettler, editor; Robert Büchler, designer; Emil Ruder, contributor and adviser
No. 2
February 1960

Front covers.

Ken Garland (1929–2021) became art director of *Design* in 1956, having spent eighteen months learning most of what there was to know about the technical side of publishing at *Furnishings* magazine straight after graduating from the Central School of Arts and Crafts (now part of the University of the Arts London). He would remain at *Design* until 1962, when he established Ken Garland & Associates.

In Garland's hands, the layout of *Design* became a sophisticated amalgam of cool restraint and playful agitation. Colour was rarely available for inside pages, but Garland's cover designs were an exceptionally seductive mix of play, planning and pleasure. Although an admirer of Swiss typography, he rejected its 'formulaic tendencies' and, despite pressure from fellow designers, did not resort to the use of a sans-serif typeface for text. In an article titled 'Structure and Substance' for *The Penrose Annual* in 1960 (vol. 54), Garland compared Swiss and American typographic design, specifically the work of Karl Gerstner (Swiss) and Saul Bass (American). He argued that British typography should take its cue from both – the reductive methodology and rational production values of Swiss design, and the freer, more playful approach of American designers – and, in this way, 'make the best of both of them'.[3]

Garland's description of the contrasting merits of European and American typographic design has substantial validity. Most of the important European design magazines established before 1939 – notably, in Germany, H.K. Frenzel's *Gebrauchsgraphik* and, in France, Charles Peignot's *Arts et métiers graphiques* – closed before or during the Second World War. The Swiss journal *Typographische Monatsblätter*, however, was an exception.

Typographische Monatsblätter was first published in 1933 by the Schweizerischer Typographenbund (Swiss Typographers' Association), Berne. The promotion of vocational training had always been a cornerstone of the Swiss book-printers' unions, together with a remarkable liberal attitude to working with designers – and this had also been the case with German print unions before 1933 (the year the Bauhaus was forcibly closed and the trade union movement was outlawed by the Nazi Party). *Typographische Monatsblätter* reflected this egalitarian approach. Its content was aimed at book printers, compositors, manual and machine typesetters, and especially young printers and typographic designers. Although its primary aim was to encourage a closer working relationship between independent typographers and the printing trade, the journal took great pains to promote education, and played an important role in the transmission of practical knowledge specific to the activities of the typographic designer. Methods of teaching specialized skills were conveyed through regular detailed displays of what was deemed to be sound practice and satisfactory outcomes. Technological progress – in terms of manufacturing processes of type and their implications for the printer – was a regular feature, and was often earnestly illustrated in diagrammatic form.

After the war, *Typographische Monatsblätter* incorporated two rival publications: *Revue suisse de l'imprimerie* (*RSI*) in 1948, followed at the end of 1951 by *Schweizer Graphische Mitteilungen* (*SGM*). Thereafter, the journal was known by the initials *TM*. The key figures were the editor from 1952 to 1981, Rudolf Hostettler, who had previously been co-editor of *SGM* alongside Hermann Strehler,[4] and the typographers Robert Büchler, who was designer of *TM*, and Emil Ruder, a regular contributor to *SGM* who became a leading influence at *TM*.

Ruder (1914–1970) grew up in Zurich and at the age of fifteen began a four-year compositor's apprenticeship in Basle. In the late 1930s he went to study in Paris,

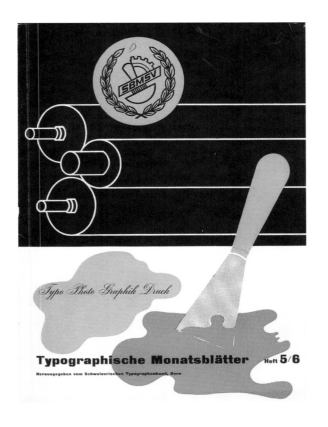

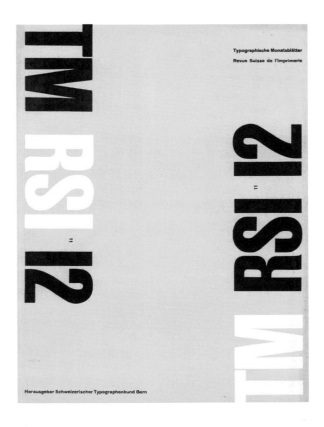

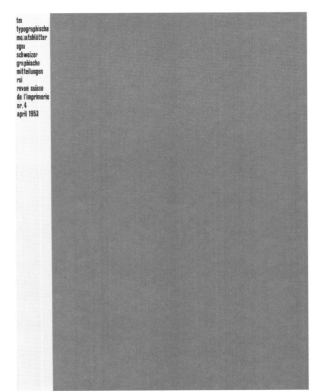

Neue Grafik 16
Josef Müller-Brockmann,
founder and co-editor
Carlo Vivarelli, cover designer
Hans Neuburg, layout designer
July 1963

Front cover and spread.

Neue Grafik
New Graphic Design
Graphisme actuel

Internationale Zeitschrift für Grafik
und verwandte Gebiete
Text dreisprachig
(deutsch, englisch, französisch)

International Review of Graphic
Design and related subjects
Issued in German, English and French

Revue internationale du graphisme et
des domaines annexes
Parution en langue allemande,
anglaise et française

16

Hans Neuburg, Zürich

Thomas Maldonado und Gui Bon-
siepe, Ulm
Peter Mächler, St. Gallen
Richard P. Lohse, Zürich

Georg Radanowicz, Zürich

Margit Staber, Zürich

Peter Lehner, Bern
LMNV

Richard P. Lohse, Zürich

Margit Staber, Zürich

Ausgabe Juli 1963
Inhalt
Schweizer Plakate der letzten vier
Jahre
Ein Zeichensystem für elektro-
medizinische Geräte
Fortschrittliche Wahlpropaganda
Werbung für eine Londoner Möbel-
firma
Arbeiten von Robert Praed
Reine Foto-Grafik
Fotoklasse der Kunstgewerbeschule
Zürich
Ausstellung für Asbeströhren (Eternit)
von Max Bill
SWB Form Forum 1962
Braun-Ausstellungsstände

Buchschutzumschläge aus den
dreißiger Jahren
Ein Maler als eigener Plakatgrafiker

Issue for July 1963
Contents
Swiss Posters of the past four years

A Sign System for Electromedica
Instruments
Progressive Elections Notices
Publicity for a London Firm of
Furniture

Pure Photo-Graphic Design
Photo-graphic class of the Kunstgewerbeschule
Zürich
Exhibition of Asbestos Pipes

SWB Design Forum 1962
Permanent Braun Pavilion
on an Exhibition Site
Book jackets of the Thirties

A Painter is his own Graphic
Designer

Juillet 1963
Table des matières
Affiches suisses des quatre années
écoulées
Un système de signes pour appareils
électromédicaux
Propagande électorale d'avant-garde
Publicité pour une maison
d'ameublement londonienne

Photo-graphisme pur

L'exposition des tubes de ciment
d'amiante
Forum 1962 de la forme ASAI
Pavillon Braun permanent
sur l'esplanade d'une foire
Couvertures de protection
des années trente
Un peintre-graphiste

Einzelnummer Fr. 15.–

Single number Fr. 15.–

Le numéro Fr. 15.–

Herausgeber und Redaktion
Editors and Managing Editors
Éditeurs et rédaction

Druck/Verlag
Printing/Publishing
Imprimerie/Édition

Richard P. Lohse SWB/VSG, Zürich
J. Müller-Brockmann SWB/VSG, Zürich
Hans Neuburg SWB/VSG, Zürich
Carlo L. Vivarelli SWB/VSG, Zürich

Walter-Verlag AG, Olten
Schweiz/Switzerland/Suisse

---

before returning to Zurich to attend the Kunstgewerbeschule during 1941–42. It was there that Ruder discovered Jan Tschichold's New Typography and the design principles of Bauhaus.

Ruder's work in *TM* exemplifies the restraint to which Ken Garland was referring when comparing European and American typographic design. Ruder, along with Armin Hofmann, Karl Gerstner, Herbert Matter, Max Bill, Carlo Vivarelli, Josef Müller-Brockmann and others, came to exemplify the Swiss design style of the 1950s and '60s. In his 1967 book *Typographie*, Ruder explained that 'Typography has one plain duty before it and that is to convey information in writing. No argument or consideration can absolve typography from this duty. A printed work which cannot be read becomes a product without purpose.'[5] Ruder's typography, and indeed the Swiss International Style in general, are characterized by the use of a simple and clearly defined grid structure, asymmetrical layouts and sans-serif typefaces limited to lower case, and often include geometric

---

58

**A Painter Who Is
His Own Graphic Designer**
Margit Staber, Zurich

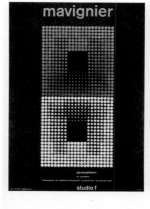

As a painter Almir Mavignier belongs to the group of constructivist artists who are loosely bound together by similar interests and who by employing more or less objective methods have made structure such the purpose and vehicle of the design. They include Heinz Mack and Otto Piene in Germany; François Morellet in France, and Piero Dorazio in Italy. Mavignier came to Europe from Brazil in 1951, studied from 1953–1958 in the department for visual communication at the Ulm School of Design and then settled in Ulm. During this '"European decade"' Mavignier worked predominantly with dot structures and within this restricted technique pursued a kind of basic research. Mavignier describes the field in which he is working in the following way: 'I created my first dot pictures in 1953, basing them on an idea of Klee's—where two lines meet there occurs a dot or point of energy containing the action of the one against the other. Basic course of instruction Frau Nonne-Schmidt, School of Design.' The colour sequence followed the dot concentration – optical deformation of geometric shapes through the progression of dots – contrast of tachist structures by direction and limitation – merging colours – separated colours.' Mavignier regards Josef Albers and Max Bill as his principal masters. As a graphic artist he designed the posters for all his own recent exhibitions. Mavignier incorporated the elements of his painting in a logical manner in all these posters, a process to which constructivist painting is peculiarly suited and which is perhaps only legitimate with this kind of painting. It has nothing to do with the reproduction of a picture on a poster. In these image-making processes Mavignier is concerned with the organization of like elements in the flat, and thus with the resolution of the problem of colour. With painting this kind of organization leads to visual autonomy while in poster design it assumes the character of something which can be visually reproduced: it becomes informative about art by representing the definitive fragments of this art. The dividing lines, it is true, sometimes approach dangerously near to one another in an experiment in which secondary creative effects are provoked by their own creator.

Un peintre-graphiste
Margit Staber, Zurich

En sa qualité de peintre, Almir Mavignier appartient au groupe des peintres structuraux, donc d'artistes que réunissent des intentions similaires et qui, au moyen de méthodes plus ou moins objectives, ont érigé la structure en tant que telle au rang de moyen et de but de leur effort créateur; citons dans ce sens en Allemagne Heinz Mack et Otto Piene, en France François Morellet et en Italie Piero Dorazio. Originaire du Brésil, Mavignier vint en Europe en 1951 et étudia à la section «Communication visuelle» de l'École supérieure des arts graphiques à Ulm de 1953 à 1958. Depuis, l'artiste a élu domicile à Ulm. Au cours de cette «décade européenne» le peintre Mavignier a travaillé avant tout avec des structures ponctuées et, dans le cadre de cette thématique, à procédé à une sorte de recherche sur les fondements. Esquissant le champ de son activité, Mavignier écrit: «1953, première image constituée de points, d'après une idée de Klee – la rencontre de deux lignes crée un point, un point d'énergie, qui renferme l'action d'une ligne contre l'autre (1er cours élémentaire Madame Nonne-Schmidt, École supérieure des arts graphiques). Développement coloré par concentration ponctuelle – déformation visuelle d'objets géométriques par progression d'un point – contrôle de structures «tachistes» par la direction et la délimitation – scintillement de couleurs – points plastiques – points lumineux – mélange de couleurs – séparation des couleurs.» Mavignier considère avant tout Josef Albers et Max Bill comme ses maîtres. Mais il n'est pas seulement peintre, il est également graphiste. Comme graphiste il a créé lui-même les affiches pour ses expositions des dernières années. Ces affiches sont une mise en application graphique conséquente d'éléments de sa peinture structurale, un procédé qui n'est probablement justifié que dans ce cas précis et qui n'a rien à voir avec la reproduction d'une image sur une affiche.

La préoccupation essentielle de Mavignier consiste dans l'arrangement d'éléments semblables sur une surface donnée, donc dans la résolution de problèmes de couleurs.

Dans sa peinture, cette organisation aboutit à l'autonomie visuelle alors que dans la conception de ses affiches elle prend le caractère d'aspect visuel susceptible d'être reproduit; elle devient informatrice sur l'art par la représentation des moments qui déterminent cet art. Il est vrai que parfois les lignes de partage se rapprochent dangereusement; mais l'artiste créateur tait cette expérience dans laquelle il provoque sciemment la manifestation des effets secondaires de son œuvre de création.

Offset
J.C.
Müller
AG.

Plakate
Prospekte
Etiketten
jedes Format
jede Auflage
jede Farbe

hergestellt
mit den neuesten
Offsetmaschinen

Zürich 8
Seefeldstrasse 111
Telephon
051/24 47 77

---

elements. Equally impressive were the unflinching confidence and veracity of Swiss typographers when conveying the value of their work to the reader.

Neue Grafik was initiated by Müller-Brockmann in 1958. It described itself as an 'International review of graphic design and related subjects', although there was very little 'international' content. It did, however, effectively present Swiss typographic design as an international authority (the text was set in three languages). It was published in eighteen issues, the last appearing in 1965, by an editorial collective consisting of Müller-Brockmann, Richard P. Lohse, Hans Neuburg and Carlo Vivarelli. The severely simple design of the cover of the first issue, set in Univers by Vivarelli, was maintained throughout the journal's existence, and came to represent the mature face of the Swiss International Style. The four columns depicted on the cover precisely reflected the gridded internal layouts designed by Neuburg.

Despite its celebrated design merits, *Neue Grafik* did not carry the broader cultural weight of *TM* (which finally closed in 2014). The distinguished typographer Helmut Schmid described *Neue Grafik* as being concerned primarily with promoting Swiss typographers and typography, whereas '*TM* was basically an educational magazine for young typesetters, printers, and apprentices. It was not only about typography, it was also about printing techniques, book binding … The *Neue Grafik* … was a promotional magazine for Zurich designers, in my opinion.'[6]

In North America the first magazine to focus on graphic design was *Print* in 1940, describing itself as 'A Quarterly Journal of the Graphic Arts'. However, the first issue, rather boldly, did not include a title or any other information on its front cover, just inky fingerprints (designed by Howard Trafton). Until 1953 there remained no fixed masthead

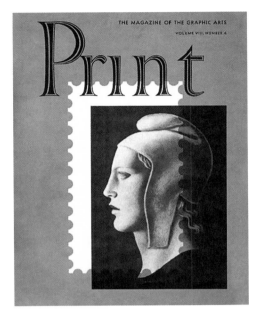

Print
Leo Lionni, art director and co-editor
Vol. VIII, no. 6
1954

Front cover. Lionni's masthead is a variation of Chisel.

Chisel
Robert Harling
1939

Sample.

Gebrauchsgraphik International Advertising Art Juli 1966 B 3149 E

design, thus its cover designers had maximum creative freedom. *Print*'s first established masthead was credited to Leo Lionni, who was art director and co-editor of the journal as well as art director of *Fortune*. He amended a typeface called Chisel, designed by Robert Harling. From its inception until the end of 1973, *Print* was, like its Swiss counterparts, set in metal type, using Caledonia for text and Bulmer for titles.

The German journal *Gebrauchsgraphik*, which had closed in 1944, was relaunched by Eberhard Hölscher in Munich in 1950. As its title ('Commercial graphics') suggests, *Gebrauchsgraphik* covered advertising and graphic design. Although typography was a consistent presence, it was not often discussed in detail.

The relaunch of *Gebrauchsgraphik* may have been encouraged by the remarkable success of *Graphis*, a Swiss bi-monthly journal established in 1944 by Walter Herdeg. The fact that its text was in English, French and German meant that *Graphis* was truly international in content, and it became a presence in every art-college library across America, Europe and the UK. For the most part, the content consisted of portfolios showcasing current designers, with reports of developments from major centres around the world. The covers of *Graphis* generally displayed the predominant illustrative style of German and Swiss graphic design: loose, garish and vaguely cartoonish in nature – the antithesis of the contemporaneous Swiss International Style.

LEFT, TOP
Gebrauchsgraphik
Eberhard Hölscher,
editor
No. 5
May 1958

*Front cover by
Pino Tovaglia.*

LEFT
Gebrauchsgraphik
Eberhard Hölscher,
editor
No. 7
July 1966

*Front cover (designer
unknown).*

graphic art; advertising art; applied art
freie graphik; gebrauchsgraphik; angewandte kunst
arts graphiques; arts appliqués; publicité

Alan Fletcher

Graphis 92
Walter Herdeg,
editor
November/
December 1960

*Front cover by
Alan Fletcher.*

Métro DUPLEIX
LA MOTTE-PIC

Cours : JOUR - SOIR (

BIEN

M^r ET
Professe
2 fois 2^e

TOUTES les

Leçons tous les jours de

127, Rue de
Métro : POMPE-VICTOR-HU

Méthode facile et rapide

ARS   N
PAVILLON
Métro

RS   NUIT
PAVILLON D'
Métro : POR

RS   NUIT
PAVILLON D
Métro : PO

L SIM
ASSE

Kunstgewerbemuseum Zürich
Ausstellung

deFilm

10. Januar bis 30. April 1960

Offen: Montag 14-18, 20-22
Dienstag-Freitag 10-12, 14-18, 20-22
Samstag-Sonntag 10-12, 14-17

POSTERS

During the Second World War consumer advertising was radically cut, while paper rationing and a reduction in printing facilities meant that the production of books and magazines was adversely affected or even curtailed. The only field that was protected, and indeed thrived, was poster design. Distinguished, even iconic, work was produced in every war-torn country, although it could be argued that much of what was achieved was built on the pioneering work of the 1930s. What distinguished posters designed between 1939 and 1945 was their purpose: they were less about persuading people what to buy and more about what to do – or not do. The need to inform gave poster designers a new identity, direction and elevated status, while their posters were required to communicate in a way that was decisive and unambiguous.

Such an approach was encapsulated in the extraordinary airbrush skills of Abram Games (1914–1996), who was appointed Official War Poster Designer in 1942 and produced around 100 educational and instructional wartime posters by 1946. After the war, Games resumed his freelance practice and broadened his output, creating advertising campaigns for the British Overseas Airways Corporation (BOAC), British European Airways (BEA) and Guinness, and covers for Penguin Books. Two other influential poster designers in the UK during the war were Hans Schleger (aka Zéró, who had emigrated to London from Germany in the 1930s) and Tom Eckersley (1914–1997). After 1945 Schleger, like Games, gave more attention to corporate identity and advertising, but Eckersley, influenced by A.M. Cassandre and Edward McKnight Kauffer, continued to concentrate on posters and in the late 1940s and the 1950s emerged as one of the foremost international poster designers. Perhaps his most memorable work was for the Royal Society for the Prevention of Accidents (RoSPA), but his extensive list of clients included the United Nations Children's Fund and the World Wide Fund for Nature.

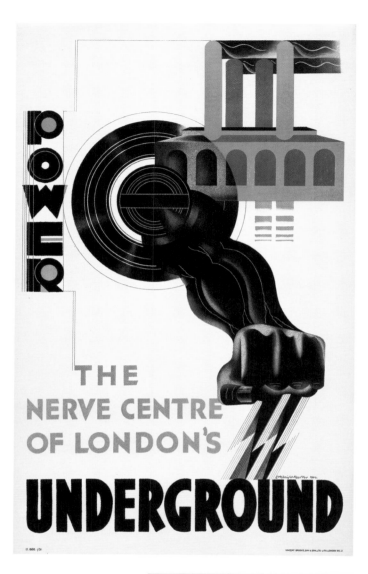

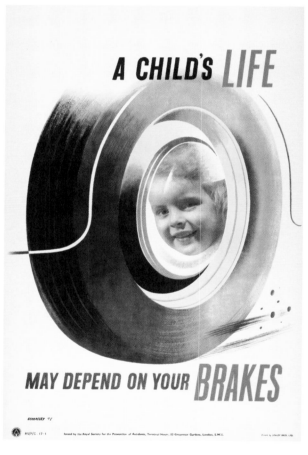

Edward McKnight Kauffer
Power, the Nerve Centre of London's Underground
1930

For the Underground Electric Railways Company of London.

Tom Eckersley
A Child's Life May Depend on Your Brakes
1948

For the Royal Society for the Prevention of Accidents.

Hans Schleger (Zéró)
Hands at Your Service (Ticket Collector)
1946

For the London Passenger Transport Board.

Alan Fletcher
Pirelli Tyres
1961

Fletcher spent a brief period working in the Pirelli design studio in Milan before returning to London to establish Fletcher/ Forbes/Gill.

Dennis Bailey
Architecture Today
1961

For an exhibition at the Arts Council Gallery, London.

architecture
today

an exhibition arranged jointly by
the Arts Council and the
Royal Institute of British Architects

Arts Council Gallery   28 June - 29 July 1961
4 St James's Square London SW1   Mondays, Wednesdays, Fridays,
                                 Saturdays: 10 am - 6 pm
                                 Tuesdays, Thursdays: 10 am - 8 pm

                                 admission 1s 6d

Romek Marber
The Moving Earth
1964

For the London Planetarium.

He also designed posters for domestic British organizations, such as the Imperial War Museum, situated around the corner from the London College of Printing (now the London College of Communication), where he taught from 1954 to 1977.

Any commission to design a poster remained highly prized among typographers and graphic designers. A poster requires no purchase or other physical interaction in order to function, which makes it a particularly attractive though demanding medium. The fact that it can be taken down and reused – even framed and hung on a wall – is also a significant factor in its appeal.

The broad appreciation and popularity of poster design (often referred to as 'poster art') had encouraged the appearance of specialist magazines, especially during the early decades of the twentieth century. In Switzerland, a federal annual national poster award was established in late 1941 and launched the following year. By February 1943, a total of 159 posters had been evaluated and reduced to the twenty-four 'Best Posters of the Year 1942'. The winners were announced in the daily newspaper *Neue Zürcher Zeitung* and displayed in popular public places in cities across Switzerland. In subsequent years, the number of entries increased and a brochure listing the winners alongside images of their work was published; the brochure also featured a commentary on the year's poster production. The text included criticism as well as praise, and often offered direct advice for improvement.

The remarkable level of interest in poster art during the 1940s culminated in 1949 with the appearance of the *International Poster Annual*, published by Zollikofer of St Gallen, Switzerland. The first four issues were published in consecutive years, their appearance much anticipated. Inclusion was

Die besten Plakate 1943 *(The best posters of 1943) exhibition in Basle.*

International Poster Annual '48–'49
W.H. Allner, editor and designer
Zollikofer
1949

Front of jacket of the first issue of the International Poster Annual, *the only book devoted to contemporary poster design. Text and captions in English, French and German.*

considered a gauge of a nation's global status in graphic design and advertising. Designed and edited by W.H. Allner under the art direction of A.M. Cassandre, the annuals initially contained work from fifteen or more countries, with text and captions in French, English and German. Not surprisingly, Swiss posters were particularly well represented.

The aim of posters was to provide unambiguous clarity in communication. In Switzerland, and earlier in Germany, clarity was equated with a super-realistic style of illustration and the rejection of all superfluous (or 'ornamental') material, even lettering where possible. Designers such as Herbert Leupin, Peter Birkhäuser and Otto Baumberger designed posters that depicted everyday products in spectacular detail, aided by the excellence of Swiss printing, to create stunning *trompe l'œil* effects. The heightened sense of objective reality – described at the time as 'magic realism'[1] – represented in these

RIGHT, TOP
Otto Baumberger
Marque PKZ
1923

For the Swiss clothing company PKZ. The ultimate 'object poster', requiring no additional text to explain or extol the product's qualities.

RIGHT
Peter Birkhäuser
Bata Shoes
1947

Birkhäuser achieved a clarity of image far superior to what could be done photographically. It was described as 'magic realism'.

RIGHT
Herbert Leupin
Bell
1939

In true 'object poster' style, Leupin avoided adding text to the poster by inscribing the name of the meat company Bell on the chopping board. The resulting demand for Bell-branded chopping boards sealed the poster's success, and others followed.

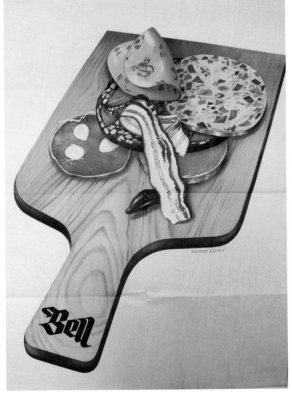

Herbert Matter
Schweiz –
Winterferien –
doppelte Ferien
(Switzerland – winter
vacations)
1934

For the Swiss Tourist
Office.

'object posters' gave them immense visual power, and the fact that they were hand-drawn added another level of fascination. They were created by drawing directly on to lithographic stones – the culmination of a traditional process that became commercially obsolete in the 1950s with the manufacture of lightweight metallic lithographic plates. The quality of Swiss translucent printing inks enabled the designer to build up images and lettering by overprinting an unlimited number of colours. The use of pens, crayons and brushes to apply an oil-based inky substance on to the stones (the artwork for each colour had to be applied to a different stone) offered a much subtler range of possibilities than those that could be achieved at the time by printing from line or half-tone blocks. A virtuoso level of technical skill was required to achieve such results. Ironically, it was these same skills that became the prime target for criticism. The suggestion by modernist designers, also described as 'avantgardists' in Switzerland, was that the sheer brilliance of the technical skills displayed by 'magic realist' artists had become the subject of the poster – to the detriment of the product that it depicted.

The change in direction was most dramatically announced by posters designed by Herbert Matter for the Swiss Tourist Office in the mid-1930s. This range of posters changed perceptions of both printing and graphic design through the subtlety of Matter's sophisticated juxtaposition of photographic images and minimal use of typography. Although Matter left to work in the United States in 1936, Josef Müller-Brockmann (1914–1996), Armin Hofmann, Emil Ruder and others continued to develop what became known as the Swiss International Style – epitomized by Müller-Brockmann's series of posters begun in 1950 for the Zurich Tonhalle.

The preferred typeface was a neutral sans serif. Paul Renner's 'mechanistic' Futura and Eric Gill's 'humanistic' Gill Sans were

Emil Ruder
Die Zeitung
(The newspaper)
1958

*For an
exhibition at the
Gewerbemuseum,
Basle. The coarse
half-tone and large
'headline' letter
Z replicate the
characteristics of
newspapers at that
time.*

Gewerbemuseum Basel
Ausstellung «die Zeitung»
9. April bis 18. Mai 1958
Geöffnet
werktags 10-12 und 14-18
sonntags 10-12 und 14-17
Eintritt frei

die
Zeitung

Gewerbemuseum Basel

Ausstellung

Das Holz als Baustoff

6. September bis 5. Oktober

Täglich geöffnet:

10 bis 12 und 14 bis 18 Uhr

Eintritt frei

**Josef Müller-
Brockmann**
Musica Viva
1959

*For a concert at the
Tonhalle, Zurich.
The typography
represents the
orchestra and the
abstract forms the
music.*

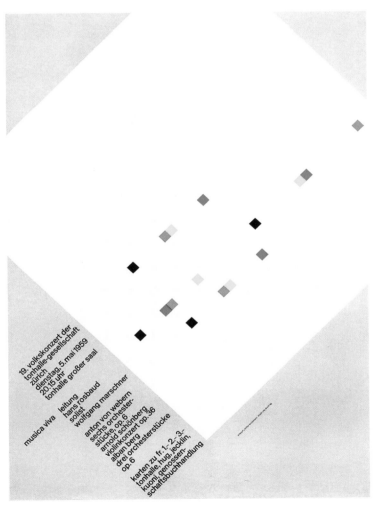

19. volkskonzert der
tonhalle-gesellschaft
zürich
dienstag, 5. mai 1959
20.15 uhr
tonhalle großer saal

musica viva   leitung
hans rosbaud
solist
wolfgang marschner
anton von webern
sechs orchester-
stücke, op. 6
arnold schönberg
violinkonzert op. 36
alban berg
drei orchesterstücke
op. 6

karten zu fr. 1.– 2.– 3.–
tonhalle, hug, jecklin,
kuoni, genossen-
schaftsbuchhandlung

Armin Hofmann
Das Holz als Baustoff
(Wood as a building
material)
1952

*For an
exhibition at the
Gewerbemuseum,
Basle.*

rejected as too distinctive and therefore distracting. The preferred typeface was Akzidenz-Grotesk (released in 1896 by the Berthold type foundry) until the appearance in 1957 of Univers and Neue Haas Grotesk – both of which later came to epitomize the visual clarity that was the hallmark of the Swiss poster. Using Akzidenz-Grotesk in combination with an elementary grid, it was possible to create a unified design that, so it was argued, placed the focus of the poster on its content – the product or service – not the designer.

The result was a strictly codified approach that was instantly recognizable and quickly adopted in many parts of the world to create a genuine International Style. However, outside Switzerland its interpretation tended to be less restrained, more exuberant and, overall, distinctly celebratory as the 1950s dawned and normality returned to everyday life. A more positive outlook began to emerge as long-planned rebuilding programmes were implemented, and many designers sought to express this optimism in their work.

From 1946 Milan became an attractive destination for Swiss graphic designers, perhaps because they felt less inhibited outside their home country. Most stayed there only briefly, but as the Italian economy improved and design became increasingly important within Italian culture, several Swiss designers made the city their home. Max Huber (1919–1992), having trained in metropolitan Zurich (where he met Max Bill and Müller-Brockmann), had spent a short period in Milan before the war and returned to live there permanently in October 1945, running his own design practice and accepting commissions from the prestigious Studio Boggeri and many others. Other influential Swiss designers, such as Carlo Vivarelli, Massimo Vignelli and Walter Ballmer, would also work at Boggeri at various times.

OPPOSITE
Max Bill
USA baut (USA builds)
1945

For an exhibition on American architecture and engineering at the Kunstgewerbemuseum, Zurich.

Ezio Bonini and Max Huber
Sirenella
1946

Sirenella was a restaurant in Milan with live music and a large dance floor.

Hans Neuburg
Konstruktive Grafik
1958

For an exhibition of works by Richard P. Lohse, Hans Neuburg and Carlo L. Vivarelli at the Kunstgewerbemuseum, Zurich.

Max Bill (1908–1994) was a huge influence on Huber. Bill had been a student at the Bauhaus in Dessau, where he was taught by Wassily Kandinsky and Paul Klee. He established the Allianz group, a collection of Swiss artists who advocated the Concrete art theories of the Dutch artist and designer Theo van Doesburg. In essence, Concrete art contains no spatial, figurative or symbolic references and, as a result, is generally restricted to geometric forms and patterns; it is also often described as geometric abstraction. The intention was to create an independent and self-contained form of art, one that focused exclusively on itself. By the 1950s, Concrete art had become an internationally recognized movement across Europe, Britain and, before the end of the decade, Latin America. Huber joined the Allianz group in 1942 and exhibited paintings with them. Other designers, including Müller-Brockmann, Vivarelli, Richard P. Lohse and Hans Neuburg, were deeply influenced by Bill's theories regarding objective form and, just as importantly, its clarity.

While the intention of Concrete art was to create a painting or sculpture whose only reference was to itself, a poster had to refer to something else, whether a product, service or event. When Müller-Brockmann made use of the same elemental 'Concrete' forms in his posters for the concert hall in Zurich (which later became known as the 'Tonhalle Series' or 'Musica Viva'), they were accompanied by text describing a specific composer and the music to be played. Inevitably, this text instilled the accompanying forms with emotive signification, evoking the spirit of the music in the viewers' minds. It was the viewers and their act of participation that effectively provided the final, highly potent statement.

By the end of the 1950s, prompted by criticism from Vivarelli for his continued reliance on geometric form,[2] Müller-Brockmann began designing posters using only sans-serif type. He used the placement, size and weight of type to achieve the same effect as his previous work. The best of these, *Der Film*, for the Kunstgewerbemuseum in Zurich in 1960 (p. 64), encapsulates what film is, means and creates, without recourse to anything other than the exhibition's title, which is set in Akzidenz-Grotesk.

Unlike many of his contemporaries, Müller-Brockmann never lived outside Switzerland but, after serving as professor of graphic design at the Kunstgewerbeschule in Zurich from 1957 to 1960, he became guest lecturer at Max Bill's Hochschule für Gestaltung in Ulm, south-western Germany, from 1963. He was also the author of several important books on typographic design, and in 1958 he was the initiator and co-editor of the journal *Neue Grafik*. Through these publishing activities Müller-Brockmann became the leading exponent of the Swiss International Style. He remained remarkably close to the tenets of Bill's Allianz group, although he was never a member and indeed dismissed any attempt to link himself or his work with that of the artist, explaining, 'as a result of my ruthless self-critical analysis I saw that I possessed no essential artistic talent beyond the ordinary, and the creativity of a mediocre person is of no general interest. You can't learn to become an artist, but you can learn to become a useful graphic artist.'[3] Others, Huber included, were less reticent.

In Milan, Huber undertook a broad range of work: he was appointed creative director of the Giulio Einaudi publishing company, in addition to designing advertising campaigns and large-scale corporate-identity programmes. But it was his poster work – the best known being the posters for the Grand Prix at the Autodromo Nazionale Monza from 1948 – that became emblematic of an exuberant positivity for everything modern. Milanese modern typography, especially that used on posters, was recognized as breaking

Max Huber
Gran premio dell'Autodromo
1948

For the Monza Grand Prix.

**Henryk
Tomaszewski**
Obywatel Kane
(*Citizen Kane*)
1948

*For the film's Polish
release.*

new ground, and the general graphics journal *Graphis* (see pp. 60–61) offered Huber, and Italian graphic design generally, an international audience – notwithstanding that the publication was only in black and white. No audience was more attentive than that in North America, where *Graphis* was influential in encouraging the crucial shift in creative power within the advertising industry from copywriters to art directors.

Geographically close but politically beyond reach, designers in post-1945 Poland, now under the control of the USSR, were impeded by what were intended to be impenetrable ideological strictures. Commercial advertising, the mainstay of poster designers, had been removed from all aspects of public life because, so it was argued, it facilitated what was newly defined as a degenerate form of consumerism. Cultural events, however, were exempt from such strictures, so short-run film, theatre, music and circus posters were able to thrive, despite censorship.

Censorship required that poster designs be vetted before going into production, so designers had to ensure that any political comment that might be construed as critical of the state was hidden under a cover of artifice (the same applied to music composers, authors and theatre directors). The idea of a poster having a secondary, ulterior meaning added considerably to public interest in the medium, and the fact that posters were freely displayed on abundant stretches of wooden boardings surrounding derelict buildings was an intriguing bonus. While restrictions on the activities of art galleries were rigorously imposed, artists discovered that posters offered an alternative creative outlet as well as the possibility of an income. Thus, many Polish painters, and also those originally trained as designers and architects, began to focus on poster design.

Henryk Tomaszewski
Czarny narcyz (Black
Narcissus)
1948

*For the film's Polish
release.*

Waldemar Świerzy
*Bulwar zachodzącego
słońca* (Sunset
Boulevard)
1957

*For the film's Polish
release.*

Jan Młodożeniec
*Szajka z
lawendowego
wzgórza* (The
Lavender Hill Mob)
1956

*For the film's Polish
release.*

**Franciszek
Starowieyski**
Upał (Heat)
1964

Film poster.

Roman Cieślewicz
Cyrke (Circus)
1962

Circus poster.

Roman Cieślewicz
Lecą żurawie (The
cranes are flying)
1957

Film poster.

Technical challenges also played a part. The relatively primitive state of printing precluded the conventional use of photographs, so the artists (in Poland, poster designers were always referred to as 'artists') were obliged to find alternative ways to present images. Isolation from artistic currents in the West was in many ways an advantage, allowing Polish artists to establish their own working methods, which, in turn, meant that the appearance of the Polish poster remained idiosyncratic, entertaining and constantly surprising. Joseph Stalin's death in 1953 brought a more liberal faction of Polish communists into power, and beneficial social reforms were instituted, but poor governance impaired the potential for economic growth over the following decade. For the general public, posters continued to represent the preservation and encouragement of cultural life through the difficulties of the 1950s.

Henryk Tomaszewski (1914–2005) designed posters for theatres and circuses, but most importantly for the state-run film-distribution agency. He became responsible for negotiations between the agency and the Ministry of Culture, and argued for an easing of restrictions on the artists' means of expression. It was agreed that, while censorship of content would remain in place, greater freedom in matters of style – for example, a less 'realistic' depiction of people, objects and/or their juxtaposition – would be permitted. As a result, Polish poster artists, notably Roman Cieślewicz (who later became art director of *Elle* magazine in Paris), Jan Młodożeniec, Franciszek Starowieyski and Waldemar Świerzy, were allowed to introduce a new, strikingly inventive and intriguingly abstract sensibility – one more akin to the kind of design that appeared in the West on book covers – to provide a more intimate, more reductive presentation. The intelligent use of irony, sarcasm, visual metaphor, 'hidden' meanings and symbolism was greatly admired at the beginning of the 1960s by a new

Atelier Populaire
Université Populaire:
Oui
1968

The initial idea was to sell posters to support the student protests in Paris. But the students themselves grabbed the posters and began pasting them up on the street. The purpose was changed, and production radically increased.

Saul Bass
Vertigo
1958

Film poster.

generation of designers who were growing tired of modernist imperiousness. (Polish posters for films made in the West have additional attraction and curiosity because they can be compared with their original, distinctly more commercial and generally less contemplative versions.)

The 1960s were a decade not only of increased consumer spending but also of consumer criticism, cultural pessimism and scepticism towards commercialization, mass culture and the cultural industry. The art of the Polish poster was perceived across Europe, Britain and America as a positive counter-image to the growth of what many were beginning to consider the insidious self-aggrandizement of corporate design. In the United States, this questioning of attitudes, particularly of the idealized portrayal of 'Post-war America', contributed to the rise of the countercultural movement in the 1960s and was epitomized by the work of Push Pin Studios. Push Pin was set up in New York in 1954 by Seymour Chwast, Milton Glaser and Edward Sorel. Their eclectic approach – reinterpreting historical styles, utilizing popular culture and celebrating the vernacular peculiarities of everyday city life – would later be called postmodernist. Although Glaser was the most prolific poster designer, Chwast's anti-war poster *End Bad Breath* (1967) perfectly encapsulates the less formal, more colloquial influences of American visual culture as it drew away from the Swiss International Style.

Capable of communicating without recourse to language, Polish poster work – and undoubtedly the work of Push Pin Studios too – directly influenced the artists of the Atelier Populaire, whose political posters supported the student riots in Paris in 1968.

Seymour Chwast
Push Pin Studios
End Bad Breath
1967

*Created in response
to the US bombing
of Hanoi during the
Vietnam War.*

Milton Glaser
Push Pin Studios
Mahalia Jackson
1967

*For an Easter Sunday
concert at the Lincoln
Center, New York.*

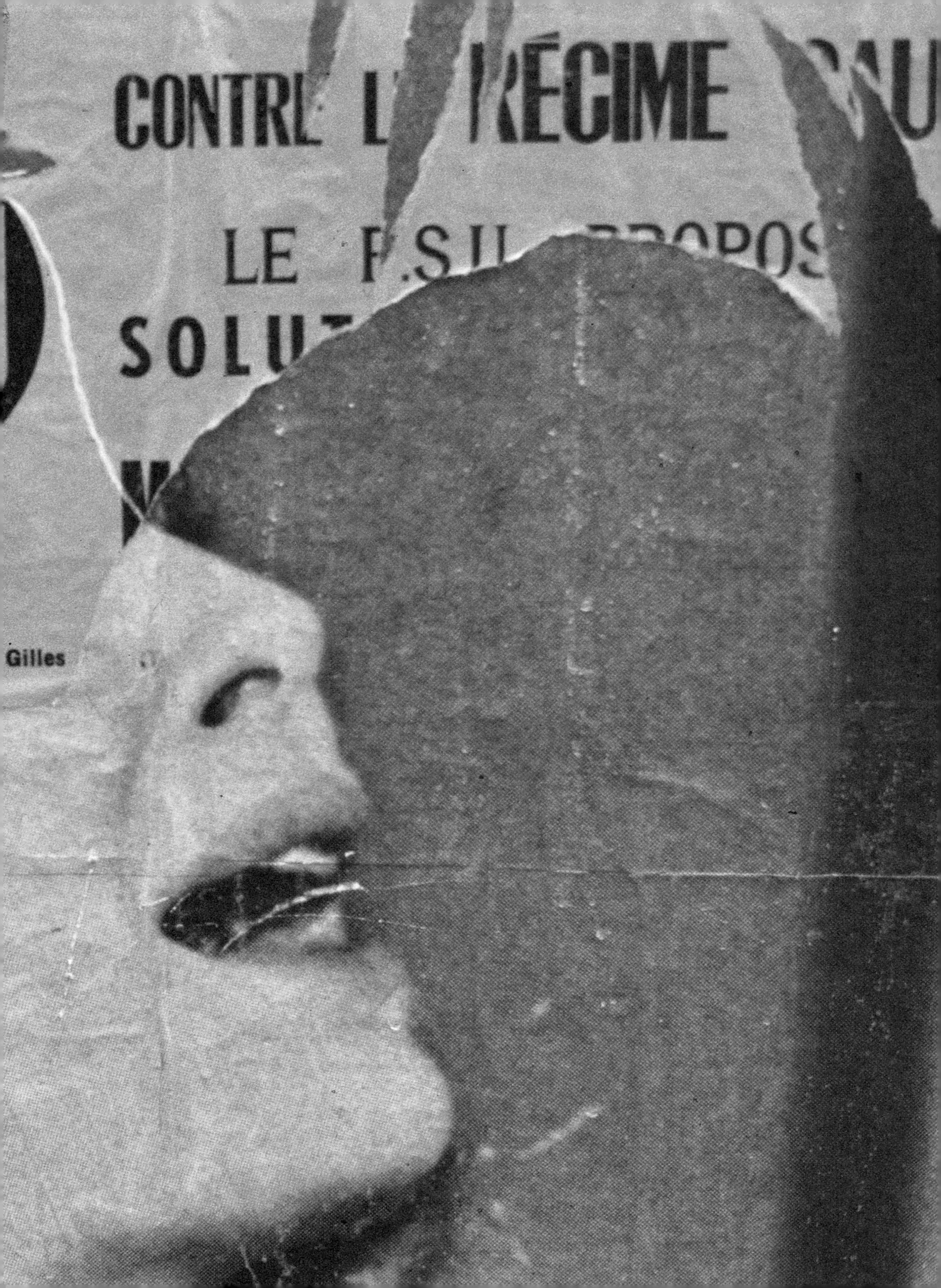

CONTRE LE RÉGIME

LE P.S.U. PROPOS

SOLU

Gilles

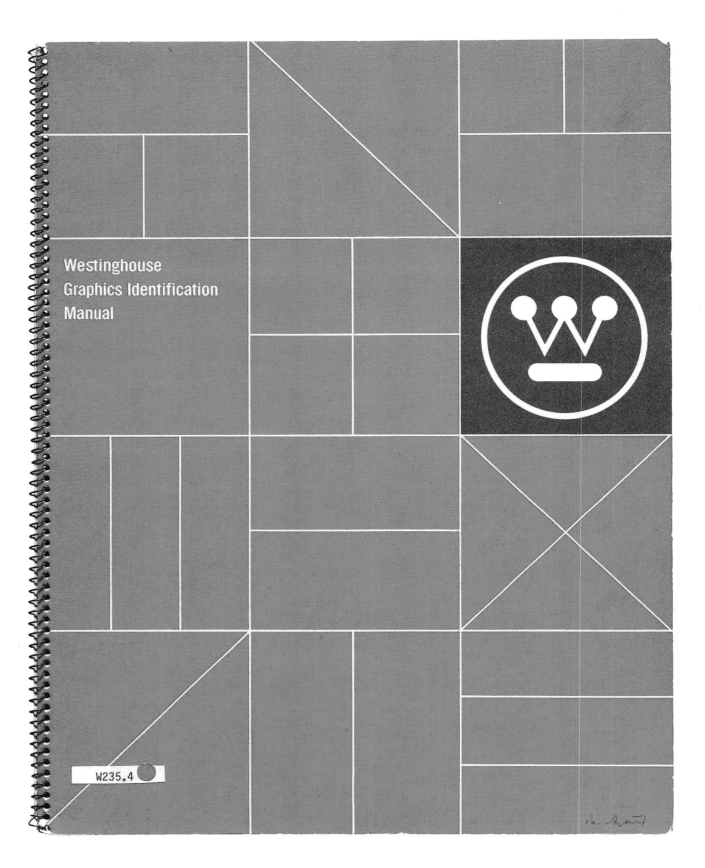

Westinghouse
Graphics Identification
Manual

W235.4

CORPORATE IDENTITY

The earliest corporate identities are generally considered to be Henry van de Velde's work for the food manufacturer Tropon in the 1890s. From 1907 Peter Behrens was designing everything for the Allgemeine Elektricitäts-Gesellschaft (AEG), including products, notepaper and even the company building. F.H.K. Henrion could claim to have been one of the first (certainly the first in Britain) to carry out a corporate communications programme of any size in the modern (post-war) era. It was created in 1952 for Fisons, a firm that would grow to become a multinational pharmaceutical company. Henrion's solution was thorough but also audacious, requiring the company's vehicles to be painted green on one side and cream on the other.

Henrion (1914–1990) was born in Nuremberg, and worked briefly in Paris as a poster designer (he was a huge admirer of A.M. Cassandre's work). In 1936, while in Palestine, where his work was on display at a trade fair, he was offered a job by the British Crown Agencies and moved to London. In 1940 he was employed as a graphic designer by the Ministry of Information and the US Office of War Information, producing posters and other informational material. From 1945 Henrion worked as an exhibition designer for the 1951 Festival of Britain,[1] and it was his success in that role that spurred him to set up his own design consultancy, Henrion Design Associates (HDA). Fisons was his first client.

Henrion was in his mid-thirties when he established HDA. He was blessed with a strong personality, beguiling charm and political acumen with which he could persuade a conservative, sceptical and combative boardroom that the service of a good designer was what its company required. This ability, born out of an unshakable self-belief, was a trait also associated with the New Yorker Paul Rand, who, like Henrion, began work on his first corporate-identity project in the early 1950s, and with Roger Excoffon in Paris, whose work for Air France began in 1957–58. All three made huge contributions to the acceptance and viability of corporate identity, but it is Rand – in large part because of the subsequent growth, longevity and international reach of the companies for which he worked – who dominated the field during the 1950s.

F.H.K. Henrion
Fisons
1952

Logo (below); vehicle livery (right).

F.H.K. Henrion
Blue Circle Cement
1966

Logo (below); photograph showing it in use and unchanged more than half a century later (right).

Henrion was thinking in terms of corporate identity in the late 1940s, some years before he gained his first commission. Large companies rarely had any one person, let alone a department, responsible for the public image of their goods and services. Such material would be farmed out in a piecemeal fashion by department managers to various jobbing printers, with little or no coordination with an existing 'standard'. In 1948 Henrion wrote an article titled 'Design' for the journal *Art & Industry* in which he explained (perhaps with possible future clients rather than fellow designers in mind), 'Designers working for commerce and industry must meet businessmen and industrialists on their own terms and on their own ground. Refusal to do so is sentimental escapism, permissible to artists, or the illustrator, but not to the specialist designer or design consultant.'[2]

In 1958 the Dutch airline KLM (Koninklijke Luchtvaart Maatschappij, or Royal Aviation Company) set out to discover what its logo and its application conveyed to the public, and whether a greater clarity of purpose might be achieved. A simplified logo was introduced, but in 1961 David Ogilvy (see pp. 110–11) was approached to carry out further research on KLM's image. He reported that the airline scored highly on 'cleanliness, punctuality, hospitality and friendliness', but that 'technical capability' and 'modernity' were lacking.[3] Concluding that 'reliability' should be a key public perception of its service, KLM decided to enhance this aspect of its current identity through the introduction of another new logo. The airline contacted HDA, and Henrion met with the board and other relevant departments at the KLM head office in The Hague. On his flight back to London, he began making preliminary sketches on a serviette.

The letters KLM remained as sans serifs but were redesigned to have a stronger, upright

1959

1963

1972

F.H.K. Henrion
KLM
1963

*From left to right:
previous KLM logo,
Henrion's redesign and
updated version; drawing
from 1970s corporate-
identity manual showing
logo's construction grid,
and a 1960s logo (below).*

F.H.K. Henrion
LEB
1971

*Previous London
Electricity Board
logo (top); Henrion's
'lightning-bolt' logo,
introduced in 1971
(above, left and right).*

stance. More radical was the new depiction of the crown. Its design, reduced to a stripe, four dots and a cross, remained eminently recognizable and, just as importantly, coupled it firmly with the letters KLM. Henrion was able to prove not only that his new logo was clearer, in both large and small formats, but also that it remained legible in adverse weather conditions.

When Henrion presented his solution to the board of KLM in 1963, he demonstrated the rationale behind the design by showing its metamorphosis through fifteen variations, analysing each for impact and legibility and demonstrating how each was tested and adapted, before eventually revealing the final version of the logo. In other words, he did what most designers actively avoid: he demystified the creative process and brought it into the boardroom. Although Henrion's solution was accepted in full, the implementation of coordinated change across such a large organization took time. The KLM corporate identity – from the tail fins to the cutlery and glasses used on board the aeroplanes – was finally completed and a new 'house-style manual' distributed in 1964.

In 1957–58, around the same time as KLM was reviewing its corporate design, Air France appointed Roger Excoffon as its artistic director to take responsibility for the redesign of its identity. Excoffon had only recently formed his own Paris-based design and advertising consultancy, Studio U+O (Urbi et Orbi), while continuing to design typefaces in his role as art director at Fonderie Olive. One such typeface, Nord – whose design had been prompted by the commercial success of such recent 'neo-grotesque' typefaces as Folio,

Roger Excoffon
Air France
1959 (top), 1964

Two posters, one showing elegance and sophistication,

the other speed and power. With amendments, the latter was also used to promote Concorde in the 1970s.

Neue Haas Grotesk and Univers (all 1957) –
was used (with minor modifications by José
Mendoza) for the new Air France identity.
Marcel Olive, director of Fonderie Olive,
astutely waited until Air France had loudly
and lavishly announced its newly designed
corporate identity before releasing Nord to
the public.

The first public viewing of Excoffon's new
livery on an Air France aircraft was in May
1959, and it has remained in use to the present
day. In other material, most notably posters,
supporting images were created by Excoffon,
showing his fascination with the dynamism
distilled in the gestural abstract paintings of
Georges Mathieu and Hans Hartung that he
had discovered as a student. His depiction
of the jet plane on Air France posters is
still distinctive today. Excoffon's gestural
brushstrokes were also used effectively on the
corporate identity he designed for the 1968
Winter Olympic Games in Grenoble.

Airlines are an obvious example of
the globalization of services and
trade during the 1950s and of the need for
organizations to be 'intelligible' across an
increasing number of unfamiliar markets.
Effective mass communication – controlling
the way an organization was perceived by the
public of different countries – fell to relatively
few high-profile graphic designers. The use of
terminology associated with the boardroom
rather than the design studio caused the public
perception of design and the designer to shift.
It was also a shock to many in the design
profession. Before 1945 a graphic designer
could describe his or her role as being that of
a principled, independent communicator – a
facilitator, acting in the service of the public

Roger Excoffon
Air France
1959

*Menu and brochure.
Illustration by Guy
Georget.*

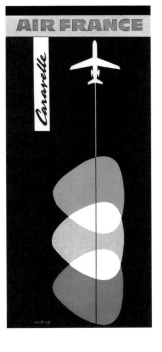

Roger Excoffon
Air France
1969

*One of a series of
press advertisements.*

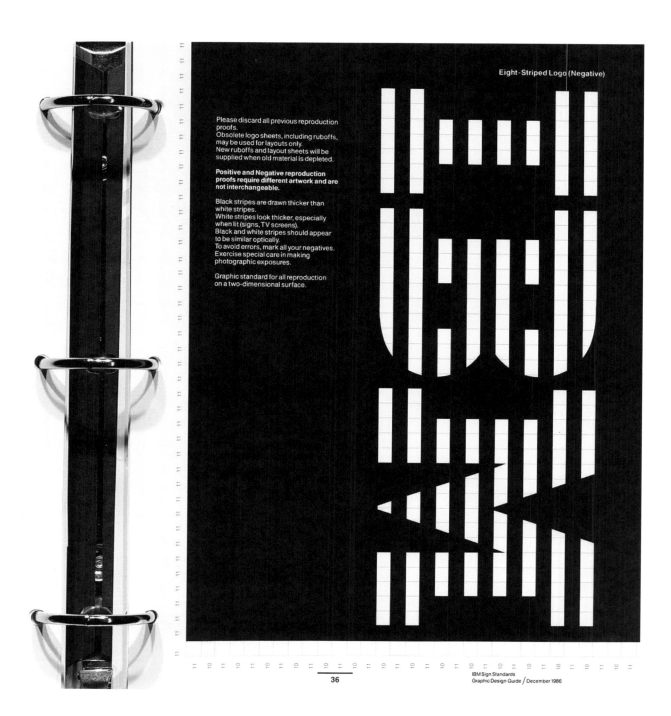

Please discard all previous reproduction proofs.
Obsolete logo sheets, including ruboffs, may be used for layouts only.
New ruboffs and layout sheets will be supplied when old material is depleted.

Positive and Negative reproduction proofs require different artwork and are not interchangeable.

Black stripes are drawn thicker than white stripes.
White stripes look thicker, especially when lit (signs, TV screens).
Black and white stripes should appear to be similar optically.
To avoid errors, mark all your negatives.
Exercise special care in making photographic exposures.

Graphic standard for all reproduction on a two-dimensional surface.

36

IBM Sign Standards
Graphic Design Guide / December 1986

Paul Rand
IBM
1972

Rand began working on the IBM corporate identity in 1956. The eight-bar logo was launched in 1972. This page is from the 1986 updated manual.

as much as commercial organizations. By the 1950s that role had dramatically changed: graphic design was now perceived to be in the service of the commercial sector. The discipline had evolved, 'grown up' some might have said, while others might have claimed that objectivity had been lost along with innocence. The fact that commercial organizations were paying large amounts of money for such a service did not go unnoticed, either – nowhere more so than in the buoyant post-war economy of the United States.

Paul Rand (1914–1996), more than any other American designer, represents this celebrated period. His earliest successes were in publishing, but what transformed his status, certainly within the business community, were his hugely successful corporate identities, many of which remain in use today. IBM, ABC, UPS and Enron, among many others, owe their graphic heritage to Rand. The magazine covers designed by Rand may have been lauded by his peers in the media, but the unequivocal influence he attained was due to his access to the nation's industrial boardrooms. As in the case of Henrion, Rand's strength was his ability to explain to leaders in the business community the necessity of design and the role of the designer in solving challenges of mass communication. According to the graphic designer Louis Danziger, 'He almost singlehandedly convinced business that design was an effective tool ... Anyone designing in the '50s and '60s owed much to Rand, who largely made it possible for us to work. He more than anyone else made the profession reputable. We went from being commercial artists to being graphic designers largely on his merits.'[4]

In the 1950s the International Business Machines Corporation (IBM) had established itself as one of the leading data-processing companies in the world. IBM's president, Thomas Watson Jr, was one of the earliest believers in the role of design as an essential process in the modern business landscape. He

Paul Rand
UPS
1961

UPS commissioned Rand to restyle its shield. He then added the package tied with a bow, which became the crucial element that explains what the company does.

Paul Rand
ABC
1962

The logo was updated to signal the arrival of colour television in 1966 and then more radically with the arrival of high definition in 2007. However, the key elements of Rand's design have been retained.

Paul Rand
Cummins
1976

The letters of the company name are derived from Helvetica Neue, but with a customized capital C, a repeat of the principal C of the logo.

ordered a complete overhaul of IBM's graphic communications and, quite specifically, commissioned Paul Rand to do it. Rand was in his early forties but at the top of his profession. In 1937 and barely out of design college, he had gone from creating magazine spreads on a freelance basis to the position of art director at *Esquire* magazine. Perhaps inevitably, Rand was drawn into New York's renowned advertising agencies on Madison Avenue, and in 1941, aged twenty-seven and with just a few years' art-direction experience behind him, he was offered the role of art director at the newly formed ad agency William H. Weintraub (see pp. 106–108).

Influenced by the European design he discovered through such magazines as *TM* and *Gebrauchsgraphik* and the work of such modern artists as Matisse and Picasso, Rand brought a simpler, more visually direct form of communication that was not reliant on text for its authority. His work was bright and confident, and although carefully composed, it had a refreshingly carefree, egalitarian air about it – very different from the standard authoritative, 'this will be good for you' mode of advertising at the time.

From 1956 onwards, Rand created for IBM the most thorough and celebrated post-war corporate-identity system. Starting with the redesign of the logo – itself requiring a lengthy process of strategic incremental changes – he developed a design vocabulary that informed all applications of the IBM identity across the entire company to give the monolithic corporation a visual sense of purpose and direction. The results were implemented in everything from letterheads and package design to showroom interiors and company offices. Executives from other companies watched what was happening at IBM and recognized that it was someone called a 'graphic designer' who was responsible. For the remainder of the 1950s

Dennis Bailey
International Design Congress
1961

Back and front cover of report. The congress was arranged by the Council of Industrial Design to discuss 'Design policy for corporate buying'.

and throughout the 1960s corporate identity was considered by many to be the holy grail of design consultancy work, and the multifaceted aspect of its implementation would, over time, drive the creation of multidisciplinary design consultancies.

One of the earliest of these consultancies was Total Design (TD), founded in 1963 in Amsterdam. Three designers were among the five founders: the graphic designer Wim Crouwel (1928–2019), the industrial designer Friso Kramer, and Benno Wissing, who worked in both graphic and spatial design. Brothers Paul and Dick Schwarz were responsible for management and finance. They were quickly joined by Ben Bos, an experienced copywriter and graphic designer. The range of design skills and knowledge that TD had at the top of the organization enabled it to take on complex design problems and to provide a truly unified multidisciplinary – total – solution. Before Total Design, The Netherlands did not have a design company considered 'business-like' enough or of sufficient scale and breadth of experience to understand, let alone tackle, international communication difficulties. As a result, large Dutch corporations were contracting their major design projects to agencies outside the country. Particularly galling was KLM's decision to commission Henrion's design consultancy in London to redesign its corporate identity. In 1962 Crouwel, Kramer and Wissing went on a fact-finding trip to the UK and visited Henrion's studio to ask why the KLM job had gone to an English rather than a Dutch design company. Henrion's response was incisive: 'Institutions like to talk to institutions.'

Creativity may be an integral part of a design consultancy's work, but Crouwel, Kramer and Wissing realized that, if they were to attract major clients, they had to look the part and use the same language. The TD team explained that their approach to solving

design problems was 'systematic', something
leaders of industry, trade and transport, as
well as of government and cultural sectors,
could readily appreciate and understand. Their
range of design expertise meant that corporate
identity became Total Design's speciality;
major Dutch clients included Schiphol Airport,
De Bijenkorf (exclusive department stores),
Randstad (employment agency) and SHV
(energy distribution), while Olivetti and the
Belgian General Bank were among the foreign
clients. However, it was TD's work for small
but highly prestigious clients, such as the
Stedelijk Museum Amsterdam, that had the
most significant and long-lasting cultural
impact. Crouwel took sole responsibility
for the design of all the museum's visual
communications from 1963 until the mid-
1980s. When Crouwel left Total Design in
1985, his reputation far exceeded that of
the company he had helped to form. The
'corporate' business with which TD elevated

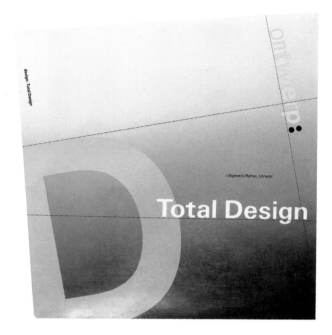

Dutch design on to the global stage was now too often banal and characterless – perhaps a reflection of what the clients demanded. The memorable moments – such as posters for the Stedelijk Museum, the experimental but nevertheless controversial New Alphabet typeface (1967), the Dutch Pavilion for Expo '70 in Osaka, stamps for the Dutch Post Office (PTT, 1976) and the innovative, all lower-case PTT telephone directory of 1977 – were all the work of Crouwel.

Another design office that Crouwel, Kramer and Wissing visited in London in 1962 was that of the newly formed Fletcher/Forbes/Gill. Still in a fledgling state, it consisted of graphic designers Alan Fletcher (1931–2006) and Colin Forbes (1928–2022), and illustrator Bob Gill (1931–2021), plus a receptionist and her dog. What little work they had was confined to *Time* and *Life* magazines, Penguin Books and Pirelli. To attract attention and promote their expertise, they wrote, designed and published a soft-bound book, *Graphic Design: Visual Comparisons* (1963), which sold well enough to encourage them to follow it up in 1970 with *A Sign Systems Manual* (by Crosby/Fletcher/Forbes, the new name for the partnership). The partners astutely used both books to enhance their authority and reputation. At the end of their second year they published a portfolio titled *Fletcher/Forbes/Gill 1962/3*. It contained fifty-six pages printed in black and white, and the text was set in English, German and French. The authors' ambitious plans were set out in the introduction:

We believed ... that within our specific interests and abilities, our organization would be unique and that it could provide a service to industry from total corporate image to individual graphic solutions. Although we have designed theatre sets, television commercials, film titles, packages and exhibitions, we are primarily

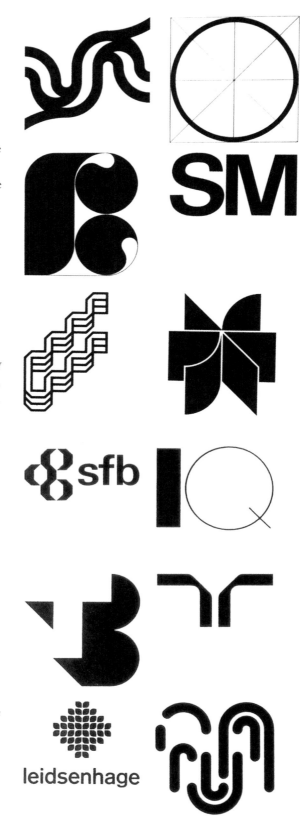

Total Design
Logos

A selection of the logos featured in Ontwerp: Total Design. *From top, left to right: District of Rijnmond, 1968; Teleac, 1964; Leeser Fashion, 1966; Stedelijk Museum Amsterdam, 1964; Dutch Municipal Building Fund, 1974; Kluwer, 1968; Social Building Fund, 1972; Intomart Qualitative, 1980; Thyssen-Bornemisza, 1971; Randstad, 1966; Shopping Centre Leidsenhage, 1970; Amsterdam Creative Team, 1972.*

Fletcher/Forbes/Gill
*Graphic Design:
Visual Comparisons*
Studio Books
1963

Front cover of a book
ostensibly about
graphic design, but in
reality an opportunity
to showcase the
work and practice
of Fletcher, Forbes
and Gill.

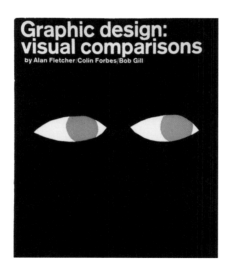

graphic designers. *We feel that any one visual
problem has an infinite number of solutions;
that these solutions should derive from the
subject matter; that we have no pre-conceived
graphic style.*

The architect Theo Crosby joined in 1965,
the idea (perhaps following the success of Total
Design) being that the addition of 'building
and interiors' expertise in the partnership
might provide not only more but also larger
design opportunities. (Gill decided to leave at
this point.) This supposition proved correct,
and higher-profile clients such as Shell, Arthur
Andersen, Reuters and Cunard began to
arrive. By the end of the 1960s each of the
three partners had a team of assistants and, as
planned, collaborations between design partners
were becoming a reality. When the product
designer Kenneth Grange and one of their own
associate designers, Mervyn Kurlansky, became
partners in 1971 (making five in total), the
company was renamed Pentagram and quickly
began to blossom. An office in New York (with
Forbes in charge) was opened, and other new
offices followed. The partners were now doing
what they had always dreamed of, designing
multidisciplinary, multinational corporate
identities – such as the Commercial Bank of
Kuwait – involving every possible aspect of a
complex organization's visual manifestation.
That London became a hub of corporate activity
during the 1970s was due in no small measure
to the verve of Pentagram. The other design
consultancies, often referred to as 'supergroups',
who dominated British design during the late
1960s and throughout the 1970s and '80s
included Wolff Olins, Minale Tattersfield, Fitch
& Company, Michael Peters & Partners, and
Conran Design.

While these ambitious, fast-growing
companies captured the media's
attention, independent designers were creating
corporate-design solutions of equal and often

**Fletcher/Forbes/Gill
Colin Forbes**
D&AD
1963

Forbes glued each of
the four characters
to the sides of
a wooden cube,
photographed it and
then gave the print
to Wolf Spoerl, who
drew the artwork for
the logo. Forbes was
a founding member
of D&AD (Design and
Art Direction).

**Fletcher/Forbes/Gill
Colin Forbes**
International Die
Casting Conference
1966

The two sixes of the
logo represent the
positive and negative
of a mould.

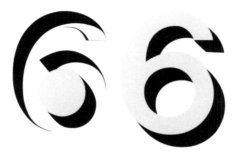

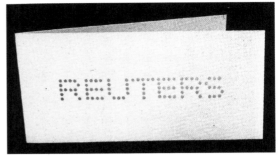

Fletcher/Forbes/Gill
Reuters
1965

Corporate identity for the international news agency Reuters, as featured in Pentagram's book Living by Design *(1978).*

Wolff Olins
BOC
1967

BOC provides specialist gases for medical and industrial use. Wolff Olins was able to specialize in corporate-identity work from its beginnings in 1965, thanks, in part, to the pioneering work of Fletcher/Forbes/Gill.

Romek Marber
Barnards
1960s/1970s

Logo (below); leaflet (right). Marber had a knack of finding elegance in the most mundane of manufactured products. He won an award for the logo in 1972. Plastic-coated chain-link fencing never looked better.

Barnards Barnards plastic covered
chain-link fencing for
maximum protection at minimum cost. Available in a range of colours, the PVC coated high-tensile, bright wire core remains resilient and tarnish-free for years. Our service organisation from whom full specifications are available provides swift and expert advice.
Barnards Ltd: Salhouse Road, Norwich: Norwich 47321; Birmingham, Midland 3555; London, Mansion House 8597

Romek Marber
Education Resource
Development Trust
Date unknown

Sketches and a later trial drawing show the underlying structure on which Marber built this appropriately vibrant and complex logo. It is not known if it was ever used.

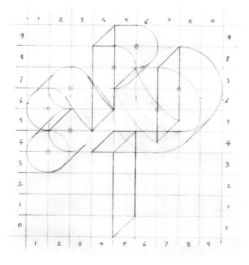

superior quality, albeit for more modest-sized organizations. Of these, two designers, Romek Marber and Ken Garland, stand out.

Marber (1925–2020), born in Poland to a Jewish family, arrived in Britain in 1946 after a traumatic childhood.[5] He studied commercial art at St Martin's School of Art and then, in 1953, secured a place at the Royal College of Art. When his friend and fellow student Alan Fletcher was planning to leave his job as assistant to Herbert Spencer, he recommended Marber to take his place. Spencer, editor of the influential journal *Typographica* (see pp. 49–53), had a profound effect on Marber, who gained invaluable professional knowledge and experience working with the distinguished typographer. In the late 1950s he established his own independent studio and living space in Harley Street, central London.

One of Marber's first clients was Robert Nicholson, who had just designed an office partition system called Cunic. Marber was commissioned to provide a branding design that would give the product an identity encompassing modernity and flexibility. It was the first of many such commissions. From the beginning, Marber had an intimate understanding of modernist design ideology, but his work, even in the more rarefied, marketing-led field of corporate identity, always retained a curiously human, even playful quality that illuminated the quirkiness of ordinary things. A prime example might be his response in the 1960s to Barnards, a manufacturer of plastic-coated chain-link fencing – an efficient but otherwise utterly mundane product. Marber did not shy away from the product itself or its elemental purpose, and in so doing created a logo that made the ordinary appear rather exceptional.

Ken Garland had been a student at the same time as Fletcher (and Colin Forbes), but at the Central School of Arts and Crafts during 1952–54. Unlike them, however,

Cunic partition system

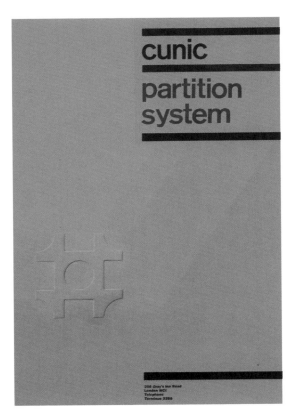

cunic

partition system

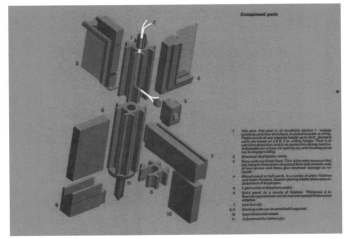

Romek Marber
Cunic
1958–62

*Marber based the
Cunic identity on the
'post' of the partition
system, which served
as a conduit for
power cables and as
a means of securing
partitions.*

*Posters. Garland
was not interested
in making the logo a
sacred cow; instead,
he enjoyed playing
around with its
words, letters and
colours – a mindset
wholly appropriate to
Galt Toys.*

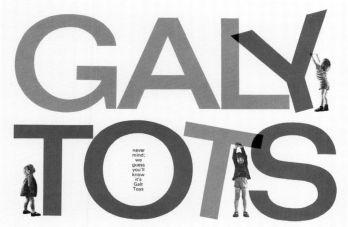

Garland had little interest in wearing crisp suits and skinny ties, and even less in seeking work from large corporations. (Years later, Paul Rand put Garland's name forward to handle the UK end of IBM. Before a meeting was arranged, Garland sent a copy of his book *Ken Garland and Associates: Designers – 20 Years Work and Play 1962–82*, in which he said he 'had never had any taste for working for multinationals'. To no one's surprise, IBM cancelled the proposed meeting.[6]) Garland set up his studio in the family home in Camden Town, a less chic part of London, in the same year as Fletcher, Forbes and Gill established themselves in a central London mews studio off Baker Street. Needless to say, Ken Garland & Associates was not on Crouwel's list of design companies to visit.

The results of Garland's aesthetic influences – Swiss typographic simplicity combined with the colour and energy of mid-century American graphic expression – would not have looked out of place in the Fletcher/Forbes/Gill portfolio book, or in a book of Rand's work for that matter, especially the work he created for Galt Toys, manufacturers of immaculately made educational wooden toys and games. With a playful use of sans-serif Folio Medium Extended and striking photography, Garland and his small team (there were never more than three – and never a receptionist) designed every aspect of the Galt Toys identity, including its change of name (previously James Galt and Company), packaging and promotion, and even contributed to the development of new games. Galt became a leader in its field, renowned for the sturdy manufacture of intelligent, colourful toys.

Garland's distaste for what he considered the self-serving behaviour of his contemporaries was distilled in a manifesto titled 'First Things First', which he, irreverent and provocative as ever, delivered at a meeting in November 1963 of the Society of

Industrial Artists and published the following year. The manifesto called on designers to question their role in the nascent consumer culture, especially the vacuous pitches made by the design profession's 'status salesmen': 'We are proposing a reversal of priorities in favour of the more useful and more lasting forms of communication. We hope that our society will tire of gimmick merchants, status salesmen and hidden persuaders, and that the prior call on our skills will be for worthwhile purposes.' The solution was to focus design on educational public service and on tasks that promoted the betterment of society – preoccupations, Garland suggested, that were more worthy of a designer's skills. The manifesto was co-signed by twenty-one like-minded practitioners – none, of course, from the larger design groups of that time.

Garland's 'alternative' outlook in the early 1960s mirrored the beginnings of a wider cultural rejection of the 'big is better' premise on which corporate identity depended. 'First Things First' attracted much attention: it received the backing of more than 400 graphic designers and of Tony Benn, the radical left-wing MP and activist, who reprinted it in its entirety in his weekly column in *The Guardian* newspaper. It also lured so-called 'fringe' clients, including cultural organizations such as the St Pancras Arts Festival and the Science Museum. Garland had worked with the Campaign for Nuclear Disarmament (CND) since 1962, and during the next four years designed a highly effective campaign. Updated versions of the manifesto, edited by others, were published in the early twenty-first century.[7]

A manifesto

We, the undersigned, are graphic designers, photographers and students who have been brought up in a world in which the techniques and apparatus of advertising have persistently been presented to us as the most lucrative, effective and desirable means of using our talents. We have been bombarded with publications devoted to this belief, applauding the work of those who have flogged their skill and imagination to sell such things as:

cat food, stomach powders, detergent, hair restorer, striped toothpaste, aftershave lotion, beforeshave lotion, slimming diets, fattening diets, deodorants, fizzy water, cigarettes, roll-ons, pull-ons and slip-ons.

By far the greatest time and effort of those working in the advertising industry are wasted on these trivial purposes, which contribute little or nothing to our national prosperity.

In common with an increasing number of the general public, we have reached a saturation point at which the high pitched scream of consumer selling is no more than sheer noise. We think that there are other things more worth using our skill and experience on. There are signs for streets and buildings, books and periodicals, catalogues, instructional manuals, industrial photography, educational aids, films, television features, scientific and industrial publications and all the other media through which we promote our trade, our education, our culture and our greater awareness of the world.

We do not advocate the abolition of high pressure consumer advertising: this is not feasible. Nor do we want to take any of the fun out of life. But we are proposing a reversal of priorities in favour of the more useful and more lasting forms of communication. We hope that our

society will tire of gimmick merchants, status salesmen and hidden persuaders, and that the prior call on our skills will be for worthwhile purposes. With this in mind, we propose to share our experience and opinions, and to make them available to colleagues, students and others who may be interested.

Edward Wright
Geoffrey White
William Slack
Caroline Rawlence
Ian McLaren
Sam Lambert
Ivor Kamlish
Gerald Jones
Bernard Higton
Brian Grimbly
John Garner
Ken Garland
Anthony Froshaug
Robin Fior
Germano Facetti
Ivan Dodd
Harriet Crowder
Anthony Clift
Gerry Cinamon
Robert Chapman
Ray Carpenter
Ken Briggs

Published by Ken Garland, 13 Oakley Sq NW1
Printed by Goodwin Press Ltd, London N4

Ken Garland
'First Things First' manifesto
1964

The influence of the manifesto quickly reached a broader audience when it was printed in The Guardian, *which led to*

Garland appearing on television. It was subsequently published in numerous journals, magazines and other newspapers.

ALDERMASTON TO LONDON EASTER 62

| Aldermaston Good Friday 12 noon | Reading Easter Saturday 9am | Slough Easter Sunday 9.30am | Acton Green Easter Monday 9.30am | Hammersmith | Kensington |

RALLY HYDE PARK [near Hyde Pk Corner] 12.30–3PM
FINAL MARCH: Hyde Pk Corner / Sloane St / Victoria St / Whitehall

Ken Garland
Campaign for Nuclear Disarmament
1962

Poster. Garland had always been politically active. He was a member of CND and produced material for the organization between

1962 and 1968. It was during this time that he redesigned the CND logo that now symbolizes the peace movement.

MIKRON - Le macchine Olivetti si distinguono per l'eccezionale nitidezza e la costante uniformità della scrittura

ELITE - Le macchine Olivetti si distinguono per l'eccezionale nitidezza e la cos

PICA - Le macchine Olivetti si distinguono per l'eccezionale nitidez

STAMPATELLO ELITE - LE MACCHINE OLIVETTI SI DISTINGUONO PER L'ECCEZIONALE NITID

STAMPATELLO - LE MACCHINE OLIVETTI SI DISTINGUONO PER L'ECCEZIONALE

SIMPLICITAS - Le macchine Olivetti si distinguono per l'eccezionale

ITALICO - Le macchine Olivetti si distinguono per l'eccezionale nit

ELITE PICA - Le macchine Olivetti si distinguono per l'eccezionale

IMPERIAL - Le macchine Olivetti si distinguono per l'eccezion

MEDIO ROMANO - Le macchine Olivetti si distinguono per l'eccezion

CARATTERI
olivetti

ADVERTISING

European advertising agencies rarely expanded overseas even after the Second World War, despite the opportunities offered by the reopening of international trade borders. But while in Europe agencies felt linguistically and culturally tied to their own domestic markets, American agencies thought the opposite, and expanded existing overseas offices and opened new ones. This expansion generally followed the advancement of their clients as they expanded operations into a Europe that was attempting to rebuild itself.

The services provided by advertising agencies included market research, media planning and the purchase both of space in printed media and on billboards and of time on television and radio and in the cinema. The creation of strategies and their visual interpretation may be crucial, but they are in fact a remarkably small part of an advertising agency's business. In addition, the critical scrutiny of a proposed creative 'solution' by the plethora of 'experts' within an agency, all with a legitimate claim for their views to be heard, inevitably waters down any individuality the designer's work might once have borne. The general consensus of the time was that Americans

OPPOSITE
Costantino Nivola
Olivetti
c. 1965

Leaflet advertising the range of typefaces available for Olivetti typewriters.

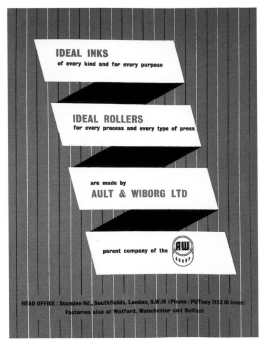

Designer unknown
Staybrite
1943

Designer unknown
Ault & Wiborg
1949

Press advertisements placed in specialist magazines: Staybrite steel in The Architectural Review *and Ault & Wiborg printing inks and rollers in* The Penrose Annual.

Lester Beall
Rural Electrification
Administration
1939

*Lithographic and
silk-screen printed
poster.*

Alvin Lustig
Knoll
1945

*Full-page press
advertisement
placed in* Arts &
Architecture,
July 1945.

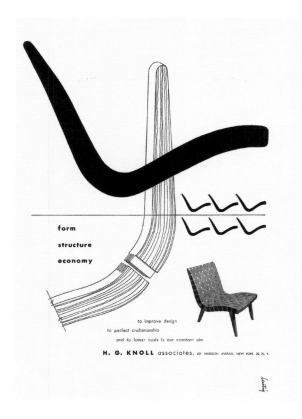

preferred tradition: text-heavy adverts using a serif type, ornamentation with illustrations, the frequent use of humour and a tendency towards hucksterism. The best pre-war advertising in Europe – simple, to the point and without adornment – was a dramatic contrast, and several young American designers were taking note.

From 1941 to 1955 Paul Rand worked as art director of the William H. Weintraub advertising agency in New York. Weintraub had been a senior partner at the magazine publisher Esquire-Coronet, where Rand had also been working, and when Weintraub cashed in his shares to set up his own advertising agency in the Rockefeller Center, he took Rand with him. Weintraub was the consummate salesman, but he acknowledged that a major reason for his success was Rand's creative direction and his stipulation that he maintain complete autonomy in the running of his department.

Rand kept the art department at Weintraub small, recruiting many designers he had known at *Esquire*. Of these, some were made associate art directors with responsibility for specific accounts. However, Rand rarely delegated new conceptual work, and so all the advertising generated at the agency was effectively his own – an aberration in the industry.

The distinctive appearance of Rand's work came initially from his interest in European design when he was a student in the early 1930s. He took every opportunity to study the commercial arts journals in the college library from Britain, Germany and Switzerland, and was particularly enamoured of the 'object posters' of such Swiss designers as Herbert Leupin and Otto Baumberger. Along with several fellow young American designers – Lester Beall and Alvin Lustig, among others – Rand experimented with the solemn restraint of European poster work, infusing it with vernacular American functionalism, wit and optimism. This was achieved by combining collage, hand lettering, drawing and photography. Rand collaborated with the copywriter William (Bill) Bernbach (they would meet in art galleries to talk through concepts) to create advertisements in which text and images were integrated to produce a simple but effective and engaging message. Bernbach (1911–1982), like Rand, was keenly aware that the way his words were presented was just as important as the message itself. By paring down copy and using white space in his designs, Rand created advertisements that stood out from the rest of the page. He embraced wit and humour, developing, for example, friendly hand-drawn characters for the aperitif-maker Dubonnet (made famous by A.M. Cassandre, a designer much admired by Rand), Coronet Brandy and the cigar company El Producto. Rand insisted on signing every advertisement that left his art department, and threatened to quit

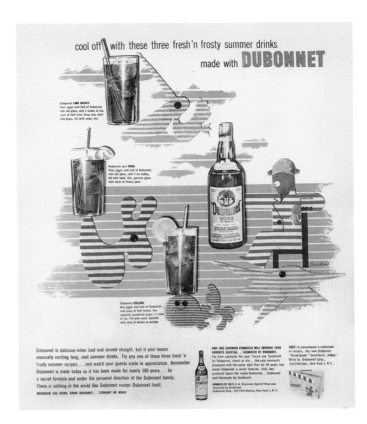

Paul Rand
William H. Weintraub
El Producto
c. 1952

Press advertisement.

Paul Rand
William H. Weintraub
Dubonnet
1944

Press advertisement. Early in his career Rand was a prolific illustrator, and often used cut-and-paste montage techniques. All three clients on this page benefited from his drawing skills, each commissioning endless variations.

Paul Rand
William H. Weintraub
Coronet Brandy
c. 1945

Press advertisement. Rand designed the character with a brandy-glass-shaped head. The distinctive background was intended to suggest bubbles.

BELOW
Numa Rick
Publicité
1946–47

BOTTOM
Pierre Monnerat
Publicité 7
1953

Cover designs.
Publicité *was an
annual review
of advertising
and the graphic
arts, published in
Switzerland from
1944.*

when Weintraub questioned this procedure.
Weintraub backed down.

Across the industry, Rand helped to
initiate the shift in creative authority away
from the copywriter and towards the art
director, and in doing so laid the groundwork
for what became known as the 'Creative
Revolution' (or the 'Big Idea') in advertising
in the 1960s. Rand brought ideas and
intelligence to the industry, yet he himself
claimed that his attitude and approach
had little to do with advertising as such
and considerably more to do with creating
effective communicative design. Indeed, his
approach to the creation of an advertisement
was much the same as his design of a
magazine or book cover – a creative field
in which he had already proved himself the
consummate expert.

The Weintraub agency specialized in
mass-market product advertising, not the
huge-scale corporate projects sought by the
larger agencies. Weintraub's work appeared
in weekly magazines and daily newspapers
with the intention of moving commodities
from retailers' shelves. Rand was keenly aware
that such work had limits for himself, and
as the 1950s progressed he witnessed other
designers creating corporate logos and posters,
'and not posters for cornflakes, either'.[1] For
almost every new account, before designing
what inevitably would be a string of variously
themed adverts, Rand would develop a
discernible trademark look – a colour, pattern
or shapes that would provide a visual link
between advertisements.[2] Clearly aware of
developments in graphic design, Rand was
becoming less enthralled by the advertising
industry, and in 1955 he left Weintraub.

Bill Bernbach had left Weintraub around
1943 and, following war service, was hired
by Grey Advertising as a copywriter and
in 1947 promoted to creative director. He
became good friends with James Edwin Doyle
and Maxwell Dane; Doyle was an account

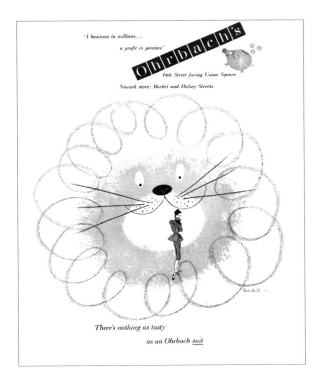

**Bill Bernbach and
Paul Rand**
Grey Advertising
Ohrbach's
1946 onwards

*Full-page
weekly press
advertisements
for Ohrbach's
department store.*

The Rolls-Royce Silver Cloud—$13,995

"At 60 miles an hour the loudest noise in this new Rolls-Royce comes from the electric clock"

*What __makes__ Rolls-Royce the best car in the world? "There is really no magic about it —
it is merely patient attention to detail," says an eminent Rolls-Royce engineer.*

1. "At 60 miles an hour the loudest noise comes from the electric clock," reports the Technical Editor of THE MOTOR. Three mufflers tune out sound frequencies–acoustically.

2. Every Rolls-Royce engine is run for seven hours at full throttle before installation, and each car is test-driven for hundreds of miles over varying road surfaces.

3. The Rolls-Royce is designed as an *owner-driven* car. It is eighteen inches shorter than the largest domestic cars.

4. The car has power steering, power brakes and automatic gear-shift. It is very easy to drive and to park. No chauffeur required.

5. The finished car spends a week in the final test-shop, being fine-tuned. Here it is subjected to 98 separate ordeals. For example, the engineers use a *stethoscope* to listen for axle-whine.

6. The Rolls-Royce is guaranteed for three years. With a new network of dealers and parts-depots from Coast to Coast, service is no problem.

7. The Rolls-Royce radiator has never changed, except that when Sir Henry Royce died in 1933 the monogram RR was changed from red to black.

8. The coachwork is given five coats of primer paint, and hand rubbed between each coat, before *nine* coats of finishing paint go on.

9. By moving a switch on the steering column, you can adjust the shock-absorbers to suit road conditions.

10. A picnic table, veneered in French walnut, slides out from under the dash. Two more swing out behind the front seats.

11. You can get such optional extras as an Espresso coffee-making machine, a dictating machine, a bed, hot and cold water for washing, an electric razor or a telephone.

12. There are three separate systems of power brakes, two hydraulic and one mechanical. Damage to one system will not affect the others. The Rolls-Royce is a very *safe* car—and also a very *lively* car. It cruises serenely at eighty-five. Top speed is in excess of 100 m.p.h.

13. The Bentley is made by Rolls-Royce. Except for the radiators, they are identical motor cars, manufactured by the same engineers in the same works. People who feel diffident about driving a Rolls-Royce can buy a Bentley.

PRICE. The Rolls-Royce illustrated in this advertisement—f.o.b. principal ports of entry—costs $13,995.

If you would like the rewarding experience of driving a Rolls-Royce or Bentley, write or telephone to one of the dealers listed on the opposite page.

Rolls-Royce Inc., 10 Rockefeller Plaza, New York 20, N. Y., CIrcle 5-1144.

David Ogilvy
Ogilvy, Benson &
Mather
Rolls-Royce
1959

Press advertisement.

Ford quieter than Rolls-Royce?

"Dammit, sir! Those upstart American car-makers just don't know their place..."

– London Daily Mirror. October 26, 1964

J. Walter Thompson
Designer unknown
Ford
1965

*Press advertisement.
Ogilvy's advert for
Rolls-Royce (above)
still resonated six
years later and
was mirrored by
J. Walter Thompson
to promote the new
Ford Galaxie 500.*

director at Grey, while Dane was running his own, much smaller agency. Bernbach also established with Bob Gage, an art director at Grey, a working relationship similar to the one he had enjoyed with Rand. In fact, Rand (as design consultant while employed by Weintraub) and Bernbach worked together on the account of one of Grey's clients, Ohrbach's, a New York department store for which they created a stream of weekly newspaper advertisements. Nathan Orbach, the store's owner, was impressed by Bernbach's work and encouraged him to quit Grey and set up his own agency with Orbach as the first client. Bernbach was reticent until Orbach confided that he was planning to move his account away from Grey anyway. Bernbach, having persuaded Doyle and Dane to join him, decided to leave Grey,[3] and Doyle Dane Bernbach (no commas – 'nothing will come between us') opened its doors for business in June 1949.

The previous year, David Ogilvy (1911–1999) had set up his advertising agency in New York with the backing of the London agency Mather & Crowther, which was run by his elder brother, Francis. The New York agency was called Hewitt, Ogilvy, Benson & Mather.

Ogilvy had been a copywriter and then account executive at Mather & Crowther, and in 1938 he persuaded the company to send him to the United States for a year to work for George Gallup's Audience Research Institute in New Jersey. Ogilvy's agency was built on principles learnt at Gallup – in particular, the principle that the success of advertising, regardless of the product or service, will always be based on information about the consumer. His celebrated advert for Rolls-Royce in March 1959 – with the headline 'At 60 miles an hour the loudest noise in this new Rolls-Royce comes from the electric clock' – encapsulates Ogilvy's traditional, literary and immaculately researched approach.

The headline was supported by a 450-word text arranged in three columns, outlining thirteen features unique to the car. Ogilvy created adverts that included such narrative tropes as 'the man in the Hathaway shirt', whose eyepatch was a mysterious prop used to generate curiosity and suggest an untold backstory. This approach, complex and erudite, was effectively the antithesis of that applied by Bernbach, yet both were equally successful during the 1950s.

The 1950s were the decade in which the American advertising industry consolidated and then transformed itself. Although no new large agencies were created, expansion, especially into South American and European markets, greatly accelerated. In every case, the agencies were simply opening offices to correspond with their clients' global development plans; they could serve their clients' needs by adapting publicity created in the USA to national and regional requirements. South American markets were relatively easy to enter, as was Britain, thanks in large part to there being no language problems,[4] but mainland Europe proved more resistant. There, most advertising was still handled by manufacturing companies and service providers in-house, some of which – Olivetti, for example – were outstanding.

Advertising in Britain and Europe for much of the 1950s remained firmly grounded in the aesthetic culture of interwar poster work and then in the modernist graphic work emerging from Switzerland. The sense of purpose, service and optimism – encapsulated in 1931 in the Futurist Fortunato Depero's assertion that 'the art of the future will inevitably be advertising art'[5] – was still pertinent in Europe during the post-war years. The idea that advertising not only had a responsibility to its clients but also had broader cultural ambitions was demonstrated

Giovanni Pintori
Olivetti
1959

Pamphlet. Pintori joined the Olivetti design studio in 1936. Outside commissioned work was often done in consultation with Studio Boggeri, Milan, with which Max Huber had maintained connections.

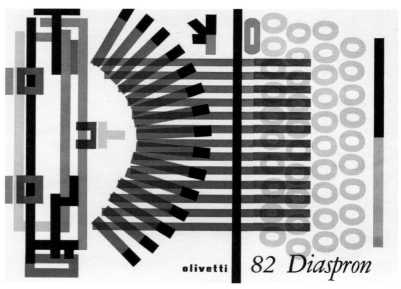

Max Huber
Olivetti
c. 1948

Pamphlet.

Ashley Havinden
W.S. Crawford
Liberty
1949

*Poster, from a series
for the iconic Liberty
store in London.*

by Ashley Havinden (1903–1973), who was made art director at the London agency W.S. Crawford in 1929. Havinden had worked in Berlin during the previous year, directing the European campaign for Chrysler, and this was probably when he became aware of modernism, specifically the New Typography of Jan Tschichold, as well as the design work of A.M. Cassandre, Edward McKnight Kauffer and other luminaries of poster art.

Impeccably connected to the cultural zeitgeist, Havinden took typographic advice from Stanley Morison and drawing lessons from Henry Moore, and was close friends with Ben Nicholson and Barbara Hepworth. He also met Walter Gropius and László Moholy-Nagy when they lived for a brief period in London before finally leaving for New York. In the catalogue of an exhibition at the National Gallery of Scotland, the curators describe Havinden's work as 'a quintessentially English presentation of Modernism, combining rigid geometric planes and lines with biomorphic motifs'.[6] The optimism associated with modernism is reflected in the spirit of Havinden's early work, particularly, for example, in the compelling energy he gave to the Chrysler campaign and the photomontage campaign for Dewar's whisky from the same pre-war period. After the war, Havinden's work was tempered with a little more caution. The celebrated campaigns for the Milk Marketing Board, Eno's fruit salt and Wolsey socks were characterized by a retreat from formal innovation towards a combination of Havinden's own brush-script lettering and cheery caricature. However, his work for DAKS, from post-war to 1956, with its clever use of overlapping photographs and type, remains remarkably fresh and alluring.

In the post-war period it was common for Havinden to design not only the advertising but also the packaging and in-store promotional material for a product,

LEFT
Ashley Havinden
W.S. Crawford
DAKS
1947

Press advertisement.

BELOW
Ashley Havinden
W.S. Crawford
Wolsey
1951

Press advertisement. Havinden's irreverent use of the client's product for humorous effect is not dissimilar to Paul Rand's early work (p. 107). However, the softer lines and use of Gill Sans Italic maintain a distinctly British feel.

Nylon re-inforced at heels and toes!

Guaranteed not to shrink!

Wolsey CARDINAL SOCKS

DAKS being a prime example. Similarly, Charles Loupot's agency Les Arcs and Roger Excoffon's Studio U+O, both in Paris, made little distinction between advertising and graphic design, as Loupot's work for St Raphaël aperitif and Excoffon's for Air France (see pp. 88–89) and the 1968 Winter Olympic Games in Grenoble testify. In general, the distinction between the businesses of advertising, graphic design and typography was far less pronounced than it would become by the 1960s.

In mainland Europe, there was a strong sense that localized cultural traditions and aesthetic principles should not be swept away by what some perceived as a wave of 'aggressive US imperialism'.[7] In this, France was particularly defiant, and its markets remained heavily regulated to repel foreign interests.[8] However, from an American political perspective, Italy was different from its European neighbours because it

was considered to be at risk of electing a communist government. As a result, the US government decided to invest in propaganda activities, or 'information services', in Italy during the immediate post-war years.[9] During the 1950s, American advertising agencies were encouraged by the cooperative activities of, for example, the Committee for Economic Development and the Advertising Council, to open offices in Italy as a means of propagating capitalism.[10] This association with subversive politics tainted advertising, and when reports of the experimental use of subliminal advertising were published from 1952 onwards,[11] it was generally assumed that they were true. Such reports of unethical practice led to trust in the advertising industry sinking to an all-time low – and the most vehement criticism emanated from the graphic design community. 'Advertising sells, graphic design tells' was the common, if simplistic, refrain. Nevertheless, what at the beginning of

Charles Loupot
Les Arcs
St Raphaël
c. 1948

Press advertisement, from Loupot's almost abstract series for St Raphaël's quinquina-based aperitif.

Roger Excoffon
Studio U+O
X Olympic Winter Games
1968

Poster, from a series for the Winter Olympics held in Grenoble.

GRENOBLE 1968
FRANCE
X[es] JEUX OLYMPIQUES
D'HIVER

the 1950s had been a minor ideological fissure between design and advertising was, by the decade's end, a seemingly unbridgeable chasm.

However, none of this impeded the international growth of the advertising industry as it followed the global success of its clients. By the late 1950s, all the pre-eminent (mostly American) agencies had offices in major cities around the world. Essentially, an advertising campaign would be created in the head office and then tweaked by each sub-office to fit local norms. This internationalist approach meant that design became a less significant factor, giving way to a 'concept' that was universally adapted to make it fit localized social conventions. Quirky local characteristics that had once been part of a company's identity were replaced by what was called an 'unrestrained' marketing strategy, meaning one that worked worldwide – 'US imperialism' by another name.

Quirky characteristics were what the Volkswagen had in excess. The 'People's Car' had played an integral role in the *Kraft durch Freude* (Strength through joy) programme of the German National Socialist (Nazi) Party in the late 1930s. When VW launched in the United States shortly after the war, it faced several unique problems. First, it was selling a single mass-market car, the Beetle (officially, the Volkswagen Type 1), at a time when American automakers were offering an extensive range of styles and optional features. Secondly, not only was it a European car, it was German, and given its history, it was understandably referred to as 'Hitler's car'.

Volkswagen's initial attempts to market the car in the United States were unsuccessful, and in 1958 only 150,000 were sold in what was probably the biggest automobile market in the world. That all changed when Carl Hahn took charge of VW's US division in 1959. Hahn had a relatively small budget with which to expand sales and met with several agencies over a

Designer unknown
KdF-Wagen
1938

Sales brochure for the first-generation Volkswagen, part of the Nazi campaign for car production.

You can get color prints like this in 60
seconds with a Polaroid Color Pack Camera.
Is there any other way to take pictures?

Prices start at under $60.

three-month period, but was not impressed.
He complained that the advertising industry
was governed by research and think tanks,
yet its solutions were always predictable.

One of Volkswagen's distributors knew of
Doyle Dane Bernbach (DDB) and suggested
that Hahn should meet with the firm. During
the 1950s DDB had forged a reputation as a
maverick agency through its work for such
companies as Polaroid and Levy's rye bread
(although it was DDB's superior work for
these same clients in the 1960s that would
help to cement the company's repute for
innovation). When Hahn met Bill Bernbach,
he was impressed by his modest office and
distinct lack of personal bravado. Bernbach
did not presume to know the product or
the client, and consequently did not make
an ostentatious presentation of speculative
Volkswagen work, explaining that it could not
possibly be an honest representation of the
product. Hahn appointed DDB to the account.

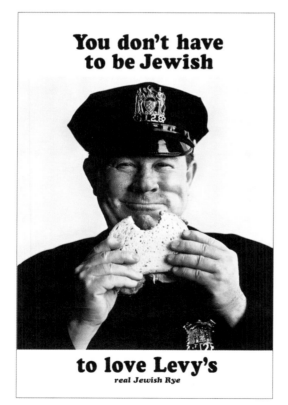

**You don't have
to be Jewish**

to love Levy's
real Jewish Rye

**You don't have
to be Jewish**

to love Levy's
real Jewish Rye

The Volkswagen account team comprised Helmut Krone (art director) and Julian Koenig (copywriter), plus, of course, Bill Bernbach. Krone, perhaps uniquely, was able to conflate graphic design and advertising. He had the perfect background to achieve this, having discovered the work of designers Paul Rand and Lester Beall in his student days, and attended classes with Alexey Brodovitch during the late 1940s while working at *Esquire* magazine. He then moved to Sudler & Hennessey to work in Herb Lubalin's design department, where he met and became friends with George Lois. He joined Doyle Dane Bernbach in 1954 as one of four art directors.

For Volkswagen, Krone used black-and-white photographs designed to exude a true and uncomplicated single image. There were no aspirational settings (large house, happy family); in fact, the car was usually shown with no background at all. Koenig wrote copy that was brief, matter-of-fact – even self-effacing – and infused with deadpan humour. To complement this 'no frills' approach, Krone set the text in Futura, a German sans-serif typeface. He asked Koenig to keep his sentences short and to reduce each paragraph to just two or three sentences – or even one. This was done to keep the text open, unstuffy and less authoritarian in appearance; Krone described what he wanted as 'Gertrude Stein-y' (the American modernist author).[12]

The role of Carl Hahn should also not be underestimated. Krone's speculative first headline was 'Wilkommen'. Hahn rejected it and pointed to 'Think small', the last line in Koenig's initial copy, asking, 'Could that be the headline?'

The same quirky self-deprecation and simplicity were applied to the Volkswagen

Doyle Dane Bernbach
Volkswagen
1959 onwards

Press advertisements.

Will we ever kill the bug?

What if you only need part of a Volkswagen?

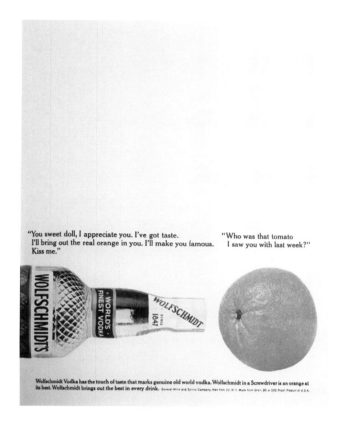

"You sweet doll, I appreciate you. I've got taste. I'll bring out the real orange in you. I'll make you famous. Kiss me."

"Who was that tomato I saw you with last week?"

Wolfschmidt Vodka has the touch of taste that marks genuine old world vodka. Wolfschmidt in a Screwdriver is an orange at its best. Wolfschmidt brings out the best in every drink. General Wine and Spirits Company, New York 22, N.Y. Made from Grain. 90 or 100 Proof. Product of U.S.A.

"John, is that Billy coughing?"

"Get up and give him some Coldene."

television adverts. For example, a famous sixty-second advert of 1964 included barely ten seconds of voice-over: 'Have you ever wondered how the man who drives the snow plough drives to the snow plough? This one drives a Volkswagen. So you can stop wondering.'

Krone remained at Doyle Dane Bernbach for the rest of his illustrious career, but Koenig joined with George Lois, who had worked at CBS under William Golden before becoming an art director at DDB, to form Papert Koenig Lois (again with no commas) in 1960. Lois's campaigns for Xerox, Wolfschmidt vodka, Coldene and scores of other products had a distinct and simple street-smart manner seasoned with a strong wit – even biting satire – making them some of the most memorable of their time.

Both Papert Koenig Lois (PKL) and DDB opened offices in London in the early 1960s, their innovative approach fitting neatly with the lively experimentation in music, fashion, photography and graphic design that was occurring in the UK. The leading London-based advertising agency was Collett Dickenson Pearce (CDP), founded in 1960 by John Pearce and Ronnie Dickenson when they bought Pictorial Publicity, an agency owned by John Collett. Pearce described British advertising as 'terminally dull', yet its fervent young creatives would hurry to their newsagent as soon as such American magazines as *Esquire* and *The New Yorker* were released to see the best – sharp, funny, insightful – adverts. In this way, the American advertising revolution had crossed the Atlantic ahead of the appearance of PKL and DDB in London. But it was CDP that would create what would later be acknowledged as

LEFT, TOP
George Lois
Papert Koenig Lois
Wolfschmidt
1960

Press advertisement.

LEFT
George Lois
Papert Koenig Lois
Coldene
1961

Press advertisement.

RIGHT
D'Arcy Advertising
Illustrator unknown
Coca-Cola
1948

*Poster. D'Arcy
Advertising was
Coca-Cola's
advertising agency
from 1906 to 1956.
'It's the Pause That
Refreshes' had
been Coca-Cola's
official slogan since
1929, but affiliated
European agencies
were allowed to
interpret it to suit
their own markets.*

Illustrator unknown
Coca-Cola
France
1955

Poster.

Illustrator unknown
Coca-Cola
Germany
1955

Poster.

Herbert Leupin
Coca-Cola
Switzerland
1956

Poster.

John Donegan
*The Sunday Times
Colour Section*
4 February 1962

*Front cover of the
first edition of The
Sunday Times Colour
Section. The grace of
the footballer Jimmy
McIlroy (photographed
by John Bulmer) is
compared with that
of the fashion model
Jean Shrimpton
(photographed by
David Bailey).*

Romek Marber
The Observer colour
supplement
11 April 1965

*Front cover. The
Observer's colour
supplement
was launched in
September 1964.
Marber was hired to
work on the dummy
issues and was then
made art director.*

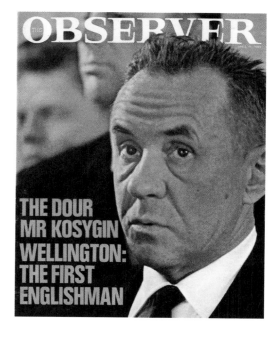

the golden age of British advertising during
the 1960s.

The clients CDP attracted did not have
the lavish budgets enjoyed by their American
counterparts, but Pearce recognized that
there was a demand in Britain for bolder,
attention-grabbing and, above all, intelligent
advertising. In its initial years the agency
showed plenty of promise; enough to persuade
DDB to try to buy it just two years after its
creation, but Pearce was disinclined to sell,
despite the fact that at that point CDP was
still debt-laden and struggling. One of the key
factors that saved the agency was the launch
in 1962 of *The Sunday Times Colour Section*,
the first colour magazine to be offered free
with a British newspaper. Other newspaper
supplements followed.

With his background in publishing, Pearce
realized that the magazine would be the
perfect placement for the witty wordplay that
CDP so often incorporated in its advertising.
Colin Millward was the agency's creative
director and imaginative force. He began his
career in the creative department of Mather &
Crowther and then moved to Colman Prentis
& Varley, where he met John Pearce. It was
Pearce who persuaded him to join CDP in
1960. Undoubtedly influenced by the work
of Bernbach and Lois, Millward and CDP
played a major role in London's cultural shift
during the 1960s, and the agency would go
on to blossom in the 1970s with a surfeit of
imaginative print and television advertising
for clients that included Heineken, Harveys
Bristol Cream, Hovis, Benson & Hedges and
Hamlet cigars. The allure of CDP as a creative
powerhouse was demonstrated by the quality
and range of the creative talent it attracted,
including, for example, Charles Saatchi,
Ridley Scott, Alan Parker, Frank Lowe and
David Puttnam. It is probably no exaggeration
to say Doyle Dane Bernbach and then Collett
Dickenson Pearce salvaged and transformed
the reputation of the advertising industry.

Make Hovis
your daily bread.

They obviously felt like
shooting each other.

Heineken. Refreshes the parts other beers cannot reach.

34 NEW
SCHEMES FOR
THE SOUTH

LATE NEWS
FOR LEGS:
THE
SHIMMERING
STOCKINGS

GIFTS: THE
THOUGHT IS
THE THING

DECEMBER 1959
60 CENTS

MAGAZINES

In post-war Europe, letterpress still dominated magazine production, although its position was under threat. Letterpress enabled type to be printed beautifully, but it could not offer high-quality full colour. The half-tone dot was too large and therefore too coarse to show fine detail, so four-colour letterpress printing presses were never developed to enable full-colour work to be produced in a single pass. This was necessary in the days before humidity control, without which paper could distort between print runs, making precise registration impossible. However, gravure, a relatively new process in commercial printing, was capable of printing photographic images of a consistent quality at high speed and in large print runs. And because gravure could transfer a generous amount of ink to the paper (helped by the development of quick-drying inks), it was possible to achieve remarkable levels of colour density and tonal range. The only disadvantage of gravure was that *all* printed areas, including type, were printed using very small dots. But since a magazine editor's priority was the photographic image, gravure became the printing process of choice.

While many designers who had been working in Germany in 1933 fled to Switzerland to escape persecution, others sought refuge in the United States, in New York in particular. However, one of the most influential émigrés, Alexey Brodovitch (1898–1971), had fortunately been lured

to America several years before Europe's political upheaval.

In 1930, Brodovitch, a Russian by birth, was working successfully as a graphic designer and photographer in Paris when he met John Story Jenks, a trustee of the Pennsylvania Museum and School of Industrial Art. Impressed by Brodovitch's design for print, Jenks offered him a job as head of the school's advertising design department, the expectation being that Brodovitch would bring European modernism to American advertising design. By 1934 his students' work and his own freelance work were attracting attention, and Brodovitch came into contact with Carmel

OPPOSITE
Henry Wolf
Harper's Bazaar
December 1959

Cover photograph
by Richard Avedon.
Wolf succeeded
Brodovitch as art
director of the
magazine in 1958.

A.B. Imrie
Shelf Appeal
February 1934

Front cover. Shelf
Appeal *was a
monthly magazine
'devoted to
planning, designing,
manufacturing
and display of the
package', although
its content was
often far broader and
reflected the way
graphic design, then
still a blossoming
profession, was
growing in stature.*

125

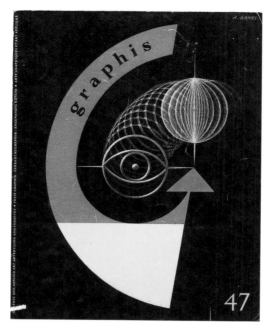

Abram Games
Graphis 47
1953

Front cover. This issue includes a wide-ranging feature about Games's work to date.

Charles Peignot
Arts et métiers graphiques 57
March 1937

Front cover. Peignot was director of the French type foundry Deberny & Peignot, and this journal was published to promote his foundry's type. It featured examples of work submitted by designers using Deberny & Peignot typefaces.

Snow, the recently appointed editor-in-chief of *Harper's Bazaar*. Snow had already begun to move the magazine away from being a sop to elite Parisian haute couture towards a more American-focused, broadly based cultural review. She wanted the emphasis to be on modern lifestyle, and needed a designer who could reflect this transformation in the magazine's layout. Snow offered Brodovitch the job of art director, and he moved to New York. He remained at *Harper's Bazaar* for the next twenty-four years.

Brodovitch took full advantage of the flexibility offered by the essentially photographic process of gravure. The arrangement of type was made not by compositors working at a Linotype or Monotype keyboard, but rather by designers at their own desks; the text was cut from printed proofs and moved about experimentally before being pasted into position. This method encouraged designers to design both headlines and text in new and playful ways alongside or within images. It was Brodovitch, using Surrealist-like strategies, who brought an invigorating sense of ebb and flow, scale and tone to provide cinematic effect, and in so doing revolutionized magazine design. The result was such that Brodovitch established the role of the art director (also often known as the art editor) as being, at the very least, equal to that of the editor.

At the height of his success at *Harper's Bazaar*, Brodovitch took on the additional challenge of designing *Portfolio*, a new magazine conceived by George Rosenthal, publisher of the photography magazine *Minicam*, and Frank Zachary, *Minicam*'s editor. With meagre funds, the two friends established *Portfolio* as a review of the fine and applied arts, but with an emphasis on graphic design. It was to be in the same eclectic mould as Charles Peignot's celebrated *Arts et métiers graphiques*, published in Paris before the war.

There were few serious graphic design (let alone typography) magazines being published in the United States at that time – an exception being *Print*, which although aimed primarily at the printing industry did offer space for the culture as well as the business of print (see pp. 59–60). *Portfolio* was something entirely different. The aim was to extend the cultural sphere of design and printing by examining progressive directions in art, design and technology, by discussing modernist designers, painters, photographers and illustrators, and by celebrating the American vernacular.

A year before starting *Portfolio*, Zachary had written an article in *Minicam* on Brodovitch (who he was happy to discover had been an occasional designer for *Arts et métiers graphiques*) and now considered him to be the best magazine art director in the United States. He asked Brodovitch to work on *Portfolio* for almost nothing, but with the enticing promise that he would be given unrestricted freedom in its design. It was an irresistible offer, and in *Portfolio* Brodovitch created what is often referred to as the ultimate rendition of American modernism. The format was unusually large – 30.5 × 22.75 cm (12 × 9 in.) – and incorporated a variety of inserts, including wrapping and wallpaper samples, printed specimens and 3D glasses with which to view a special section on stereoscopy. The intention was to create 'an American *Graphis*, but done in such a way that the magazine itself would be a model of design and at the same time communicate the contents in a very original, innovative and inspirational manner'.[1]

First published in 1950, *Portfolio* was a masterpiece of sequential pacing. In this, it had the extraordinary advantage of containing no advertisements. Rosenthal and Zachary were concerned that adverts would detract from Brodovitch's design, and of course they were right. However, sales alone were never

Alexey Brodovitch
Portfolio
Vol. 1, no. 1
Winter 1950

Back and front cover.

Mehemed Fehmy Agha
Vogue
27 October 1928

Front cover. Agha was art director of Vogue Berlin *before moving to* Vogue's *New York office in 1929. His design work revitalized the magazine as well as its sister publications* Vanity Fair *and* House & Garden.

going to be sufficient to keep *Portfolio* afloat, and the third issue, in 1951, was the last.

The 1950s were a golden period for American magazine design, and although Brodovitch undoubtedly led the way, his rapid progress at *Harper's Bazaar* was made smoother by the pioneering work of Mehemed Fehmy Agha (1896–1978), art director of Condé Nast Publications in New York. Agha, born in Ukraine, was art director of *Vogue Berlin* before being persuaded to move to New York to take over the American edition of the magazine in 1929, and he remained there until 1943. Agha cut down *Vogue*'s fussy appearance by removing extraneous elements such as borders around photos, column rules and sidebars. He also introduced sans-serif typefaces, popularizing Paul Renner's Futura, while widening margins to make space for the

text to play a more distinctive role alongside the images. When Carmel Snow appointed Brodovitch, it was in the hope that he would emulate Agha's remodelling of *Vogue*. He far exceeded expectations.

Cipe Pineles (1908–1991) began as a design assistant to Agha at American *Vogue* in 1932 and over the next decade developed her characteristic style, working for *Vogue* in both the New York and London offices. In 1942 Pineles became art director of *Glamour* before going on to the same role at *Seventeen*. Helen Valentine, founder and editor of *Seventeen* (assisted by the promotion director, Estelle Ellis) is credited with establishing one of the first magazines to treat teenage girls as thoughtful and serious.[2] When Pineles joined *Seventeen* in 1947, it was a little over three years old, its layout having been designed in consultation with Agha, whom Valentine knew from her days at *Vogue*. Typographic design on the fiction pages followed a traditional, book-like layout, allowing the artwork to dominate, while the typography on the editorial and fashion pages was open and playful, showing an early trend towards a more expressive use of type.

Valentine and Pineles remained with *Seventeen* until 1950, when Valentine was asked by the publishers Street & Smith to revamp a failing fashion magazine called *Charm*. Valentine kept the name but, in partnership with Pineles, transformed it into 'The Magazine for Women Who Work' – twenty-two years before *Ms.* – and effectively the first feminist magazine by providing a more realistic visual presentation of women's lives and options. Pineles later explained, 'We tried to convey the attractiveness of reality, as opposed to the glitter of a never-never land.'[3] (Unfortunately, such material had to compete on occasions with advertisements promoting traditional and more limited roles assigned to girls and women at the time.) *Charm* was incorporated into *Glamour* magazine when it

Cipe Pineles
Charm
January 1954

Front cover. Pineles was among the most prominent designers in the publishing industry and one of the first female art directors of a major magazine.

Cipe Pineles
Glamour
March 1945

Cover photograph by Constantin Joffé.

Cipe Pineles
Seventeen
July 1949

Front cover.

was bought by Condé Nast Publications in 1959.

Fashion magazines led the field in the use of innovative typography, photography and layout design, but there were other notable specialist periodicals. One such example was the monthly doctors' magazine *Scope*, published by Upjohn Pharmaceuticals. Will Burtin, born in Cologne, had built a career as a designer in Germany before hurriedly emigrating to the United States in 1938. He was commissioned to design the first issue of *Scope*, which appeared in 1941. From the second issue onwards, Burtin's colleague Lester Beall took over the art direction until the return in 1948 of Burtin, who was by then art director of *Fortune* magazine and a freelance designer with a raft of design-oriented clients such as Knoll, Herman Miller, Eastman Kodak, IBM and Upjohn itself. Through the use of photomontage, collage and cut-out paper in combination with

photography and economical line drawing, Burtin and Beall simplified complex topics and brought a calculated new kind of beauty to American publishing.

In the fields of specialist design, *Interiors*, *Industrial Design* and *Arts & Architecture* stand out. *Interiors* was designed by Czech-born Ladislav Sutnar, who, as an advocate of New Typography, developed a strict though adaptable typographic grid system, which in its composition and unremitting use of sans-serif type provided a functional look stripped of ornament. *Interiors* featured a regular column dealing with industrial design products – principally those associated with the home – but its publisher, Charles Whitney, realized that this could be a viable and far broader subject in its own right. *Interiors* had earned a reputation for the quality of Sutnar's design, and Whitney believed that, if it were to succeed, *Industrial Design* would also need to be led by design.

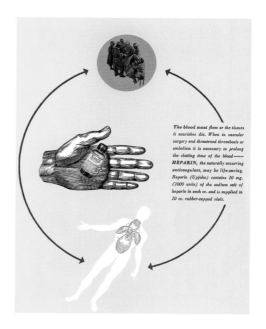

Alvin Lustig, a brilliant young American typographer and designer, was, like Sutnar, a modernist, and Whitney chose him to be the magazine's art editor. Lustig had already gained a reputation for his work on numerous magazines, including *Perspectives* and *Interiors*, as well as the masthead for *Arts & Architecture*.

Lustig's cover designs for the first two issues of *Industrial Design*, published in February and April 1954, became icons of American modernity and marked the beginning of a hugely successful publishing business for Whitney. However, they also proved to be the summation of Lustig's own distinctive style of modernism; he died from diabetes the following year, aged just forty.

Although Lustig's covers for *Industrial Design* were later celebrated as landmarks of American design, his work was not appreciated at the time by the magazine's co-editors, Jane Fisk and Deborah Allen.

Arnold Saks
Interiors
March 1959

Front cover. After the early death of Alvin Lustig, Saks designed many covers for Interiors *and other magazines, including* Graphis. *He established the design partnership Ward & Saks in 1958.*

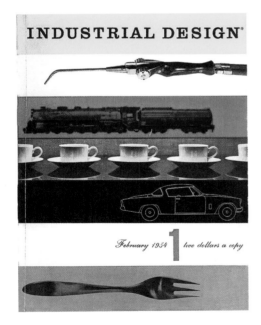

Alvin Lustig
Industrial Design
Vol. 1, no. 1
February 1954

Front cover.

Alvin Lustig
Industrial Design
Vol. 1, no. 2
April 1954

Front cover.

They considered the design of the cover and its interior spreads to be disconnected from the content. Their criticism is valid: Lustig dealt with text by strictly adhering to his predetermined grid, and in this sense he came closer to the immaculacy of the Swiss International Style (at the height of its influence in Europe at this time) than any other American-born designer. However, there can be little regret that Lustig was able to resist the editors' attempt to add coverlines to his front-cover designs.

European attitudes towards American magazines were mixed. Although admired by some for what was commonly called the 'slick' quality of the design, these magazines were also viewed as being blatant 'American propaganda'; for example, the USA's long-standing social problems of race and poverty were never covered. This was the time of the 'Cultural Cold War' with the Soviet Union, and many magazines – the arts- and culture-based quarterly *Perspectives* in particular – wilfully presented a sanitized version of

American life. *Perspectives*, published from 1952 to 1956 and titled *Perspectives USA* in America, was supported by funds from the Ford Foundation to promote American values abroad, with editions in French, German and Italian.

In their own defence, the editors and art directors of the magazines discussed here argued that their principal audience was the American people and that their aim was to promote design as a subject in its own right – something that the still-emerging fields of design thought both culturally and commercially necessary. Their impact abroad was undeniable: it was noted that during the design and construction of the Festival of Britain in London in 1951, the content of *Arts & Architecture* was closely scrutinized.[4]

Arts & Architecture began in 1929 as *California Arts & Architecture*. John Entenza became both publisher and editor (until 1962) in 1938 and changed the magazine's title in 1944. Entenza then masterminded the sponsoring of the now-famous Case Study House program, which brought many Los Angeles architects to international attention, among them Charles Eames, Richard Neutra and Craig Ellwood. Herbert Matter designed most of the covers, but Alvin Lustig, Ray Eames and others were also commissioned. Perhaps not surprisingly, the magazine rarely paid attention to the work of designers outside the United States, and when it did look elsewhere, it was generally towards Mexico rather than Europe or the UK.

In Britain, *The Architectural Review*, founded in 1896, covered much of the same ground as *Arts & Architecture*, but featured a broader and far more eclectic range of material. To a large extent, the character of the review, arguably at its best in the 1950s and '60s, was embedded during the 1930s, when its editors and their assistants (including John Betjeman, 1930–35) sought

Alvin Lustig
Arts & Architecture
April 1945 (right),
November 1946
(below, left), January
1946 (below, right),
December 1945
(bottom)

*Front covers and
spread. Lustig
designed the
masthead using a
grid of letterpress
squares and quarter
circles to create
and then print the
characters.*

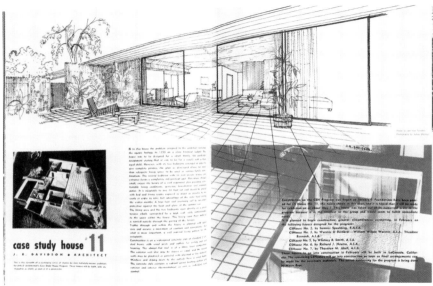

contributions from other artistic fields and adjusted the magazine's architectural focus to reflect a view of built environments from street level.

Articles in *The Architectural Review* ranged from features on neglected architectural curiosities – windmills, follies, lighthouses and seaside piers – to extended reviews of modern developments from around the world, if they were deemed interesting enough to be included. But the true focus was on urban or townscape development rather than individual buildings – an approach that was very much to the fore post-1945, not only in Britain but also across most of Europe. The magazine benefited from having several assistant and/or co-editors (among them Nikolaus Pevsner, Hugh Casson and Osbert Lancaster), each with his own distinctive opinions and interests, while James Richards, editor from 1937 to 1971, encouraged the diversity and international outlook that these men brought to the review.

As in the case of *Arts & Architecture*, the covers of *The Architectural Review* only occasionally displayed images of actual buildings. But whereas *Arts & Architecture* commissioned graphic designers who took the open brief as an opportunity to produce odes to modernism – or as Herbert Matter might have explained, a synthesis of modern art, design and architecture[5] – from 1943 *The Architectural Review* pointedly used a heterogeneous mix of artists, illustrators, graphic designers and photographers whose cover designs made a conscious connection, directly or indirectly, with the content of each issue. The other, more significant difference was in the design of the inside pages.

This aspect of almost every magazine is often difficult to credit accurately because the nature of the process means that sections may be distributed among the studio designers available at the time. Nevertheless, at *Arts & Architecture* John Follis, the magazine's art director, and Matter certainly had overall responsibility for the internal layout.

Despite *Arts & Architecture*'s firmly held modernist credentials, the grid, predominant in Swiss and German magazines, was often barely perceptible inside the cover. The typeface Spartan (ATF's version of Futura), set to a justified measure, gave the typography a strong presence, but the text placement was arbitrary, differing from page to page to fit around the architectural drawings.

In contrast, the art editors of *The Architectural Review*, Gordon Cullen and Kenneth Browne, had a grid system that gave the text a cogent, structured appearance from front to back cover. Justified text was set in Clarendon, in one, two or three columns per page, with carefully judged amendments in type size and within tight margins to the edges of the page and between columns. Tightly constructed but never dull, these textural areas – usually printed on uncoated, variously coloured paper – provided a dramatic contrast with the open spaces that helped to announce the beginning of a new article or topic. The choice of a fine Edwardian script on the contents page solely for the regulation issue number and date of publication suggested a playful mocking attitude to formality that the magazine managed to sustain throughout the 1950s and into the '60s.

Like Britain, Italy was preoccupied with rebuilding throughout the 1950s. But Italy had endured nearly twenty years of Fascism under Mussolini before the war, and Fascist support of modernism was now, post-war, a problem. The answer for Italy's new generation of progressive young architects was found in Nikolaus Pevsner's ideas expressed in *The Architectural Review* and elsewhere, in which he described the British peculiarity of giving importance not only to the geographical but also to 'the historical, social and especially the aesthetic character' of a site.

Gordon Cullen
The Architectural Review
October 1946

Front cover of special issue on industrial design, featuring the new Swedish flat-pack 'Priva' chair.

Gordon Cullen and Kenneth Browne
The Architectural Review
March 1959

Spreads.

Gordon Cullen and D. Dewar Mills
The Architectural Review
August 1951

Front cover of special issue on the 'South Bank Exhibition'.

This, he explained, 'may indeed be called the principle of tolerance in action, and there is no more desirable element of Englishness than tolerance'.[6] After the strictures of Mussolini's brutal, 'stripped-back' modernism, Pevsner's so-called 'English Picturesque' theories were particularly attractive in Italy.

Shortly after 1945, there was a spate of Italian cultural magazines centred on architecture, among the most important being the Rome-based *Metron*, which promoted 'organic architecture'. None of these publications survived for long. The 1950s were the decade of reconstruction and a golden period for Italian magazine design. *L'architettura*, aimed at the burgeoning architectural profession, resembled *The Architectural Review* internally, although its covers were generally more abstract than informative. More influential was *Domus*, which had been running since 1928 but, after a brief cessation during the war, resumed publication in 1946 with a revitalized look. It covered architecture, interior design, furnishings and domestic products, with an emphasis on materials and craftsmanship. Importantly, some of the text was set in three languages and so *Domus* became the standard choice of libraries around the world, and as such promoted Italian design as a cultural force.

Stile industria was created as an offshoot of *Domus* in 1954, the same year as *Industrial Design* was created as an offshoot of *Interiors* in the United States. While *Domus* was giving space mainly to interiors and domestic products, and *Casabella*, edited by Ernesto Nathan Rogers, was focusing on architecture, the editor of *Stile industria*, Alberto Rosselli, chose to concentrate on mass production. The range of products under review was extensive: alongside chairs, tables, kitchenware and packaging, Rosselli examined toilets, cars, measuring instruments, truck tyres and prefabricated

Designer unknown
Domus 404
July 1963

*Front cover and
opening spread
from an article on
the design of a
motor yacht, from
its construction to its
interior design, lighting
and furnishings.*

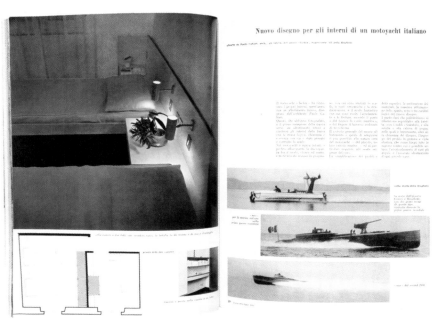

Designer unknown
Casabella continuità
213
November/December
1956

*Front cover and
spread. The
magazine, which had
several changes of
name, focused on
traditional housing
and architectural
renovation.*

materials used in construction. He invited people such as Max Bill, Gillo Dorfles, Bruno Alfieri, Misha Black, Sori Yanagi, Angelo Mangiarotti and Ettore Sottsass to show how different fields of design created both beauty and function in objects capable of enhancing efficiency and pleasure in everyday life. Rosselli's magazine also introduced the Italian public to innovative student work at, for example, the Institute of Design in Chicago, the Hochschule für Gestaltung in Ulm and the Royal College of Art in London, in addition to reporting on international design conferences around the world.

Equally important was the way these topics were presented. Michele Provinciali, the art director of *Stile industria*, would analyse a product by carefully displaying its functional effectiveness and aesthetic assets across double-page spreads, enabling the reader to look closely and critically at industrial production, whether that was the

thread of a screw or the design of a yacht. Albe Steiner, Bruno Munari, Pino Tovaglia, Giovanni Pintori, Max Huber and Enzo Mari, among others, designed beautiful covers that promoted a cultured appreciation of industrial objects and made the magazine accessible not just to specialists in the field but also to the general reader. As such, Italian magazines came to epitomize sophistication and a glossy presence.

In contrast, there had been a long tradition of British weekly journalism printed on cheap newsprint with little apparent concern for design, which was considered window dressing by publishers who thought that such frippery would distract from the serious business of reading. The leaders of this kind of publication were *The Spectator* (founded in 1828), *The Economist* (1843) and the *New Statesman* (1913). To this illustrious list was added *The New Scientist* in 1956. Like

Designer unknown
New Statesman
9 April 1960

Front cover. An austere publication that resisted the idea of a separate cover.

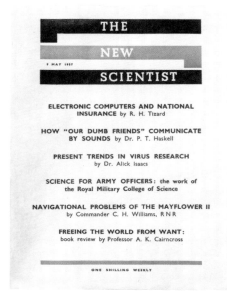

Designer unknown
The New Scientist
9 May 1957

Front cover.

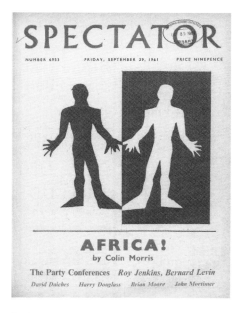

Designer unknown
Spectator
29 September 1961

Front cover.

its predecessors, *The New Scientist* was printed black only, with a second colour available for the cover. While these magazines shunned the increasingly glossy appearance of general-interest periodicals, they were not anti-populist, and avoided academic writing. Their purpose above all was the informal exposition of new research or ideas, written in a way that avoided condescension. Once established, the readership of specialist magazines remained loyal, although *The New Scientist* benefited greatly from the launch of Sputnik 1 by the Soviet Union shortly after its appearance on the news stands.

The covers of these magazines were, effectively, also the contents page. This unobtrusive approach began to change around 1960, shortly after *The Economist* appointed Peter Dunbar as its art director. Dunbar began commissioning designers to provide a cover image to communicate each issue's leading article. When *New Society* was launched in 1962 – with a format and paper quality similar to those of its competitors – its visual impact was comparatively lacklustre, causing an internal critical reassessment of both its cover and internal layout. Timothy Raison, the magazine's founding editor, wrote the design brief and commissioned Germano Facetti in 1963 to redesign every aspect. Lead articles, typeset in Linotype Times, were arranged in two columns, with an additional narrow column that could carry captions and allow illustrations to extend beyond a single column width. Other articles and reviews were set in three columns. Printed letterpress, the inside pages were black only, while the cover allowed for black and one colour, usually red. Richard Hollis was made *New Society*'s art editor in 1965, and under his direction the cover design had a bold new masthead set in Helvetica with 'NEW' in a second colour, under which was a list of selected articles in Univers Bold capitals, their

Romek Marber
The Economist
16 September 1961

Front cover.

Dennis Bailey
The Economist
15 August 1964

Front cover.

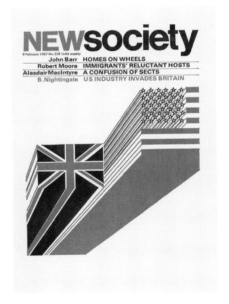

Romek Marber
New Society
9 February 1967

Front cover.

Dennis Bailey
Olympia 4
1963

*Front cover of a
short-lived Paris-
based magazine
edited and published
by Maurice Girodias.
It featured texts
by such writers as
William S. Burroughs
and J.P. Donleavy,
whose work was
censored in other
countries.*

Maurice Rickards
Man About Town
Autumn 1958

*Front cover, one
of many designed
by Rickards for the
magazine.*

titles separated by fine rules. These essential
elements took up a quarter of the cover,
leaving the rest for a distinctive image created
by a chosen designer.

Graphic design in the UK was still barely
recognized as a profession, but there was now
an emerging and dynamic post-war generation
of designers who would pioneer revolutionary
developments in British graphic design in the
1960s. The Association of Graphic Designers
London (formed in 1959) mounted an
exhibition in 1960 (see p. 210) and three years
later published a book, *17 Graphic Designers
London*. This was a slim, letterpress-printed
volume that featured an array of what were
to become illustrious names, including Dennis
Bailey, Derek Birdsall (who designed the
book), Bob Gill, Alan Fletcher, Colin Forbes
and Romek Marber, all of whom found an
outlet for their talents in the burgeoning field
of British publishing.

By the late 1950s there was full
employment in Britain, higher wages and – a
decade later than in the United States and
most European countries – an emerging sense
of modernity. The magazine industry reacted
slowly to this new affluence, but one of the
earliest to do so was the women's society
magazine *The Queen*, which was acquired
by a new owner in 1957 and dropped the
definite article from its title. In 1963 Tom
Wolsey (1924–2013) became its art director.
Wolsey had already demonstrated his interest
in modernism in his first job at the respected
advertising agency W.S. Crawford, whose art
director, Ashley Havinden, had long been an
advocate of modern art and design. However,
by the late 1950s Crawford's reputation
was on the wane, and when, in 1960, Clive
Labovitch, editor of the rather weary-looking
quarterly *Man About Town*, asked Wolsey to
redesign the magazine, he agreed. The work
was done during evenings and at weekends,
but the results were deemed a success: when
the refreshed magazine went monthly at the

end of the year, Wolsey left Crawford to become *Man About Town*'s art director.

In contrast to his experience in advertising, Wolsey relished working on a magazine: 'no endless meetings, no bullshit, great flexibility, quick decisions, great responsibility'.[7] Over the following three years, he developed an audaciously cinematic approach to layout design that underpinned an editorial policy pitched at a new generation of ambitious young men – a policy laced inevitably, given the time and place, with a generous helping of hedonism and misogyny.

Wolsey was determined to use Neue Haas Grotesk (renamed Helvetica in 1960), and travelled to Switzerland to purchase it. He adopted the typeface for almost all headings, playfully using it to generate both high drama and quiet irreverence. He created emphasis through the use of scale, placement and arrangement; added humour with visual

Tom Wolsey
About Town
September 1961

Cover photograph by Terence Donovan. The portrait – of Chita Rivera, who played Anita in West Side Story – illustrates the theme 'Anatomy of Anger'. Man About Town *was retitled* About Town *in 1961 and* Town *in 1962.*

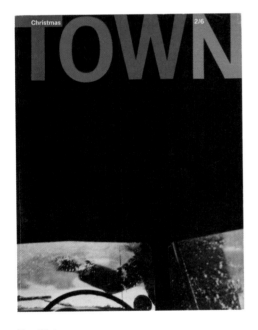

Tom Wolsey
Town
Christmas 1962/
January 1963

Cover photograph by Saul Leiter.

Tom Wolsey
About Town
April 1962

Spread with photographs by Terence Donovan.

Dennis Bailey
Town
February 1966

*Cover photograph
by Duffy. Bailey was
art director of* Town,
1965–66.

Willy Fleckhaus
Aufwärts
Vol. 9, no. 12
15 December 1956

*Cover photograph
by Horst Baumann.*

wordplay; and occasionally introduced Victorian display faces and graphic devices to change the tempo. Images and writing were 'equal and indivisible', with the dense, justified columns of text serving as a crisp counterpoint to the high-contrast, grainy photography. When the American writer David Usborne wrote about British graphic design in 1963, he said that the work of Wolsey, Bailey, Fletcher and Forbes 'could rival anything produced in America, Switzerland or Italy'.[8]

In the summer of 1963, Wolsey left *Town* (*Man About Town* had been shortened to *About Town* in March 1961, and further reduced in mid-1962) to work with the renowned editor Bea Miller on *Queen* magazine, but within months Miller left for British *Vogue*. The following year, disenchanted with the loss of editorial potency in the magazine, Wolsey departed and set up an advertising agency.

Seeking similar source material to Wolsey, Willy Fleckhaus (1925–1983), a young journalist who grew up near Düsseldorf, discovered the Amerika Haus, a US-sponsored cultural institute with a library where he was able to study such magazines as *Harper's Bazaar*, *Arts & Architecture* and *Seventeen*. He was enthralled by their visual verve. Fleckhaus edited a number of specialist publications whose subject matter ranged from religion to politics and labour relations. In 1953 he took over the editorship and design of *Aufwärts*, a youth magazine published by the German trade union movement. Fleckhaus quickly transformed what had been a staid publication into a bold and topical journal whose content regularly

OPPOSITE
Willy Fleckhaus
Twen
Vol. 4, no. 8
1962

*Front cover and spread
with photograph by
Horst Baumann.*

verged on the impudent – to the delight of its readership. 'Should girls wear long trousers?' was the lead story in his first issue.

Aufwärts was one of Germany's first home-grown lifestyle magazines, and its success led to Fleckhaus being appointed as art director of *Twen*, a new magazine for 'people in their twenties, from 15 to 30'. It was launched in 1959 as a bimonthly journal and proved so successful that in September 1961 it began appearing monthly. There was nothing uncommon about the twelve-column grid that Fleckhaus devised (with main text occupying two columns), but the way he used it – leaving large, irregular areas of white space – certainly was. These areas contrasted with headlines, often huge in scale, set in Schmalfette Grotesk, and with grainy, high-contrast photographs that were tightly cropped. While *Twen* owed something to the pioneering work of Alexey Brodovitch and other American art directors of the 1950s

RIGHT
Willi Landers
Queen
27 March 1968

Cover photograph
by Bill King.

BELOW
Derek Birdsall
Nova
September 1968

Front cover. Nova
covered once-taboo
subjects such as
abortion, birth
control, race, same-
sex relationships and
divorce. Its covers
were comparably
provocative.

such as Henry Wolf (*Esquire* from 1952), Allen Hurlburt (*Look* from 1953) and Otto Storch (*McCall's* from 1955), its look and feel were more pragmatic and could be quite dark at times. The covers, however, were almost always upbeat and often decidedly flirtatious. (*Twen* was taken to court in 1961 for showing 'no regard for society or morals', but the case was eventually dropped.)

Fleckhaus's dominant hold on *Twen* was the cause of constant internal strife. The editorship became little more than a ceremonial position, and few stayed in the job for long. As its readership matured and the issues with which it had been closely associated faded or shifted, *Twen*'s potency dwindled. In 1970 the last of many publishers forced Fleckhaus to resign, and *Twen* folded soon after.

The success of *Twen* at its height and the commanding role of the art director led to a major shift in influence within the publishing industry. One of the beneficiaries was *Nova*, a magazine established in London in March 1965. Derek Birdsall, John Blackburn and Bill Fallover all ensured that their role as art director at *Nova* was at the very least equal to that of editor. The distinctive masthead was designed by Harri Peccinotti, the magazine's first art director, who adapted Windsor Bold Condensed, a typeface designed by Eleisha Pechey and released as wood type in 1905. Its soft, curved lines made it a bold choice – indeed, the antithesis of the clean, straight lines so prevalent in popular magazine mastheads – but one that captured the zeitgeist. Peccinotti later designed a lower-case set for headlines. The text on the cover shown on this page is Cooper Black, designed by Oswald Cooper in 1922. Unlike Windsor, Cooper had the advantage of being available in a range of weights and styles and for all typesetting equipment, including Letraset, and it became the most popular headline typeface of the late 1960s. *Nova* closed in 1975.

When Britain's first newspaper colour supplement, originally titled *The Sunday Times Colour Section*, was launched on 4 February 1962, it was considered across the publishing industry to be a risky experiment, in large part because of production concerns: the huge print run coupled with severe time constraints meant that any malfunction would be a disaster. Importantly, it was printed in full colour by gravure, a process ideally suited to the reproduction of colour photography. Advertisers recognized the value of reaching the paper's wealthy readers and, after a hesitant start, took full advantage. Edited with aplomb by Mark Boxer, who had moved from *Queen*, and art-directed by John Donegan for the first year and then by Michael Rand until 1993, *The Sunday Times Colour Section* became a great success. Having seen *The Sunday Times* gain a quarter of a million new readers, other newspaper supplements followed, the most notable being that of the rival Sunday newspaper *The Observer* under the art direction of Romek Marber. More crucially, the arrival of the colour supplements demonstrated that the British press was capable of capitalizing on changes in print and advertising culture.

Phototypesetting technology became widely available from around the mid-1950s, and being a photographic process, it offered a new flexibility with regard to intermixing styles, weights and sizes of type; letter spacing and kerning; and line and word spacing, as well as hyphenation and justification. These new-found freedoms had a significant effect on typography and design – sometimes detrimental, but on occasion the results could be engaging.

Herb Lubalin (1918–1981) had worked since 1949 at Sudler & Hennessey, an important New York advertising agency and a distinguished participant in the creative revolution that took place in mid-century

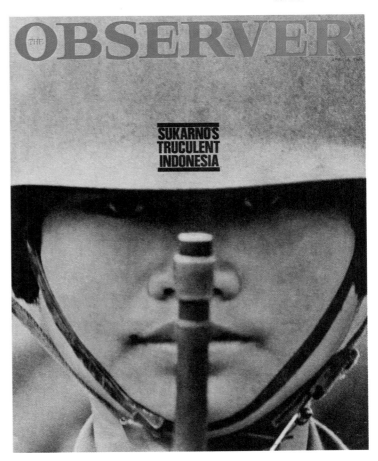

Romek Marber
The Observer colour supplement
4 April 1965

Front cover. Powerful photojournalism featured large under Marber's art direction, and his use of penetrating portraiture became a predominant aspect of his Observer *covers.*

American advertising. Lubalin left in 1964 to set up his own design studio and took on numerous wide-ranging projects, from poster and magazine design to packaging and identity solutions. Most significant, certainly most memorable, however, was a succession of magazines published by Ralph Ginzburg: *Eros*, *Fact* and *Avant Garde*.

Eros was a quarterly magazine intended to play an active part in the burgeoning countercultural movement in the United States, especially in regard to sexual liberation and racial equality. The paper and printing were of a high standard, it carried no advertising, and its size (33 × 25.4 cm/ 13 × 10 in.) provided an expansive format that Lubalin used to good effect. The subject matter no longer has the social or political impact it once had – indeed, 'Black and White in Color', a 'photographic tone poem' purportedly about interracial sex by Ralph M. Hattersley Jr. (vol. 1, no. 4, Winter 1962), appears risible today – yet Lubalin's editorial design has ensured that *Eros* remains a magazine of interest. It closed after the fourth issue, when an obscenity case was brought against Ginzburg by the US Postal Service.[9]

Undaunted, Ginzburg and Lubalin responded in 1964 with *Fact*, a more politically focused magazine whose scathingly satirical, anti-establishment views were interpreted by Lubalin with a severe, distinctly untheatrical typographic treatment, no doubt also influenced by a much-reduced budget. Its black-and-white covers, of which many were purely typographic, are quintessential Lubalin: a tightly set title and text and a distinctive use of contrasting scale and weights to create an enduring 'image'. In 1967, perhaps inevitably, *Fact* also folded in controversy, this time after Ginzburg was sued by the subject of one of the magazine's investigations. Ginzburg and Lubalin's final and probably best collaboration was *Avant Garde*, which ran from 1968 to 1971. It achieved only a modest circulation, but once more Lubalin's editorial design work proved particularly popular with America's advertising industry. The memorable masthead was designed by Lubalin and realized by Tom Carnase – by this time a partner in Lubalin's design studio. The Avant Garde typeface is characterized by geometrically perfect round strokes, short ascenders and descenders, and an exceptionally large number of unconventional ligatures. The International Typeface Corporation (ITC), of which Lubalin was a founder, released a full version in 1970 and promoted it through the ITC journal *U&lc* (*Upper and Lower Case*), which was launched in 1973 and designed by Lubalin.

The glossy sophistication of Lubalin's *Avant Garde* had yet to emerge when a swathe of new publications – hardly magazines at all, but also the antithesis of the establishment newspapers they loved to mock – irrupted suddenly, almost spontaneously on to the streets. Generically known as the underground press, these publications offered a truly alternative approach to designing for print and publishing by putting immediacy and verve above all else. Electric typewriters and Letraset provided the means to produce the words, which were cut out with scissors and stuck down with glue. The unfiltered, hands-on appearance of the publications matched their editorial policies perfectly.

The *International Times* (1966–73, quickly renamed *IT*) and *OZ* (1967–73) were the leading 'alternative' magazines in the UK. Despite their huge success, they splendidly maintained their anti-establishment credentials not only in their abrasive editorial stance (Allen Ginsberg, William S. Burroughs and Germaine Greer were contributors to both) but also in their increasingly adventurous design. This was especially the case in Martin Sharp's work for *OZ*, which had the advantage of being a monthly publication (*IT* appeared fortnightly).

Designer unknown
IT 32
31 May–13 June 1968

*Front cover and page.
This issue, with a
special feature on
'alternative society'
in Paris, was free
of charge in that
city. Price in the UK
remained 1s. 6d.*

Martin Sharp
Oz 3
May 1967

*Front cover. Sharp
had made a name for
himself in Australia
as a cartoonist, and
his covers for the
first two issues of Oz
were in that style. This
issue was the first to
combine photography
and drawing in a style
for which he became
renowned.*

In the United States, underground publications were more numerous; almost every city and college town had at least one alternative newspaper of its own. One of the most innovative was *The City of San Francisco Oracle*, designed by Gabe Katz. Katz eventually persuaded the printer, Howard Quinn, to allow him and his colleagues into the press room on Sundays to run the lithographic presses themselves. The experimental results gave *The Oracle* a unique and often sensational appearance. Having begun in 1966 with a circulation of 3000, the publication reached a peak of around 125,000 copies. It closed in 1968.

Gabe Katz
The City of San Francisco Oracle
Vol. 1, no. 7
1967

Front cover and spread. This cover features the 'split-fountain rainbow inking effect', the result of experiments by Katz when he was given free access to the presses.

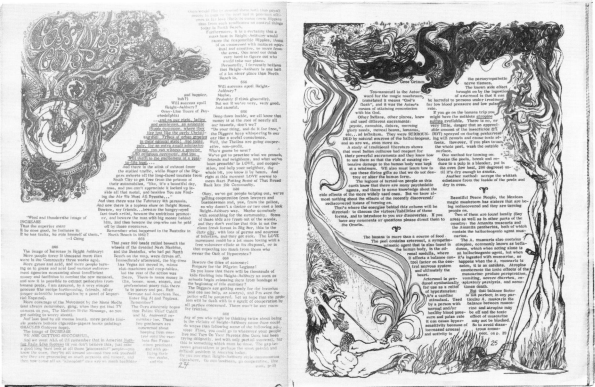

DESIGN IN

by Herbert Spencer

BUSINESS

Sylvan Press London

PRINTING

BOOKS

After the Second World War, the German typographer Jan Tschichold declared his disillusion with New Typography, whose theories he had been practising and so effectively promoting since the publication of his book of the same title in 1928. Before the visit to the Bauhaus student exhibition in 1923 that sparked his allegiance to New Typography, Tschichold had had a deep affinity with the craft and scholarship of calligraphy, typography and printing, so his infamous post-war volte-face was more a reversion – the rediscovery of a rich vein of human endeavour and accomplishment – than a rejection of the Bauhaus and modernism.

Although Tschichold's change of heart was in large part caused by the war,[1] it was also prompted by his experiences during the late 1930s, when he was invited to give lectures in Denmark and London. In Britain, the publisher Lund Humphries mounted an exhibition of his work at its London office, organized by the company's then joint managing director Eric (Peter) Gregory. This led to Tschichold being commissioned to design the 1938 volume of the celebrated *Penrose Annual*, a review of the graphic arts printed and published by Lund Humphries. Shortly after his exhibition, the journal *Typography*, edited by Robert Harling, published the first serious article on Tschichold's work to appear in the UK. This was followed by an invitation to Tschichold to give a talk to the Double Crown Club – a

dining club and society of typographers, book designers and illustrators established by Oliver Simon – the very heart of British New Traditionalism, a melding of traditional values with modern printing technologies.

The welcome Tschichold had received in England in the late 1930s, especially from Gregory, Harling and Simon (art director at the Curwen Press) – all admirers of German fine-printing culture – made it much easier for him to decide to accept the offer made by Allen Lane in 1947 to work at Penguin Books. From the start, Tschichold's work at Penguin was effectively a continuation and development of British New Traditional typography.

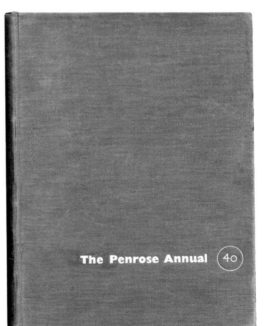

OPPOSITE
Herbert Spencer
Design in Business Printing
Sylvan Press
1952

Front of jacket. This book angered the printing industry but was greeted enthusiastically by graphic designers. Spencer was a champion of asymmetric typography and an admirer of Jan Tschichold.

Jan Tschichold
The Penrose Annual
40
Lund Humphries
1938

Front cover of green cloth with title foil-blocked in white. Published almost annually from 1895 to 1982, Penrose was a review of the graphic arts that was highly regarded by the printing industry and typographers alike.

Unlike most other forms of ephemeral graphic design (see pp. 211–25), paperback books have remained in everyday circulation in spite of their physical frailty; they are often considered too precious to throw away. Their physical vulnerability provides evidence of their continued usefulness, which, in turn, adds to their appeal. During the war years there had been a huge demand for Penguin paperback books, a demand fulfilled against all the odds by a print industry that had lost of much of its trained workforce to the war effort while dealing with a dramatic shortage of paper. ('Paperback', of course, is a misnomer, since such books had covers of at least two-sheet thickness.) By 1947 paperbacks had become a hugely successful form of mass media, and Penguin Books in particular provided readers with a wide range of exceptional and affordable literature. Lane had recently launched a new range called Penguin Classics and, no doubt aware

of the remarkable commercial success of the handsome but inexpensive Birkhäuser Classics designed by Tschichold for the Swiss publishing house, wanted Tschichold to achieve the same results for Penguin's series.

Penguin's books were printed in vast numbers (at least 500,000 sales of each title were expected) and occupied the presses of numerous printing companies scattered around Britain. Before his arrival, Tschichold requested samples of Penguin books and realized that, having been given a minimal specification by Penguin, each printer was effectively applying its own house rules to the textual arrangement of pages. As a result, Tschichold's design reform began by establishing his role as typographic designer – an independent practitioner working outside the printing industry, yet in control of every aspect of the final printed outcome. His 'Penguin Composition Rules', occupying just four A5 pages, were written as a guide for

RIGHT
Jan Tschichold
Geschichte von Romeo und Julia
Luigi Da Porto
Birkhäuser
1943

Front cover. Tschichold spent the war years in Switzerland, where he worked for several publishers. The design of this slim paperback is in stark contrast to the New Typography he had endorsed before the war. Letterpress-printed throughout.

FAR RIGHT
Jan Tschichold
Formenwandlungen der et-Zeichen
Stempel
1953

Front cover of a book on the evolution of the ampersand. Letterpress-printed throughout.

printers, and featured elemental but essential instructions on such matters as spacing for words and punctuation marks, the setting of footnotes and page numbers, and numerous other details of composition. (Tschichold had undertaken a similar task for Benno Schwabe & Co. during his exile in Switzerland in the early 1930s.) It was through these basic rules, along with the collaboration of vigilant copy editors, that Tschichold was able to establish and control typographic standards across all Penguin publications.

Through design, Tschichold sought a functional yet humanistic expression that could be suitably applied to a broad range of topics and achieve balance, consistency and clarity. In his (post-war re-evaluated) view of typographic design, adherence to the tenets of traditional typography – legibility, a balance of type styles, wide margins and simplicity, but with the careful integration of decorative rules and ornaments – was

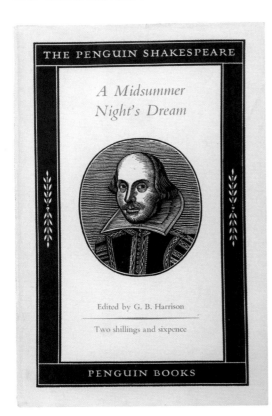

Jan Tschichold
A Midsummer Night's Dream
William Shakespeare
Engraved portrait by
Reynolds Stone
Penguin Books
Tschichold's cover
design introduced
1951

*Front cover.
Tschichold adopted
Monotype's most
distinguished
typefaces when at
Penguin, choosing
Bembo for the
Penguin Shakespeare
series.*

Penguin Composition Rules

TEXT COMPOSITION

All text composition should be as closely word-spaced as possible. As a rule, the spacing should be about a middle space or the thickness of an 'i' in the type size used.

Wide spaces should be strictly avoided. Words may be freely broken whenever necessary to avoid wide spacing, as breaking words is less harmful to the appearance of the page than too much space between words.

All major punctuation marks – full point, colon, and semicolon – should be followed by the same spacing as is used throughout the rest of the line.

INDENTING OF PARAGRAPHS

The indent of the paragraph should be the em of the fount body.

Omit indents in the first line of the first paragraph of any text and at the beginning of a new section that comes under a sub-heading. It is not necessary to set the first word in small capitals, but if this is done for any reason, the word should be letter-spaced in the same way as the running title.

If a chapter is divided into several parts without headings, these parts should be divided not only by an additional space, but always by one or more asterisks of the fount body. As a rule, one asterisk is sufficient. Without them it is impossible to see whether a part ends at the bottom of a page or not. Even when the last line of such a part ends the page, there will always be space for an asterisk in the bottom margin.

PUNCTUATION MARKS AND SPELLING

If this can be done on the keyboard, put thin spaces before question marks, exclamation marks, colons, and semicolons.

Between initials and names, as in G. B. Shaw and after all abbreviations where a full point is used, use a smaller (fixed) space than between the other words in the line.

Instead of em rules without spaces, use en rules preceded and followed by the word space of the line, as in the third paragraph above.

Marks of omission should consist of three full points. These should be set without any spaces, but be preceded and followed by word spaces.

1

Jan Tschichold
'Penguin Composition
Rules'
c. 1947

*First page of a
four-page booklet.
Resentment from
printers at being told
how to do their job
was understandable,
but Tschichold was
determined to
establish a common
standard across all
Penguin books.*

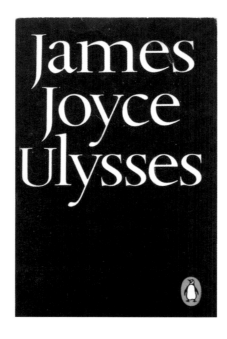

Hans Schmoller
Ulysses
James Joyce
Penguin Books
1968

*Front cover. This was
Penguin's 3000th
book, and Germano
Facetti, art director,
passed the important
assignment to
Schmoller, who
designed one of the
most iconic covers
in the publisher's
history.*

Edward Wright
This Is Tomorrow
Whitechapel Art
Gallery
1956

*Front cover of
exhibition catalogue.
Wright also designed
the exhibition graphics
and title mural for
the exhibition in
collaboration with
Theo Crosby.*

essential not only to a book's attractiveness but also to its function. The use of sans-serif type (previously a staple for Tschichold) was now a rarity. He later explained: 'By guiding the compositors of a large Basle printing office I learnt a lot about practicability. Good typography has to be perfectly legible and is, as such, the result of intelligent planning. The classical typefaces such as Garamond, Janson, Baskerville and Bell are undoubtedly the most legible. Sans serif is good for certain cases of emphasis, but is used to the point of abuse today. The occasions for using sans serif are as rare as those for wearing obtrusive decorations.'[2]

Tschichold left Penguin in 1949, and Hans Schmoller, another German typographer, took over as head of typography and design, maintaining the approach and standards set by Tschichold. Schmoller would remain at Penguin until 1976, but he relinquished the role of art director to Germano Facetti (1926–2006) in 1960. Facetti had arrived in the UK from Milan in 1950, having previously worked in the offices of the architectural practice Banfi, Belgiojoso, Peressutti and Rogers (BBPR). In London, he joined an evening class in typography at the Central School of Arts and Crafts that was taught by Edward Wright. It was experimental and anarchic, but also included letterpress printing directly from type; the creative possibilities of type proved to be a revelation to Facetti. In 1956, together with Wright, he was involved in the design of the iconic *This Is Tomorrow* exhibition at the Whitechapel Art Gallery.

Permanent employment in design was difficult to find in London, and so Facetti moved to Paris, where he worked for the SNIP advertising agency. More importantly, he also engaged in documentary film-making – a significant genre in Britain since the 1930s and now rejuvenated in Paris in the 1950s. Facetti was in the circle of directors that included Alain Resnais, Agnès Varda and

Jacques Demy. For documentary makers, photographic images provided much of the raw material for their films, and the way they were animated by panning, zooming and the use of focus fascinated Facetti and other book designers of the time. He returned to Britain and for a brief period was an art director with Rathbone – later Aldus – Books. It was shortly after this, in 1960, that Facetti was invited by Allen Lane to join Penguin Books as its art director.

By this time Penguin had several categories of book for which the only unifying element was the Penguin logo. The interior typography and layout of the books took full advantage of Monotype typefaces and technology. However, Lane was concerned that Penguin's traditional covers lacked a certain pizzazz that the public was being served by television and, increasingly compellingly, by publishing rivals. Crucial questions were raised with Facetti about the relationship between design and marketing and the extent to which a book's cover should reflect its literary content or the author's *oeuvre*. The rather alarming move from typographic to 'visual' covers was initiated.

Facetti began with the popular Penguin Crime series. He asked three designers to submit proposals, and the chosen design was by Romek Marber. By dividing the cover area with a grid derived mathematically from Penguin's classic cover format, Marber cleverly retained the character of the original and much-loved format. The Gill Sans capitals were replaced by Akzidenz-Grotesk in upper and lower case and ranged left instead of centred. Covers were printed letterpress, meaning that solid colour (not half-tone) was used, providing a distinct and crisp edge for Marber's artwork. Helvetica was increasingly adopted as it became available in the UK during the 1960s.

Following the successful relaunch of the Crime series, Facetti turned to the Penguin Classics. Again Marber's grid was used, but

Romek Marber
Penguin Crime series
1960s

Grid (1961) and various front covers (dating 1962–65). Marber illustrated around 100 titles for the Penguin Crime series, retaining the classic Penguin green but lightening the shade. The grid was based on the 'golden ratio', the ancient formula for well-proportioned design (1:1.618), as is the standard A-format paperback.

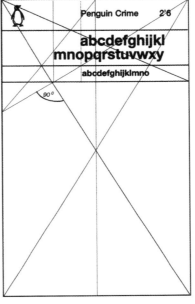

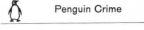

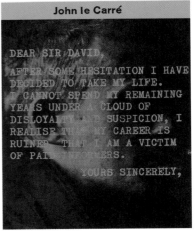

this time black was the predominant colour – to the consternation of Penguin's marketing department. Unlike the Crime series, the Penguin Classics covers were printed by lithography, so full colour was available. Facetti chose images, generally of paintings, drawings or objects from the period of the book's first publication, to provide historical context. The type, usually Helvetica or Akzidenz-Grotesk, was centred using medium-weight capitals on a black background, the author's name separated from the title by a horizontal rule. The new design was an outstanding success, and Facetti went on to design hundreds more Penguin Classics covers.

After 1945 paperback companies sprang up all over the world, and many traditional hardback publishers moved into the field. At the same time, original literature began to supersede reprints. In the United States, where Penguin was already established, the entrepreneur Robert de Graff had founded a

similar line, partnering with Simon & Schuster in 1939 to create the Pocket Books label. The first American mass-market paperback line, it was closely followed by numerous imitators. For almost the price of a magazine, it was now possible to buy a whole book. De Graff commissioned illustrators who had made their reputations designing the lascivious covers of such pulp-fiction magazines as *Man's Life*; now they brought their talent to, for example, the cover of Emile Brontë's *Wuthering Heights*. The results were startling and helped to sell one and a half million Pocket Books in the first year.

There were, however, American publishers that took an alternative route. Meridian Books approached Alvin Lustig, who proposed the adoption of an eclectic mix of typefaces, often including decorative Victorian types, in a crisp but playful arrangement on coloured backgrounds with a minimal use of imagery. The choice of type might reflect the book's

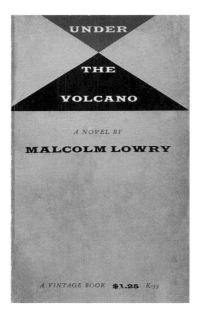

Harry Ford
Under the Volcano
Malcolm Lowry
Vintage
1958

Front cover.

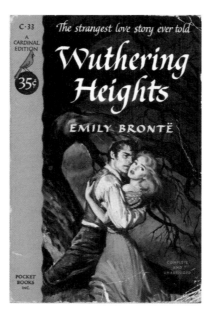

Walter Baumhofer, illustrator
Wuthering Heights
Emily Brontë
Pocket Books
1951

Front cover.

Robert Brownjohn
Journey to the End of the Night
Louis-Ferdinand Céline
New Directions
1960

Front cover.

theme or title, but there is a sense that when this occurred it was more by chance than choice. When Lustig died in 1955, aged just forty, his wife, Elaine, took over the studio. She had no formal design training but had worked in the Lustig office for seven years and successfully developed her own distinct modernist style. She specialized in book covers, including around 100 for Meridian, as well as museum and gallery catalogues and architectural signage.

The Parisian publishing house Gallimard – an offshoot of the journal *La Nouvelle Revue française* (NRF) – began publishing its paperback Collection Blanche of classic French literature in 1911. The covers were given a generic format by Edward Verbeke of the Sinte-Catharina printing company in Bruges, and have remained almost unchanged to the present day. Set in Didot, the author's name was

Elaine Lustig
Meridian Books Catalogue
1960

Front cover. Lustig successfully transitioned from office manager to designer, but it was many decades before her work received the recognition it deserved.

Alvin Lustig
The Man of Letters in the Modern World
Allen Tate
Meridian Books
1955

Front cover.

Elaine Lustig
Gods & Heroes of the Greeks
H.J. Rose
Meridian Books
1958

Front cover.

Elaine Lustig
The Scrolls from the Dead Sea
Edmund Wilson
Meridian Books
1959

Front cover.

Edward Verbeke
L'Étranger
Albert Camus
Gallimard
1942

Front cover. Until the 1960s, the belief in France was that literature should speak for itself and that an attractive cover was almost an insult to a book's content. When Gallimard launched the Idées NRF series, its covers (below), though colourful and different from one other, remained nondescript.

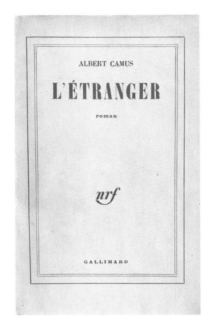

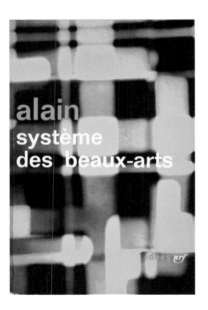

Robert Massin
Système des beaux-arts
Alain
Idées NRF/Gallimard
1963

Front cover.

Robert Massin
Gauche, année zéro
Marc Paillet
Idées NRF/Gallimard
1964

Front cover.

printed black, the title in red, and both were centred within borders of red and black on an off-white, lightweight uncoated card. These quintessentially laissez-faire covers came to represent the French preference for understatement, especially in regard to culture. A similarly austere look was created for the covers of Les Éditions de Minuit. The press was set up as an underground publisher during the Nazi occupation of France, when all forms of publishing were controlled and censored. After the liberation of Paris in 1944, its almost 'plain-wrapper' covers were retained, giving the books, certainly from a 1960s perspective, an 'alternative' aura.

In contrast, when Gallimard launched a new series of pocket books in 1962 titled Idées NRF, bold, brightly coloured and almost abstract designs were employed for its covers. Robert Massin, art director at Gallimard, commissioned the British-born, Paris-based photographer Henry Cohen to provide the images, while Massin himself designed the typography: all lower-case sans serif, ranged left across the middle of the covers, over Cohen's photographs (the type was later moved to the top). Over the next thirteen years Cohen provided some 300 cover images incorporating various photographic darkroom techniques, including solarization, shooting through layers of textured glass and the superimposition of film positives and negatives.[3] Cohen went on to collaborate with Massin on the Folio series of paperbacks for Gallimard from 1972, as well as on Massin's groundbreaking design of Eugène Ionesco's absurdist text *La Cantatrice chauve* in 1964. The result earned Massin international recognition when an American version (*The Bald Soprano*) was released in 1965, followed the next year by a version for the British market (*The Bald Prima Donna*). The high-contrast photographs and experimental typography became a prominent influence on the burgeoning underground press.

Massin's prolificacy is exceeded only by that of Pierre Faucheux (1924–1999). Both men began their careers when Paris was under Nazi occupation, but it was Faucheux who would make an impact first, as art director of the newly established Club Français du Livre from 1946. The idea of selling books by mail order to subscribers was based on such popular American book clubs as Book of the Month and The Literary Guild, which were established during the 1920s and developed memberships that ran into hundreds of thousands. But while the design of these books was standard fare, Faucheux's approach was determinedly divergent.

Faucheux trained as a printer, attending the École Estienne in Paris, where he was taught traditional typesetting, page layout and proof correction, as well as drawing and art history. When he left college in 1942 he chose not to enter the printing profession and instead sought work as a designer.

Nevertheless, his knowledge meant that when necessary he was able to make up his design work 'at the stone', composing the metal type and locking it into the chase. His skill in handling metal type not only enabled him to design more radically – knowing precisely how his intentions could be achieved – but also gave him a deep appreciation of type's aesthetic and creative potential.

Unlike the books discussed so far, Club Français du Livre books were not designed to appear as a series. They were unified only by their size – initially 20.8 cm (8¼ in.) high – and their stiff, case-bound, cloth-covered covers. Faucheux used various coloured and textured cloths, and either printed directly on to the cloth or had an image printed separately and glued into position, usually within a debossed area for protection. Internally, Faucheux's design work was unique, governed by his response to the substance of the text. Every part of the book was individually considered,

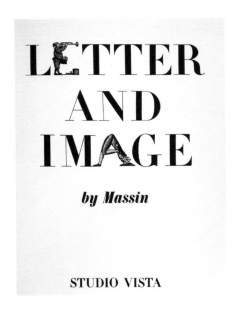

Robert Massin
Letter and Image
Studio Vista
1970

Front of jacket and spread. Published in French as La Lettre et l'image *by Gallimard.*

including folios and running heads, but especially the prelims, in which the progression of an idea might use endpapers and half-title, title and contents pages. The shape and placement of textual areas and the choice of type also varied accordingly, although Plantin, Bodoni and Garamond were most frequently used, while bold sans serifs and nineteenth-century decorative typefaces were often employed for section headings and chapter titles. Faucheux's Club Français du Livre books lacked the finesse of, for example, the Penguin Classics series, and they were not *éditions de luxe*, but they were distinctive and often experimental in nature, full of visual surprise and, inevitably, Faucheux's own personality. The idea that the book typographer should remain invisible, acting solely as a conduit between author and reader, was swept aside by Faucheux. Club Français du Livre was a huge success, and other mail-order publishing companies quickly joined the market.

Traditional booksellers decided to respond to the loss of sales to subscription-only book clubs by setting up a rival mail-order company. Established in 1954, it was called the Club des Libraires de France, and Faucheux was persuaded to join as production manager and art director. Faucheux's book designs were again very successful, and he stayed with the Club des Libraires until 1962, when he opened his own studio, the Atelier Pierre Faucheux.

Between 1962 and 1976, Faucheux's studio was producing well over 400 separate projects a year – mainly book covers for Le Livre de Poche and other publishers, but also occasionally entire books – and by the mid-1960s Faucheux employed fourteen assistant designers. As a result, originality suffered, but nevertheless the studio continued to produce some outstanding work, the best of which still looks remarkably fresh today. For example, in 1964 the independent French publisher and provocateur Jean-Jacques

Pierre Faucheux
Les Jeux inconnus
François Boyer
Club Français du Livre
1950

Front and back cover and title page. The book is case-bound and covered in dark-grey cloth. The image is created by white foil blocking debossed into the cloth.

Pauvert launched a literary series called Libertés, which he commissioned Faucheux to design. The books were tall and narrow with a cover design that was letterpress-printed using large Folio Condensed black capitals on a brown paper into which the letters were slightly debossed. Inside, the paper stock was poor, but the texts were carefully set and printed. Several colour variations followed.

The expressive potency of type, used with such enthusiasm by Faucheux and Massin in France, was likewise utilized, albeit in a subtler manner and restricted to covers, by Faber & Faber when it appointed typographer Berthold Wolpe (1905–1989) in 1941. Under Richard de la Mare's direction, the 1930s had been a distinguished decade for the publisher, a period in which it had established a format and house style with the aid of a brilliant group of freelance illustrators and designers, including Barnett Newman, Rex Whistler, Edward Bawden, Edward McKnight Kauffer, Paul Nash, Eric Fraser and Reynolds Stone. However, the new austerity demanded during the war years suited Wolpe, who was able to demonstrate how calligraphy and typography alone, often using just one or two colours on a plain ground, could replace the elaborate process work of the previous decade.

Wolpe shared his studio at Faber & Faber with David Bland, the head of the production department, which also included six production/design assistants. Although Wolpe did not design every cover, he was able to choose the covers he wanted – well in excess of 1500 between 1941 and 1975. Many of the great writers, and particularly those published in the 1950s and '60s – Auden, Eliot, Larkin, Hughes, Plath, Golding, Beckett and others – came to be defined, and their reputations enhanced, by Wolpe's calligraphic lettering and above all by the emphatic presence of Albertus, the typeface he had designed for the Monotype

Pierre Faucheux
Provinciales
Pascal
Libertés 6
J.-J. Pauvert, editor
1964

Front cover. A small double-square format, bound in heavy brown kraft paper. The black ink has a sheen in contrast to the matt brown paper. Unusually, the trimmed head, foot and fore-edge of each book are coloured black.

Pierre Faucheux
Racine polémiste
Raymond Picard
Libertés 51
J.-J. Pauvert, editor
1967

Front cover.

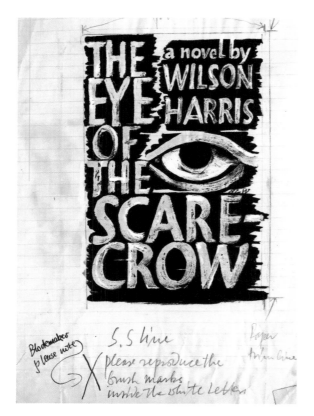

THE EYE OF THE SCARE-CROW

a novel by WILSON HARRIS

Blockmaker please note ✗ S.S. line

✗ please reproduce the brush marks inside the white letters

Paper thin line

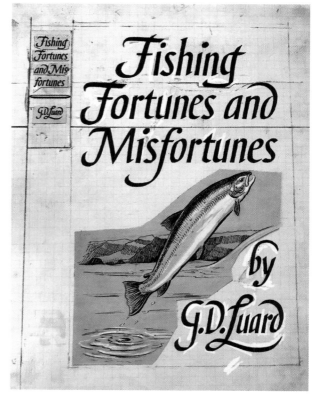

Fishing Fortunes and Misfortunes

G.D.Luard

Fishing Fortunes and Misfortunes

by G.D.Luard

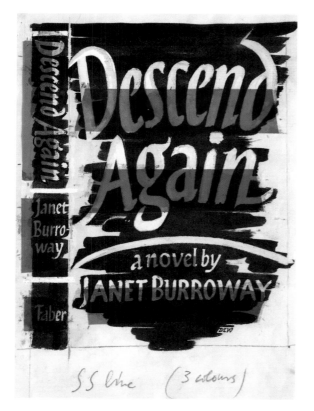

Descend Again

a novel by JANET BURROWAY

Descend Again

Janet Burroway

Faber

S.S. line (3 colours)

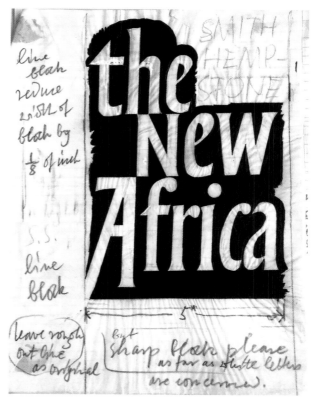

the New Africa

SMITH HEMP-STONE

line black reduce 2 S.S. of black by 1/8 of inch

S.S. line black

leave rough out line as original

but sharp black please as far as white letters are concerned.

Corporation in 1935 and first shown in *The Monotype Recorder* of Summer 1935 (lower case was added in 1940). Albertus regularly appeared, albeit in a multitude of subtle guises, on Wolpe's covers, so much so that it became known as 'Faber lettering'.[4]

Apart from books designed for young children, most publishing in the 1940s that included internal colour images – books on art, for example, where accurate colour reproduction was a necessity – required the division of pages into 'text' and 'plates', because the text was printed letterpress (black only) and the images printed in colour from (thin metal) lithographic 'plates'. It was not uncommon for lithographic-printed images to be 'tipped in' – pasted into position – separately by hand. The 1944 book *Henry Moore: Sculpture and Drawings*, co-published by Lund Humphries and Zwemmer, is a fine example. Quite apart from the aesthetic limitations that this process imposed, it also made books on art and design expensive. However, as lithographic technology improved, and with the rapid development of phototypesetting from the mid-1950s, letterpress was effectively, if slowly, phased out of large-scale publishing, enabling an unrestricted integration of text and image printed from a set of four plates (one each for cyan, magenta, yellow and black) simultaneously. Crucially, this also meant that books on art and design became affordable for a far larger number of readers. Moreover, the drop in production costs encouraged publishers to be more adventurous in their choice of subjects.

Walter Neurath arrived in London from Vienna in 1938, and initially worked as production director of Adprint, a book-packaging company established by Wolfgang Foges. (While at Adprint, Neurath designed and produced the hardback King Penguin books, published between 1939 and 1959,

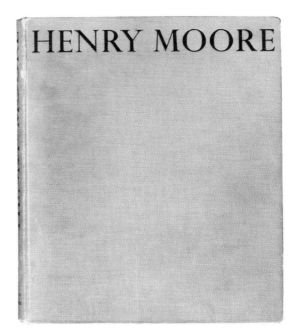

Designer unknown
Henry Moore: Sculpture and Drawings
Lund Humphries and Zwemmer
1944

Linen-covered board with foil-blocked title.

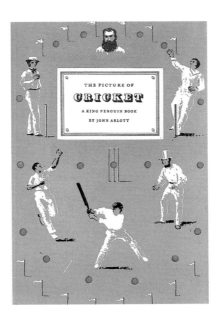

Walter Neurath
The Picture of Cricket
John Arlott
King Penguin
1955

Front of jacket of a slim, pocket-size hardback.

OPPOSITE
Berthold Wolpe
Cover layouts
1940s–60s

Hand-drawn cover layouts for Faber & Faber, marked up for the printer by the designer.

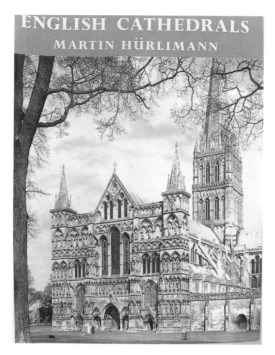

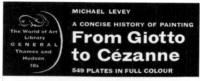

a blatant imitation of the extraordinarily successful Insel-Bücherei series published in Germany since 1912.) Together, Neurath and Foges pioneered the revolutionary concept of co-edition publishing, in which books are conceived, commissioned and produced, and then sold, minus the black-only text, to publishers in other territorial markets and languages; the new publisher simply adds its translated text in the available space. In 1949 Neurath established his own publishing house with offices in London and New York. He named the company Thames & Hudson, after the rivers in the two cities – an allusion to his plan to succeed on both sides of the Atlantic.

Thames & Hudson published ten titles in its first season in 1950, among them *English Cathedrals*, with photographs by Martin Hürlimann. The company went on to become one of the most important publishers in Europe, its reputation made principally by publishing carefully edited art books at affordable prices. Neurath was also the first to recognize the potential of the full-colour paperback. His famous World of Art series, launched in 1958, was designed to fit a student budget. Michael Levey's *Concise History of Painting: From Giotto to Cézanne*, first published in 1962 (and in paperback in 1964), is noteworthy for including more than 500 colour illustrations. As a result, it has remained on every art student's reading list and has been translated into more than twenty languages.

The ability to economically print and publish books with images in full colour encouraged art galleries to publish catalogues. Before 1945, pre-eminent national galleries had occasionally produced expensive case-bound books of their art collections in small numbers, usually in collaboration with a publisher to manage production and distribution. However, by the end of the 1950s large-format catalogues were published to accompany temporary exhibitions, serving not only as aides-memoires but also to raise the profile of a museum or gallery in terms of the seriousness of its commitment to programming.[5] One of the earliest galleries to recognize and fully endorse the possibilities of the art catalogue was the Stedelijk Museum Amsterdam.

Willem Sandberg became a curator and assistant director at the Stedelijk in 1938 and immediately after the war was appointed director, a post he held until 1962. In addition to his administrative tasks, he undertook the design of catalogues and posters for exhibitions, working mainly in the evenings. He found inspiration in the expressive letterpress work of H.N. Werkman and the Dadaists, but was also fascinated by the materials and papers he saw at the printer's premises. As both client and designer, Sandberg was able to work unhampered, creating hand-torn letterforms and incorporating heavily textured papers, vivid colours and his own distinctive handwriting. The result was a consistent, identifiable visual idiom that, over time, became renowned and helped to transform the Stedelijk into one of Europe's first truly modern art galleries.

In 1963, when Edy de Wilde took over as director, he asked Wim Crouwel to take sole responsibility for the design of all the museum's graphic material. In the following twenty-two years – until De Wilde's retirement – Crouwel designed over 300 catalogues. It was a working relationship of uncommon longevity, one that, like Sandberg, contributed enormously to the cultural status of the Stedelijk Museum. Crouwel's close association with the exceptional variety of avant-garde activities at the Stedelijk also undoubtedly augmented his reputation as an innovative typographic designer.

No other major art gallery has maintained such a high level of consistency in the delivery of printed material. Indeed, some would

Willem Sandberg
Léger: Wegbereider
Stedelijk Museum
Amsterdam
1956

Back and front cover and brown-paper spread from an exhibition catalogue on the French artist Fernand Léger.

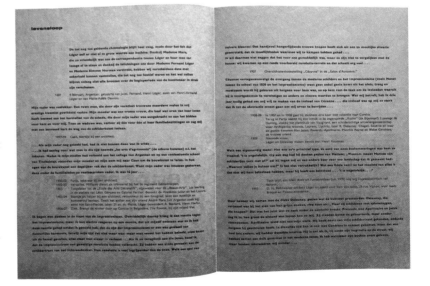

Wim Crouwel
Agam
Stedelijk Museum
Amsterdam
1973

*Front cover of an
exhibition catalogue
on the Israeli artist
Yaacov Agam,
widely known for
his contributions to
optical and kinetic art.*

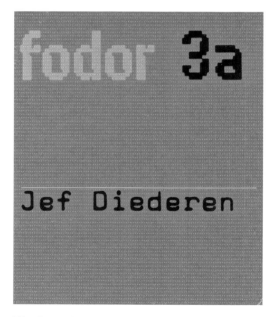

Wim Crouwel
*Fodor 3a: Jef
Diederen*
Museum Fodor,
Amsterdam
1972

*Front cover of an
exhibition catalogue,
one in a series
with a standard
cover design, each
catalogue on a
different artist.*

argue that the focus the Stedelijk placed on itself, or even on its designer, was misjudged; they suggest that the emphasis should instead have been on art and the diversity of the artists who create it. The Museum of Modern Art (MoMA) in New York, which rapidly grew in importance during the 1930s, had, from the outset, recognized the significance of print in generating international recognition: its Bauhaus exhibition catalogue of 1938 and the one for the Picasso retrospective of 1939 are good examples. But MoMA catalogues have remained eclectic, each an individual response to the exhibition that it represents, sometimes even without the gallery name on the cover. *The Machine as Seen at the End of the Mechanical Age*, in 1968, was a special case. The exhibition explored the interdependence of art and technology, and the catalogue's front cover featured the famous MoMA building on Fifty-Third Street. The cover was designed by Anders Österlin and manufactured from tin and pressed galvanized steel, which gave the image of the museum, carefully adapted from a photograph, a bright and sparkling appearance.

Books about design suffered for the same practical reasons as books about art, but had the added disadvantage of having a relatively small readership until graduate-level courses in graphic design, fashion and industrial design began to appear after 1945. However, manuals concerning typography were an exception, since they were required reading for print apprentices. There were even books on graphic design (described as 'composition' or 'page layout' to suit the terminology used in printing offices), although their purpose was to provide an immutable resolution, effectively a set of rules. But when graphic design as an independent profession grew in stature, a new generation of graphic designers sought something different.

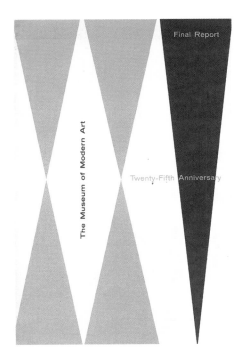

Leo Lionni
Twenty-Fifth Anniversary: Final Report
The Museum of Modern Art, New York
1954

Front cover.

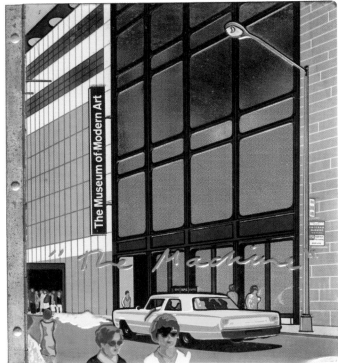

Ivan Chermayeff
The Art of Assemblage
The Museum of Modern Art, New York
1961

Front of jacket.

Anders Österlin
The Machine as Seen at the End of the Mechanical Age
The Museum of Modern Art, New York
1968

Front cover of an exhibition catalogue with steel binding and a riveted spine. The cover is a lithograph printed on to tin and then relief-stamped, after a photograph by Alicia Legg.

Richard Guyatt
Graphic Design
John Lewis and
John Brinkley
Routledge & Kegan
Paul
1954

*Front of jacket,
designed by Richard
Guyatt; book design
by John Lewis.*

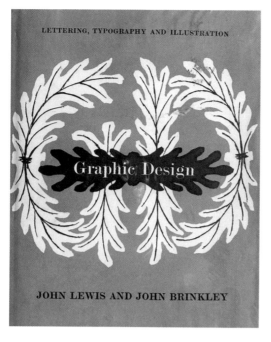

Comparing Tschichold's design manual *Die neue Typographie*, published in 1928, with the manuals that appeared in the 1950s, one is struck by the amount of technical knowledge that Tschichold was able to assume on the part of his readers. This was because he was writing chiefly for an audience of printers (*Die neue Typographie* was published by the Union of German Book Printers, Berlin), although the book also heralded the emergence of the independent graphic designer. Typography and graphic design manuals of the 1950s and thereafter had to consider a readership that had little or no hands-on experience of printing or composition of type. In fact, early handbooks and manuals for graphic designers, such as John Lewis and John Brinkley's *Graphic Design: With Special Reference to Lettering, Typography and Illustration* (published by Routledge & Kegan Paul in 1954), largely ignored the technical minutiae of typography and concentrated instead on general layout and the use of illustration, the assumption being that such details were left to the compositors, regardless of whether they were working in metal or

**Hans Neuburg and
Walter Bangerter**
*Graphic Design in
Swiss Industry*
Hans Neuburg
ABC Verlag
1965

*Front cover, without
jacket.*

photocomposition. Nevertheless, as graphic designers sought greater control (if only to avoid time-consuming errors), they needed a manual that explained the technical issues and used the correct terminology. The best such publication, Cal Swann's *Techniques of Typography* (published by Lund Humphries in 1969), is a combination of principled thinking and practical action, demonstrated by the use of distinctive images that explain not only the interrelationship between aesthetics and readability but also what the compositor should do to provide the required outcome.

The close affiliation of several key Swiss typographers with design education encouraged them to transpose their methods and ideas into print. Josef Müller-Brockmann's *Grid Systems in Graphic Design* (Arthur Niggli, 1968) and Armin Hofmann's *Graphic Design Manual: Principles and Practice* (Alec Tiranti, 1965) were designed for an international readership. They became almost instant classics and have remained in print ever since. Other books aimed at the professional designer, such as Hans Neuburg's *Graphic Design in Swiss Industry* (ABC Verlag, 1965), were also intended to attract the attention of international corporations – something they achieved with huge aplomb. They are now rare and highly prized by collectors.

Josef Müller-Brockmann
Grid Systems in Graphic Design
Arthur Niggli
1968

Front of jacket and spread.

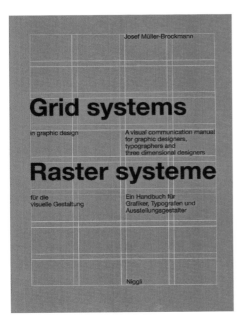

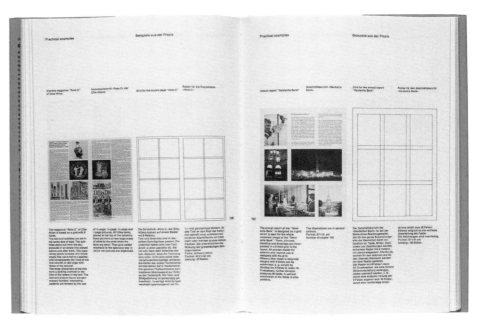

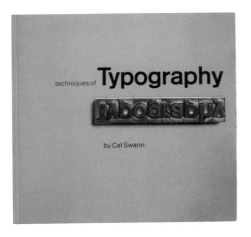

Cal Swann
Techniques of Typography
Lund Humphries
1980

Front cover and spread. Originally published 1969. Shown here is the second edition, with Swann's preferred cover design.

Design

Council of Industrial Design   152   August 1961   Price 3s

TRANSPORT

'Mile-a-minute typography' was the title of a series of photographs taken in 1961 by Herbert Spencer, designer and editor of the magazine *Typographica*. Spencer drove from central London to Heathrow Airport and took photographs of every road sign he saw along the way. Spencer's photographs demonstrated the shambolic state of British road signage: the use of different typefaces, symbols and colours, and the signs being positioned with apparently no concern for consistency. As a consequence, drivers were spending too much time looking for – and then at – signs, instead of concentrating on safety and the road ahead.

The earliest manufactured road signs were the product of automobile clubs established in the 1920s, and were erected in cities, districts and, in some instances, nationally. These clubs designed their own signs – with their insignia prominently displayed – and positioned them themselves. In Italy, this ad hoc practice extended to private companies ('Campari' on town signs was a particularly common sight) and continued well into the 1940s. After 1945 major road building became a priority across Europe – and also a symbol of modernity and a source of national pride. At this point, the creation and function of road signs became the responsibility of engineers, who viewed them as an extension of standard motorway features such as lighting and safety barriers. As a result, the typography applied to road signs was created by engineers, often

using a geometric or grid-based approach. One of the earliest and best of these typefaces was designed in Germany and was called DIN 1451 (in reference to the Deutsches Institut für Normung, or the German Institute for Standardization). It was based on a simple grid, so its forms could easily be drawn with a compass and ruler. The standard sheet *DIN 1451-Schriften* (*Schrift* means 'typeface') was first released in 1931 and then, with minor changes, re-released as the official standard in 1936, applying not only to road signs and street names but also to vehicle licence plates and house numbers.[1] When the German Autobahn system was established in 1938, DIN 1451 was used for its signs.

To encourage and enable its use, DIN 1451 was available as celluloid lettering

OPPOSITE
George Daulby
Design no. 152
Council of Industrial Design
August 1961

Front cover.

Road sign sponsored by Campari and manufactured by the Touring Club Italiano. Date unknown.

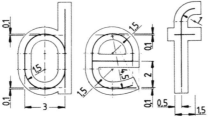

Ludwig Goller
DIN 1451
1936

Drawings from Normschriften (Standard typeface report). Goller served as chairman of the DIN committee and was instrumental in establishing DIN 1451.

stencils for smaller applications; as metal stencils for application to machinery, vehicles and airplanes; and as cast-metal lettering for street and building signage. It continues to dominate public lettering in Germany. Despite its universal application in the public realm, a DIN 1451 typeface for use in print was never produced.[2]

In the United States, the first specifications concerning the nationwide use of type in road signage appeared in *Standard Alphabets for Traffic Control Devices*, published in 1945 by the Public Roads Administration, now the Federal Highway Administration (FHWA). Although the FHWA Series, commonly known today as Highway Gothic, is the official typeface family used in road signs throughout the United States, it was never tested. Nevertheless, Highway Gothic and DIN 1451 have both been widely adopted or adapted by national transport systems around the world,[3] despite subsequent tests demonstrating that

Bilingual street signs, in German and Czech, in German-occupied Czechoslovakia, 1940.

neither performed particularly well in terms of legibility.

It is not surprising, therefore, that in 1957, when the building of Britain's first motorway caused the Ministry of Transport to realize that the current ad hoc road-signage system was inadequate, the government looked to Germany and the United States for a typographic solution. Richard 'Jock' Kinneir (1917–1994) and his assistant Margaret Calvert (b. 1936) had recently completed the signage design of London's new Gatwick Airport. This substantial project, the first signage work Kinneir had taken on, had been well received, and as a result Sir Colin Anderson, chairman of the P&O Line shipping company, commissioned Kinneir to design a baggage-labelling system, a task undertaken largely by Calvert. In 1957 Anderson was appointed chairman of a new government committee created to oversee the design of the signage for the planned British

Manual on Uniform Traffic Control Devices for Streets and Highways
American Association of State Highway Officials
1935

Page from the first edition of a manual that specifies the standards by which traffic signs, road surface markings and signals are designed, installed and used.

TOP
American road signs in Highway Gothic, formally known as the FHWA Series.

ABOVE
FHWA Series
c. 1945

From top: Series B, C, D, E and F. Purported to be based on lettering developed by Theodore Forbes for road signs in California, before being developed into a national standard by the FHWA.

RIGHT
An English pre-war signpost with directional signs from various periods.

FAR RIGHT
Pryke & Palmer
'Motor Sign Posts'
1930

From a catalogue advertising the vast range of cast-metal products manufactured by the London firm of Pryke & Palmer.

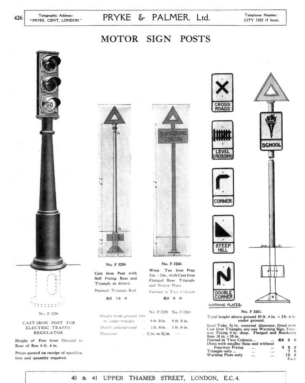

New road signs are loaded into a van at the Royal Automobile Club (RAC) sign factory in Victoria, London, 1936.

OPPOSITE
Anthony Froshaug
Design no. 178
Council of Industrial
Design
October 1963

Front cover and spread, featuring an analysis of the current state of British road signage.

motorway network, and Kinneir was duly commissioned to do the work.

Britain's first, rather short, stretch of motorway was due to open in 1958, and this became the test site for designs proposed by Kinneir and Calvert. Following European and American models, the committee had already decided that upper- and lower-case type should be used rather than capitals only – as had been used on Britain's roads since 1933. Both the American and German systems had their advocates on the committee. It had also already been agreed that white lower-case lettering on a blue background should be employed, as it had in Germany. (The United States used green.) The committee had even decided on the typeface, as Anderson explained in a letter to Kinneir following a difficult first meeting: 'I am anxious you shouldn't embark upon inventing an alphabet of a character quite "new". We have, as a committee, got into the habit of accepting the

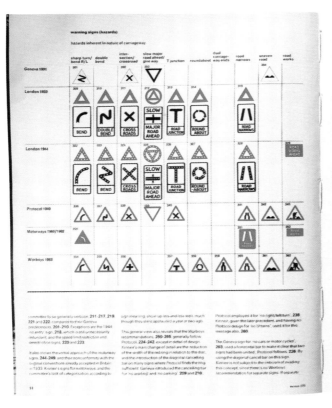

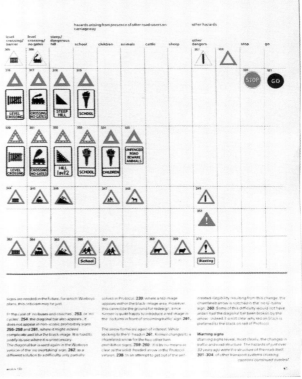

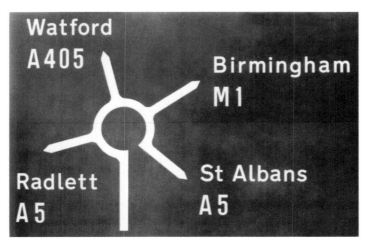

general weight and appearance of the German alphabet as being the sort of thing we need! I think therefore something on those lines is what the Committee believes it wants …'[4] Fortunately, Kinneir ignored the order, as Calvert later explained: '[We thought] that the German sans serif …, although demonstrably effective, would not sit well in the English landscape. So we started from scratch.'[5]

Akzidenz-Grotesk was a major influence on proportion and overall appearance. It had been re-released by the Berthold foundry in 1955, and a flurry of new typefaces, such as Folio (Bauer and Baum), Univers (Frutiger) and Neue Haas Grotesk (later renamed Helvetica; Miedinger and Hoffmann), followed in 1957 to compete. But Kinneir and Calvert also admired the alphabet that Edward Johnston designed in 1916 for the signage on the London Underground, and it was Johnston's influence that encouraged them to give their sans serif a more humanistic and distinctive appearance. Details such as the curve on the end of the lower-case *l*, which mirrors the curved tails of the *a* and the *t*, and the high vertex of the *M*, are all reminiscent of Johnston's Underground. The final version was officially named Transport.

The first stretch of motorway, the Preston Bypass, was formally opened in December 1958, and the signage immediately came under attack from several quarters, most notably from David Kindersley, the eminent stone engraver and lettering and type designer, who had been an apprentice to Eric Gill. Kindersley was appalled by the new signs, and *The Times* published a letter sent by a close supporter in which a series of criticisms were made,[6] the key issues being the use of upper and lower case and of a sans-serif typeface.

Kindersley argued that while upper and lower case offered a more distinctive word shape, this was helpful only when the word shape was already familiar, which was unlikely in the case of place names.

Secondly, he argued that serifs would help to reinforce the characters at those points most vulnerable to a loss of definition in poor weather conditions or the glare of headlights ('halation'). When the ministry explained, probably erroneously, that the signs were still at an experimental stage, Kindersley, without invitation, proposed his own set of letterforms – serifed and capitals only.

Using MOT Serif (perhaps with minor modifications), a typeface that he had designed for the Ministry of Transport for street signs in 1952, Kindersley had dummy signs constructed so that direct comparisons could be made with the Kinneir and Calvert signs. His proposed letterforms were designed specifically for maximum legibility, their appearance dictated by the need to ensure that each letter was distinct from every other one. In so doing, Kindersley created a set of letters that had little relation to the conventions of visual unity governing how letters relate and interact with one another. This gave his MOT Serif a distinctly homespun quality, nothing at all like the crisp, modern appearance that the committee sought for its sleek new motorway system.

Nevertheless, in true democratic fashion, tests were initiated by the Road Research Laboratory to settle the issue. Rather comically, in 1961 a small group of volunteers found themselves seated on a tiered platform on the periphery of a small airfield while a car drove towards them at 30 miles per hour with alternate combinations of signs mounted on the roof. Kindersley's MOT Serif proved to be fractionally (3%) more legible than Transport – a negligible amount given the primitive conditions governing testing, and certainly insufficient to force the committee to rethink its choice of Kinneir and Calvert's Transport. Perhaps unknown to Kindersley, international politics had been a significant factor throughout the committee's deliberations. Britain was negotiating to enter the European

IJLTFYCP SVZEXGA UKORBH DQNMW 1234567890

David Kindersley
MOT Serif
1952

MOT Serif was originally designed for use on street signs in Cambridge, where Kindersley lived and worked.

Trial sign erected on the Preston Bypass, 1958. One of the complaints by Kindersley and others was the large size of the proposed signs.

TOP
Jock Kinneir, Margaret Calvert and David Tuhill, c. 1970. Tuhill joined the studio after graduating from the Royal College of Art in 1969.

ABOVE
Jock Kinneir overseeing the production of road signs, mid-1960s.

Common Market, and Anderson knew it would be helpful if the new traffic signage system was seen to be close to European norms, hence the apparently unreserved support of the committee from the outset for the use of sans-serif, upper- and lower-case letters and a blue background. Transport was duly accepted.

Kinneir's studio (with Calvert a partner from 1964) had set the benchmark and was asked to undertake the far more complex task of designing a signage system to be applied across Britain's entire road network. At this point, European standards established by the Geneva Convention on Road Traffic regarding road signs and signals had to be accommodated, and so symbols and images (modified to suit) had to replace 'instructional' words. This meant that the urgency of having to STOP would no longer be lost during the effort to translate a wordy instruction such as 'Halt at major road ahead'. On 1 January 1965, Kinneir and Calvert's national road-signage system became law, and was widely considered to be the best in the world. A modified version of Transport, called Alfabeto Normale, was used on Italian road signs.

Throughout the rest of the 1960s and the 1970s, the firm Kinneir Calvert Associates was remarkably busy, and employed a number of additional designers. Immediately after Transport, work began on the design of Rail Alphabet, a crucial part of the new visual-identity programme for British Rail being coordinated by the Design Research Unit (DRU). The railway companies had been nationalized in 1948 but still operated as regional sectors, each holding on to its own identity. By the early 1960s it was decided that a new, all-encompassing corporate identity was needed to pull these sectors together and to eliminate the existing assortment of styles and motifs that so graphically demonstrated the confused nature of the business. British Railways (as the state-owned

Jock Kinneir and Margaret Calvert
Signs using Transport typeface
1964 onwards

Motorway signage on a blue background (left); local route signs (below).

Birmingham

Dunstable
Luton
A 505

Dunstable
Luton
A 505

↑ Northchurch 1
  Wiggington 4

← Chesham 5

Potten End 2
Gaddesden 3
Ashridge 4 ↗

Potten End 2
Gaddesden 3
Ashridge 4

Peterborough
A 47

Jock Kinneir and Margaret Calvert
Signs using Transport typeface
1964 onwards

A green background indicates a primary route (below). Erected in urban locations (right), these signs were unpopular with pedestrians but appreciated by drivers.

company was known until the rebranding in 1965) frequently used Eric Gill's Gill Sans on aluminium station signs, printed in all-capitals, generously spaced and reversed out of a darker colour – an elegant design inherited from the London and North Eastern Railway. However, type comes with certain semantic associations, and Gill Sans, highly effective when used this way in the 1930s, appeared rather austere and out of place in the more informal 1960s.

Kinneir recognized that, as in other areas of typography, a sign system should reflect something of its time and place if it is to be fully effective. It was not enough for the information on a sign simply to be clear; *how* it was said – its tone and inflection – was also crucially important. Kinneir explained: 'It has to be acknowledged that the functions of public inscriptions reside more in their content than in their form; on a utilitarian level one letterstyle could serve all purposes adequately if bleakly. Yet this apparently functional view ignores the important role of style in implying information, as well as the part which lettering plays in the environment.'[7]

Rail Alphabet has many similarities to Helvetica and, like Helvetica, has close ties to Akzidenz-Grotesk too. The typeface was also used by Kinneir Calvert Associates for the signage of Glasgow Airport, and it was adopted by other state railway companies, notably DSB in Denmark. In the UK, Rail Alphabet began to disappear in the 1990s when British Rail was privatized and split once more into a number of smaller companies. DSB used it until 1997.

The New York City Subway system, like London's Underground, was initially formed of several independent companies and had grown to be similarly labyrinthine.[8] The current New York subway system was formed in 1940, when all lines were placed under city control. (The merger of London's

underground railways took place in 1933.)
Not surprisingly, the systematic design in
Europe of signage for national road-transport
infrastructure, key modes of travel such as
railways and underground rail systems, and
major travel hubs such as airports, caused
some New Yorkers to take a critical look at
the chaotic signage that cluttered their own
city's subway system.[9]

A designed-from-scratch signage system
of particular interest was that of the first
completed (red) line of the Metropolitana di
Milano – the Milan Metro – in 1964. It was
initially planned as a three-line system: the
green line opened in 1969, the yellow line in
1990. The signage was created by Bob Noorda
(1927–2010), a Dutch designer who in 1954
had moved to Milan, became a renowned art
director at Pirelli in 1961 and then established
his own design company. Noorda's solution
involved signs designed in the form of long,
narrow enamel strips placed along the station
walls at consistent intervals. He also designed
route diagrams and neighbourhood maps. The
signage lettering was a modified version of
Helvetica drawn by Noorda himself. Notably,
this involved a new weight (between medium
and light), a reduction in the length of the
ascenders and descenders, and the design of
a system of intercharacter spacing to ensure
a standardized quality of manufacture. When
revising some of the Helvetica letters, Noorda
appears to have referenced their equivalents
in Akzidenz-Grotesk.

The new Metropolitana di Milano and
Noorda's signage design were praised by
the industrial designer William Lansing
Plumb in an article in the September/October
1965 issue of *Print* magazine in which he
compared the London, Milan and New York
subway systems and described the last as
'grimy, dingy and slumlike'.[10] At around the
same time, Massimo Vignelli (1931–2014)
moved to the United States to set up a New
York office for his newly formed company,

Kinneir and Calvert's Rail Alphabet in use at Paddington station, London, c. early 1970s.

Jock Kinneir and Margaret Calvert
British Airports Authority Sign Manual
1972

Pages showing signage for arrivals and departures in revised sign manual, originally designed in the 1960s. At that time the British Airports Authority was responsible for Gatwick and Heathrow among other airports.

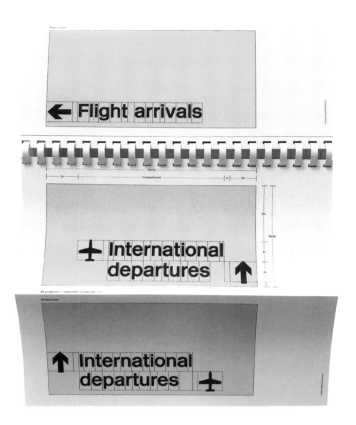

Jock Kinneir and Margaret Calvert
DSB Design Manual
1972

Rail Alphabet, as specified in the pages of the design manual of the Danish national rail company.

Unimark International. Other founding partners included Bob Noorda and Ralph Eckerstrom (former design director of the Container Corporation of America). Within months, as a result of Noorda's work on the Milan Metro, Unimark captured a significant commission: to advise on the signage of the New York City Subway. Noorda flew to New York in the summer of 1966 and spent three weeks studying commuter flow and key information points at five major subway stations. He and Vignelli then designed a modular sign system using Akzidenz-Grotesk (generally known as Standard in North America) and a colour-coding system devised the previous year by Stanley A. Goldstein after ideas for a new subway map had been considered.[11] Three sizes of type, black on a white background, were used to provide different levels of information. Noorda returned to Milan to have prototype signs made while presentation boards were drawn up in Unimark's New York offices. Noorda and Vignelli gave their presentation, were thanked for their work, and Unimark's brief, if intense, involvement in the modernization of the New York City Subway signage came to an abrupt end.

The New York City Transit Authority had decided that it would implement the design proposals itself. Unimark was not asked for a design manual nor even an explanation of the modular system (Noorda and Vignelli had assumed this would be part of the second phase of the project). Instead, the Transit Authority used its own in-house sign-making facilities. No one from Unimark was invited to inspect or advise while the signs were being made and erected. As a result, the implementation was a disaster, or, as Vignelli put it, 'the biggest mess in the world'.[12] Commuters and journalists agreed. Merely installing a few new signs, often over the top of existing ones, was not the same as implementing

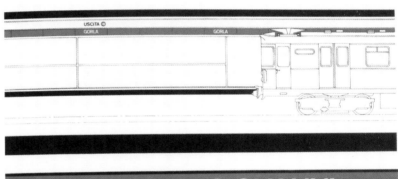

Bob Noorda
Milan Metro Design Manual
c. 1962

Details showing lettering – a modified version of Helvetica – and signage system.

Bob Noorda and Massimo Vignelli
Unimark International
*New York City Transit
Authority Graphics
Standards Manual*
1970

*Page showing
examples and
combinations of the
arrow, directional
information and
colour-coded
identification.*

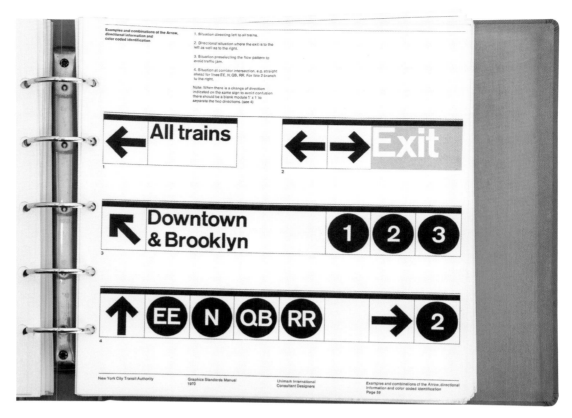

Bob Noorda and Massimo Vignelli
Unimark International
*New York Subway
Guide*
First published 1972

*The Unimark pocket
map made its debut
in August 1972 and
went through a series
of changes, most
being service-related.
The last version was
published in 1978.*

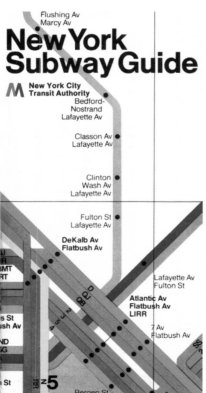

a thoroughly coordinated signage system. Recognizing these shortcomings, in the autumn of 1967 the Transit Authority announced that Unimark had been commissioned to 'devise a new system of signage' – in other words, to complete the project it had begun in 1966. The announcement was made at a symposium held at the Museum of Modern Art called 'Transportation Graphics: Where Am I Going? How Do I Get There?' Among the speakers were Bob Noorda and Jock Kinneir.

Given that the New York City Subway is now so closely associated with Helvetica, the initial choice of Akzidenz-Grotesk (Standard) requires an explanation. Vignelli was a huge advocate of Helvetica, Noorda less so. In 1966 Akzidenz-Grotesk was well established in North America, which meant that most printers (and sign-making workshops) already had a stock of it in various weights and sizes. Helvetica was released in North America

in 1963, but was not a fully viable option
for American designers until early 1965.
The decision to use Akzidenz-Grotesk was
therefore probably a practical one: the Transit
Authority's sign shop did not have Helvetica,
and 'given the costs involved and the fact
that the two faces appear indistinguishable
to most people', it would have resisted the
expense of adding it to its stock of typefaces.[13]
As a result, throughout the 1970s and '80s
printed material whose purpose was to offer
a coordinated presentation of the New York
subway continued to use a combination of
Akzidenz-Grotesk and Helvetica. It was not
until December 1989 that Helvetica finally
became the official typeface of the New York
City Subway signage system.

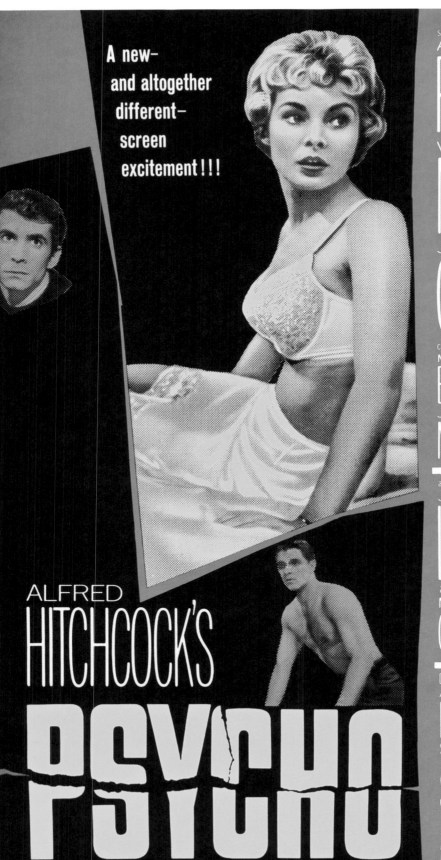

FILM & TELEVISION

By 1945 the opening titles to a film had evolved to the point where they sought to whet the audience's appetite, yet, structurally, the sequence still stood alone: titles did not advance the plot, did not contain dialogue or sound effects, and faded to black before the film itself began.

Nevertheless, typographic design and music usually gave a clear indication of the genre of film about to follow. Generic norms meant that westerns invariably opened using a bold slab serif suitably distressed to reflect the rugged, untamed nature of the subject matter. (Almost all earlier film titles were hand-drawn, often on to glass.) In contrast, comedies usually incorporated sans-serif letterforms haphazardly fashioned; the more outrageous the comedy, the more disorderly the arrangement. Shaping expectations in this predictable manner was generally considered sufficient, although sequences became longer and more complex, eventually using live action that resembled the style and narrative of the film itself. The elevation of Alfred Hitchcock (1899–1980) from intertitle-card designer to film director would become a rather common career path for would-be directors as title design became increasingly sophisticated. Saul Bass and Pablo Ferro are good examples of those who followed his lead.

Hitchcock began his career as a draughtsman and advertising designer for W.T. Henley's Telegraph Works Company in London. His skill in design earned him his first job in the movie industry, as an intertitle designer for silent films. He went on to work as a set designer for Gainsborough Pictures, established by Michael Balcon to produce B-movies and melodramas at Islington Studios. When Hitchcock was elevated to director, his working methods reflected his design background. His thorough engagement in every aspect of a film's making and visual delivery – from pre-production and detailed storyboarding to set, costume and title design, post-production editing and special effects – ensured that the film had been comprehensively designed before shooting began.[1]

OPPOSITE
Macario Gómez Quibus
Psycho
Alfred Hitchcock
1960

Poster for the film's American release. Includes Tony Palladino's hand lettering.

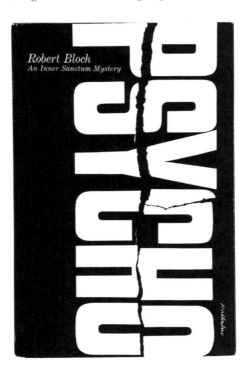

Tony Palladino
Psycho
Robert Bloch
Simon & Schuster
1959

Front of jacket.

Saul Bass
Assisted by Harold
Adler
Psycho
Alfred Hitchcock
1960

Title sequence.

Hitchcock's visual appreciation is demonstrated by his use in 1960 of Tony Palladino's typographic rendering of 'Psycho' created for the dust jacket of Robert Bloch's 1959 novel of that title, published by Simon & Schuster. Hitchcock purchased the rights to Palladino's lettering design for the film's promotion, and he probably assumed that it would be adopted for the film's title sequence. If this was discussed, it was finally rejected in favour of an alternative sans serif (predominantly Venus Bold Extended) for the famously jarring yet polished, fast-moving title sequence designed by Saul Bass (1920–1996), assisted by Harold Adler.

Hitchcock's *oeuvre* as a designer-turned-director is irrevocably linked with the American graphic designer Bass, whose work during the 1950s revolutionized the function of film opening titles. *Carmen Jones*, released in 1954, was Bass's first title sequence. Having moved from New York to Los Angeles to establish his design practice, he was contacted by the director Otto Preminger to promote the film. Bass designed the poster, and perhaps having discussed how its key features – typography, colours and textures – might be translated to the film's opening credits, Preminger suggested that Bass also direct the sequence.

Preminger's role should not be undervalued.[2] His enthusiasm for the creation of title sequences that brought an added dimension to a film had already been demonstrated in two of his previous movies, *Whirlpool* and especially *Where the Sidewalk Ends* (both 1950, designers unknown), in the latter of which the title is chalked on to the sidewalk and walked over by pedestrians. Therefore, Bass's early work seemed groundbreaking, but it was not entirely without precedent.

Bass's solution for the opening titles of *Carmen Jones* was a combination of two simple, symbolic elements: a line illustration

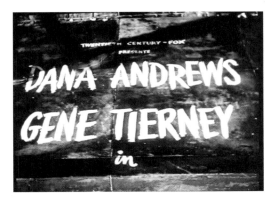

Designer unknown
Fallen Angel
Otto Preminger
1945

Title sequence.

Designer unknown
*Where the Sidewalk
Ends*
Otto Preminger
1950

Title sequence.

of a rose seen inside a live-action flame for the duration of the sequence. In retrospect, Bass's design did not do justice to the film's core themes of racism and miscegenation, but it was saved by the distinctive lettering designed and drawn by Harold Adler, a master calligrapher, lettering artist and typographer who trained at the Frank Wiggins Trade School and the original Art Center in Los Angeles. He later co-founded the Society for Calligraphy, Southern California. From 1946 Adler designed the typography for more than 100 film titles, frequently collaborating with the leading American title-sequence designers of the 1950s and '60s, including Maurice Binder and Pablo Ferro as well as Bass.

In turn, Bass (and Binder and Ferro) worked for some of Hollywood's best film directors – not just Hitchcock and Preminger, but also Billy Wilder, Stanley Kubrick and, later, Martin Scorsese. In 1955, following the success of *Carmen Jones*, Preminger

commissioned Bass to design all of the promotional material as well as the title sequence for his next film, *The Man with the Golden Arm*. Bass was now able to plan a unified scheme, so that printed material seen first outside the cinema became inextricably linked with the combined power and scale of his sound-and-motion version on screen. This was the first time such an approach had been taken, and the movie's critical and box-office success led to a major change in the way many films were marketed in the decades to come.

Bass was far bolder with *The Man with the Golden Arm* than he had been with *Carmen Jones*. White lines appear at increasingly wild angles on a black background, emphasized by Elmer Bernstein's more and more frenetic jazz score, before resolving into the disturbing shape of the jagged arm. Harold Adler cleverly assimilated this iconic final image into the lettering he

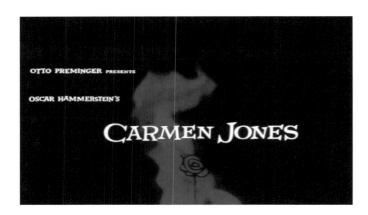

Saul Bass
Harold Adler, hand lettering
Carmen Jones
Otto Preminger
1954

Title sequence (above); film poster (right).

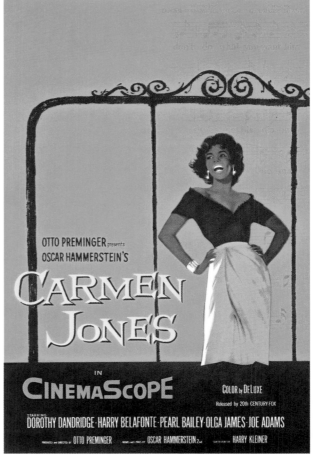

designed for the poster. However, Bass chose to use a sans serif (predominantly News Gothic, capitals only, designed by Morris Fuller Benton in 1908) for the title sequence. Bass chose a sans serif again for *Psycho*, rather than Palladino's iconic design, because the elemental letterforms were able to maintain their identity despite the constant motion of the narrow horizontal and vertical lines causing the type to be spliced in an alarming and rhythmic fashion. In this way, the opening titles to *Psycho* cleverly imply rather than illustrate the turmoil to come.

Before the end of the 1950s, Bass was offering studios a complete 'package' that included posters, main and credit titles, trademarks, film and TV trailers, trade and newspaper advertising and album-cover design. His work on the opening titles of such popular films as *Vertigo*, *North by Northwest*, *Ocean's Eleven*, *Spartacus*, *Exodus*, *Something Wild* and *It's a Mad, Mad, Mad, Mad World*

Saul Bass
Harold Adler, hand lettering on poster
The Man with the Golden Arm
Otto Preminger
1955

Film poster (below, left); title sequence (below).

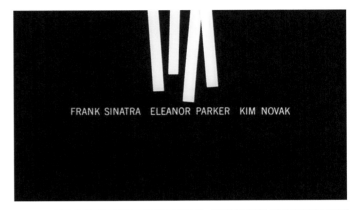

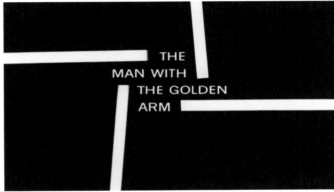

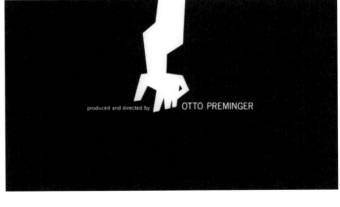

With Arnold Stang, Darren McGavin, Robert Strauss, John Conte, Doro Merande, George E. Stone, George Mathews, Leonid Kinskey, Emile Meyer, Shorty Rogers, Shelly Manne. Screenplay by Walter Newman & Lewis Meltzer. From the novel by Nelson Algren. Music by Elmer Bernstein. Produced & Directed by Otto Preminger. Released by United Artists

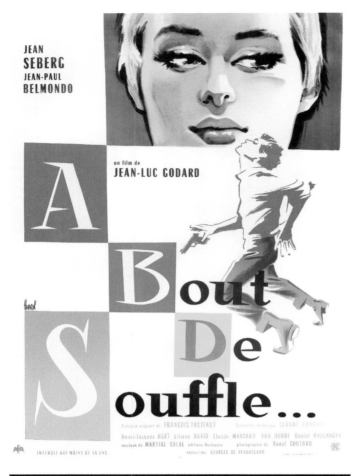

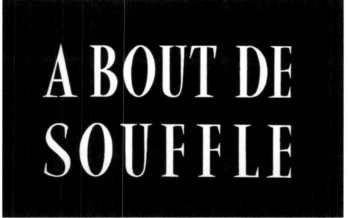

TOP
Clément Hurel
À bout de souffle
Jean-Luc Godard
1960

Poster for the film's
French release.

ABOVE
Designer unknown
À bout de souffle
Jean-Luc Godard
1960

Title sequence.

– all made within a five-year period, 1958–63 – meant that Bass became the world's best-known graphic designer. The 'package' that he provided for the film industry was effectively an adaptation of the corporate-design service his studio was already supplying to many leading American companies.

Unsurprisingly, Bass's legacy reverberated across mid-twentieth-century cinema, influencing title designers in the United States and Britain. European cinema, however, was less willing to follow suit. After the French New Wave broke through in the late 1950s, Jean-Luc Godard's first feature-length work, *À bout de souffle* (*Breathless*, 1960), made an immediate typographic statement, and it was determinedly not American.

Godard's title design reflects the New Wave method of film-making: removing the gloss by providing the audience with a movie that, on first viewing, appears still to be at the rough-cut stage. The apparently seamless transition between scenes in Hollywood films was rejected in favour of fragmented episodes that eliminated anything non-essential to the plot. The resultant 'jump-cut' sensation gave the New Wave, and Godard's films in particular, a rugged spontaneity more often associated with documentaries. Similarly, the typography in Godard's film titles has the appearance of being hand-drawn, with imperfections retained and even emphasized by his preference for bold, impactful lettering that sometimes fills the screen. The use of the red, white and blue of the French flag occurs whenever colour is available. In some cases, as in *Bande à part* (*Band of Outsiders*, 1964), the credits are layered over the top of the film, playfully but carefully positioned to fit the placement of figures or objects beneath. A sense of play also arises when the type is animated, again simply and somewhat crudely, certainly for an audience that had seen the work of Saul Bass. When words move, Godard makes the progression a little too fast or a little too slow; another reminder that this is not a Hollywood film.

By the middle of the 1960s, Godard began to use Antique Olive, a typeface designed by Roger Excoffon of Fonderie Olive in Marseilles. Excoffon's iconic display typefaces – such as Banco, Mistral and Choc of the 1950s – had played a significant part in all the New Wave films, especially those directed by Agnès Varda, François Truffaut and Godard. Long tracking shots of actors walking, cycling or driving through the Paris streets always include shop fascias, many of which display Excoffon's typefaces. Indeed, the everyday use of type, especially in newspapers, magazines, paperback books, posters and advertising in all its forms, is a prominent feature, particularly of Godard's films – something acknowledged to good effect in the poster for *Deux ou trois choses que je sais d'elle* (*Two or Three Things I Know About Her*, 1967).

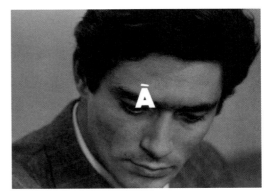

ABOVE
Designer unknown
Bande à part
Jean-Luc Godard
1964

Title sequence.

LEFT
H. Poussy
Bande à part
Jean-Luc Godard
1964

Poster for the film's French release.

Designer unknown
*Deux ou trois choses
que je sais d'elle*
Jean-Luc Godard
1967

*Title sequence and
Godard's final shot
from the film.*

Godard purportedly said, 'I wanted to include everything: sports, politics, even groceries. Everything should be put in a film.'[3] Godard's final image is a slow pull-back from a tableau of familiar packaged products arranged on grass to suggest modern apartment buildings. At the centre is a packet of Hollywood Chewing Gum.

The first James Bond film, *Dr. No*, was completed in 1962. Although a British film, its title sequence was designed by an American, Maurice Binder (with animation by Trevor Bond). Binder (1918–1991) was born in New York and worked his way up at Macy's department store to become its art director. After the Second World War he moved to the West Coast of America, where he found work designing film promotional material. By the late 1950s he was in charge of Columbia Pictures' advertising department. However, Binder designed not

René Ferracci
*Deux ou trois choses
que je sais d'elle*
Jean-Luc Godard
1967

*Poster for the film's
French release.*

only promotional campaigns but also opening titles and trailers for hundreds of films. Much of this work was uncredited, but some title sequences, such as for Stanley Donen's *The Grass Is Greener* (1960), *Charade* (1963) and *Arabesque* (1966), stood apart. Binder is best known for creating the signature style of the James Bond films. In *Dr. No*, the famous gun-barrel sequence appears first, followed seamlessly by the title credits. The circle that had been the end of the gun barrel moves and rapidly begins to change colour, dance and multiply. When the film's title appears, one of the circles becomes the full point after 'Dr.' The title appeared exactly the same on the poster. The title's four heavy-weight letters were most likely hand-drawn.

In 1963, after a disagreement with Binder, the producer Harry Saltzman approached Robert Brownjohn (1925–1970), an American typographer working in London since 1959, to design the title sequence of the second Bond movie, *From Russia with Love*. Brownjohn projected moving credits on to the body of a female dancer and filmed the results. Similarly, for the third Bond film, *Goldfinger* (1964), he projected moving images from the movie on to a gold-painted female body. (The credits themselves were arranged around the body.) The use of risqué humour, not an uncommon trait of Bond movies at that time – for example, the lining-up of a projected image of a golf putt so that the ball rolls down the model's cleavage – is a typical Brownjohn conceit. When Brownjohn fell out with Saltzman, Binder was recalled. He went on to design the opening credits of the next thirteen Bond films.

In 1964, at the height of Cold War hysteria, no film was more shocking or pertinent than Stanley Kubrick's doomsday comedy *Dr. Strangelove or: How I Learned to Stop Worrying and Love the Bomb*, in which an overzealous US general launches

Maurice Binder
Dr. No
Terence Young
1962

Title sequence.

Robert Brownjohn
From Russia with Love
Terence Young
1963

Title sequence.

DR. STRANGLOVE SHORT TYPE

AABB
CCDDD
EEFG
GHHI
JUKK
LLMM
NNOO
©

Pablo Ferro
*Dr. Strangelove or:
How I Learned to
Stop Worrying and
Love the Bomb*
Stanley Kubrick
1964

*Sample page of hand
lettering (above); title
sequence (above,
right).*

a nuclear attack against the USSR. The film's frightening absurdity is established in the opening frames of the title sequence, designed by Pablo Ferro (1935–2018). With the song 'Try a Little Tenderness' playing in the background, huge B-52 bombers engage in mid-air coitus with smaller refuelling aircraft. Overprinted on these frames are Ferro's film title and credits, filling the screen with hand-scrawled lettering squeezed or extended to an almost indecipherable degree; the sequence was certainly unlike any movie titles seen before. Ferro also edited the film's horrific concluding montage, showing atomic bombs detonating to the refrain of 'We'll Meet Again', Vera Lynn's popular hit from the Second World War. The movie launched the career of Ferro as title designer, trailer director and eventually a maker of feature films.

Before he worked with Kubrick, much of Ferro's work had been for television. During the late 1950s, he pioneered the use of moving type, often using nineteenth-century wooden display types because he considered them to be more capable of withstanding the poor definition provided by television screens at the time. It was after seeing Ferro's TV commercials that Kubrick hired him to direct the advertising trailers and teasers for *Dr. Strangelove*, and he then persuaded him to resettle in London, where Kubrick was based.

Dr. Strangelove was key to Ferro's eventual move from television to film, and working with Kubrick in London was the best possible introduction to the movie industry because it enabled Ferro to bypass the bureaucratic work practices of Hollywood. For example, once the theme of the title sequence had been chosen, Kubrick decided to film it all using models (foreshadowing his graceful spaceship choreography of *2001: A Space Odyssey* in 1968). Ferro advised against this; he found official film footage and used that instead. When Ferro proposed the screen-filled lettering, his intention was that

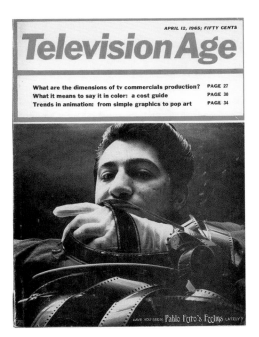

Designer unknown
Television Age
12 April 1965

Front cover, featuring Pablo Ferro.

Harold Adler
The Fantastic Plastic Machine
Eric Blum and Lowell Blum
1969

Original title-card maquette.

Geoff M. Sadler
Impact 20
September 1956

*Front cover of a
quarterly review
of advertising. This
issue is devoted to
commercial television,
which had recently
started in the UK
and was reliant on
advertising. The cover
design is based on
photograms by Ken
Simmons.*

the letters would be redrawn and refined by a
lettering artist – perhaps Harold Adler, who
had regularly done such work for him. But
Kubrick preferred the crudely drawn quality
of the hand lettering. So later, when all the
information was available, Ferro carefully
lettered the opening credits while attempting
to retain the artless quality of his original
roughly drawn visuals.

Ferro's ease of movement between
television and film, and Maurice Binder's
work for television at Columbia Pictures'
advertising department, reflect the ways in
which major film companies sought to control
and capitalize on the rising influence of
television. Film companies had always followed
media developments elsewhere: buying and
running radio stations in the 1930s, then
record labels, publishing houses and cinema
chains in the 1940s. And when television
became a potent force, film companies began

Designers unknown
The Cisco Kid,
1950–56
Hopalong Cassidy,
1949–54
The Lone Ranger,
1949–57
*The Roy Rogers
Show,* 1951–57

*Title sequences,
showing the use of
typefaces to establish
the personality of
leading characters.*

204   MID-CENTURY TYPE

to produce programming for the TV schedules. By the end of the 1950s, American film studios had become multimedia companies.

Many of the TV programmes created by the film and television studios were low-budget productions, but they were, nevertheless, remarkably popular. The success of such westerns as *Hopalong Cassidy*, *The Roy Rogers Show*, *The Lone Ranger* and *The Cisco Kid* was due primarily to their visual appeal. Dialogue was hardly necessary, with the result that these programmes were easy to sell to non-English-speaking countries. In fact, the output of the major American film studios for television would remain hugely popular outside the United States well into the 1960s and beyond.

Just as film titles were becoming longer and more sophisticated, American TV titles remained unsubtle and uncomplicated – the excuse being poor screen definition. Moreover, the fact that programmes generally lasted half an hour or less meant that their titles rarely stretched beyond thirty seconds. The title and essential credits, even for such high-profile action programmes as *The Man from U.N.C.L.E.* (1964–68) and *Mission: Impossible* (1966–73), were simply superimposed over filmed 'portraits' of key characters. The introduction of higher-definition, 625-line broadcasts (by the BBC in 1964), and later colour, had obvious benefits, although, frustratingly, the designer was obliged to consider those viewers still watching on the old 405-line monochrome sets well into the 1970s.[4]

Innovative typography therefore came relatively late to television, and a designer who stands out is Bernard Lodge (b. 1933). Lodge, who regarded Saul Bass as a major influence, joined the BBC in 1960. (The first BBC graphic designer was employed in 1954.) It was there, in 1963, that he got the opportunity to design the title sequence for a new children's series, *Doctor Who*. The swirling,

Bernard Lodge
Doctor Who
1963

Title sequence from the first series of the BBC children's science-fiction programme.

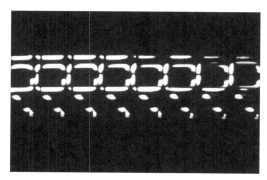

Bernard Lodge
The Late Show
1966

*Title sequence from
a BBC late-evening
arts discussion
programme.*

Bernard Lodge
Tea Party
Harold Pinter
1965

*Title sequence for a
dark and malevolent
BBC drama.*

'howl-around' visual effect seen in the original title sequence was discovered by a technical operations manager at the BBC, Norman Taylor, who pointed a camera at a monitor showing its own picture. He explained: 'I got the usual effect of diminishing images of the monitor ... when, suddenly, some stray light hit the monitor screen and the whole picture went mobile, with swirling patterns of black and white. ... Later, I repeated the experiment but fed a black-and-white caption, mixed with the camera output, to the monitor and very soon got the Doctor Who effect.'[5] This was seen by Verity Lambert, the programme's producer, who asked Lodge to take a look at what Taylor had discovered, to see if it might be incorporated into the opening titles. Lodge realized its inherent suggestion of time travel and science fiction, and created the famous title sequence. As each new Doctor was cast in the role, Lodge was able to 'update' the title sequence and take advantage of improving technology. Curiously, as the technology became more sophisticated, so the chilling sensation of danger, which remains so distinct in the original version, diminished.

Lodge produced numerous other important title sequences, including *Picture Parade* (1961, predating Binder's *Dr. No* titles), in which a pattern of circles dance and flicker to eventually form the programme's title and, in a more sophisticated convergence of image and words, Harold Pinter's *Tea Party* (1965) and the culture programme *The Late Show* (1966). Lodge left the BBC in 1977 to form his own company, which later became Lodge/ Cheesman when he was joined by his former colleague Colin Cheesman (who had become head of graphic design at BBC Television). Together they worked on TV advertising and also graphic effects for films, notably *Alien* (1979) and *Blade Runner* (1982).

Romek Marber
The War Game
Peter Watkins
1966

Animated trailer for a BBC docudrama about a nuclear attack. It was initially banned from public broadcast, although it received a limited cinema release, and was finally screened on the BBC in 1985.

graphic design : London

EPHEMERA

Every area of administrative, commercial and cultural activity generates large quantities of printed ephemera. The term 'ephemera' refers to 'the minor transient documents of everyday life',[1] and the design of such material occupies the time and skills of almost all typographers and graphic designers. However, the transiency of printed ephemera is something that a designer will attempt to delay by making the items too good to be thrown away. The amount of transient material from the period covered by this book that is now collectable suggests that designers of the time were successful. However, being transient does not mean that items of printed ephemera are unimportant; on the contrary, they are often essential. A level of trust is required that transit labels are correct when they are attached to suitcases at an airport check-in desk, and the significance of a job application form or a Valentine's card might be life-changing.

It should also be noted that not all material designed and designated as printed ephemera is, in fact, particularly transient.[2] This is often due to changes in function, such as in the case of the record cover, or to changes in attitude, as in the case of book jackets.

Printing presses have always been used to produce ephemera. Before Johannes Gutenberg printed the first book from cast-metal type in the 1450s, he raised money by printing thousands of (single-sheet) indulgences for the Catholic Church, but the mechanization

of printing during the twentieth century caused the quantity of ephemeral material to transform the printing industry and become a significant part of the typographer's output. After the restrictions of the Second World War, there was a sense that a 'throwaway' attitude was a wholly positive development – a sign, at last, of societal affluence – and that the production of disposable goods was emblematic of modernity.[3]

Items of ephemera are often designed to fulfil a specific and time-sensitive purpose, meaning that their content is predisposed towards the vernacular. The language and the use of imagery may be less guarded and so provide a more accurate reflection of social attitudes towards, for example, racism, sexism and chauvinism. When working to

OPPOSITE

Alan Fletcher
Graphic Design: London
1960

Leaflet for an exhibition of work by members of the Association of Graphic Designers London.

Tom Eckersley and Eric Lombers
Cup Final, April 30
1938

Poster explaining travel options to the FA Cup Final at Wembley Stadium, printed by the Curwen Press.

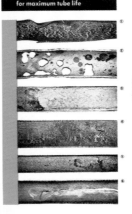

Ladislav Sutnar
Scovill Condenser Tubes
1946

Front and inside of leaflet for the Scovill Manufacturing Company.

Olle Eksell
Efficiency-Groep
1952

Front of fold-out leaflet for distribution at the Utrecht Autumn Fair.

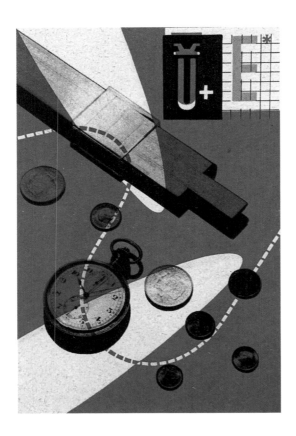

very tight deadlines, typographic designers may have resorted to solutions that provided (unintentionally) a truthful record of ways of thinking that in retrospect appear inane or naive. But it is this naivety that makes printed ephemera so informative.

Sometimes items of ephemera are difficult to define or categorize. Catalogues, brochures, prospectuses and product and price lists are names given to various types of printed matter, yet all have functions they share. Ephemera also come in a vast array of shapes and sizes, from a postcard to the packaging for a kitchen appliance, which means that storage is a particular challenge. Understandably, libraries may be deterred from collecting ephemera because of the space required and the challenges inherent in cataloguing.[4]

The context in which a large amount of ephemera is produced means that the designer is often unknown, as are the printer and date of production. Most ephemera reproduced

Romek Marber
Heal's 1957 Designs
1957

*Front cover of
catalogue for Heal's
furniture company,
London.*

Designer unknown
Schriftguss Dresden
1950

*Fold-out leaflet for
the German type
foundry Schriftguss
AG.*

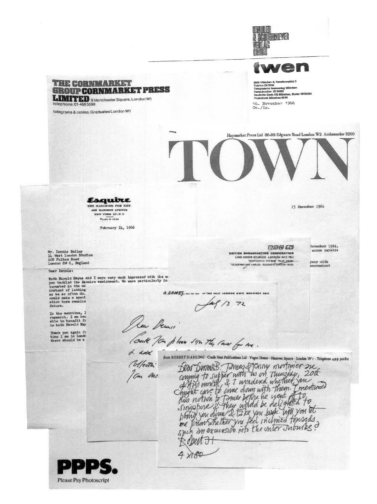

on these pages will have been designed for a company already known to the studio, for which a 'house style' had previously been established, so it was not uncommon for such work to be given to a younger, less experienced designer. Moreover, many examples of ephemera were designed by a manufacturing firm's or public service's own design studio, where anonymity was generally insisted upon.

Large corporations had 'typing pools' – hundreds of typists – that generated a huge amount of correspondence, for which a broad range of stationery was designed to aid efficiency. A standard range[5] might have included headed notepaper (or letterheads), compliments slips, quotations, orders, acknowledgements of order, advice or dispatch notes, delivery notes, invoices, statements, and credit and debit notices. Envelopes were often also designed with the business's name, the aim being to augment the company's public identity.

Increasingly, material that was once considered ephemera – book jackets,

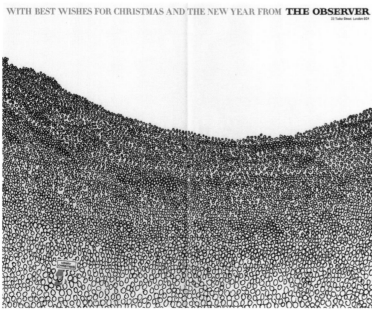

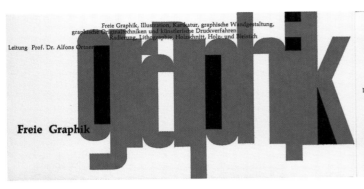

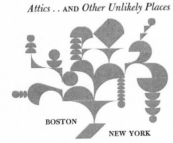

PRINTING:
UNINHIBITED

AN EXHIBITION OF WORK DONE IN
Barns . . Cellars . . Bedrooms
Attics . . AND Other Unlikely Places

BOSTON   NEW YORK

LEFT
W.A. Dwiggins
Printing: Uninhibited
1953

*Front of folded
invitation to submit
work for an exhibition.*

ABOVE
Paul Rand
Portfolio
1951

*Front of business
reply card for* Portfolio
magazine.

TOP
Designer unknown
Freie Graphik
1962

*Inside of folded
invitation to an
exhibition of graphic
design at the
Klingspor Museum,
Offenbach.*

ABOVE
Giovanni Pintori
Olivetti Quanta
1965

*Front and inside of
pamphlet for Olivetti's
electronic calculator.*

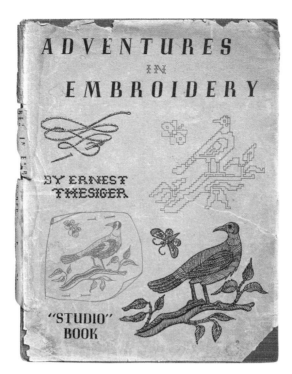

Ernest Thesiger
*Adventures in
Embroidery*
The Studio
1941

*Early example of
a dust jacket.*

Dennis Bailey
*Jonathan Cape
Autumn List*
1956

*Back and front of
publisher's sales
leaflet.*

magazines, posters, catalogues, indeed much
of what is included in this volume – has
become highly sought-after, collectable and
valuable. Changes in attitude are borne out
by the loose dust jacket, the initial purpose
of which was to protect the case-bound
book. Stripping books of their jackets was
once common practice, largely because it
was thought that their individually designed
spines made a bookshelf look untidy and
that their overtly commercial purpose was
somewhat vulgar. The dust jacket finally
gained approval in the 1940s, when libraries
began protecting loose paper jackets with
transparent, commercially manufactured film-
based jackets. The growing status of book-
cover design during the 1950s encouraged
illustrators to add a signature to their artwork.

Printed matter for the independent
traveller is among the most attractive (and
subsequently the most collected) ephemera,
and probably offers more variety than any
other genre. The middle of the twentieth
century was a golden period for rail travel,
while air travel was (literally) just taking off.
In a bid to attract new passengers, the travel
industry took great pains to ensure that all
printed material was designed to project
assurance and confidence. Tickets, security
and boarding passes, and transit labels had
to be clear and precise, but they were also
designed to alleviate passenger anxiety by
suggesting the sophistication of the upcoming
travel experience and reminding travellers of
their destination. On-board printed menus and
wine lists were required, and items that might
be bought during a flight, such as sweets and
badges, or gifts such as silk scarves, jewellery
and cigarette lighters, were branded with an
airline's logo. Air France, KLM and American
Airlines were early leaders in recognizing the
value of print in customer confidence.

The growth of the travel industry
encouraged the creation of smaller, lighter and
essentially temporary versions of common

ABOVE
Roger Excoffon
(Air France)
Unknown designers
(KLM and Prince
Hotel)
c. 1950s

*Air France boarding
pass with envelope;
KLM luggage label
and branded cigarette
lighter; Prince Hotel,
Tokyo, label.*

BELOW, LEFT
Designers unknown
The Milwaukee
Electric Railway and
Transport Co.
1940, 1945

Weekly passes.

BELOW, RIGHT
Designers unknown
Bus tickets
c. 1950s

*British bus tickets.
Punched holes
indicate date of issue
and length of journey.*

Designers unknown
Matchbooks
c. 1940s–60s

A variety of American and Canadian matchbook covers (outside and inside shown for Horseshoe and Hunt's).

 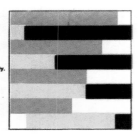

 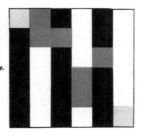

 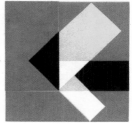

Rolf Christianson
Matchbox labels
c. 1950s

Three from a series of ten matchbox labels, Finland.

Yusaku Kamekura
Tokyo 1964
1964

Matchboxes incorporating Kamekura's logo for the 1964 Summer Olympic Games in Tokyo.

items, with plastic fast becoming the modern material of ephemerality. The archetypal mid-twentieth-century disposable printed object is probably the matchbook, the manufacture of which peaked in the 1940s and '50s. This was a small lightweight card folded to enclose ten (or so) card matches. Smoking was so widespread and matchbooks so cheap to manufacture that organizations of every kind, especially hotels, bars and restaurants, rail companies and airlines, would have large quantities produced with their name and service displayed on the cover, and gave them away to customers and clients.

The appearance and function of almost all print ephemera have constantly evolved – sometimes over centuries (the matchbook was patented in 1892) – but there are some types of ephemera that were designed to meet the needs of a product quite specific to the mid-twentieth century. One of the most prominent and significant of these was the record cover.

Before the Second World War, records were bought in uniform plain-paper wrappers, the sole purpose of which was to protect the grooves of the fragile shellac disc. There were also box sets: four-, five- or six-pocket 'albums' sufficient to contain a symphony (the normal running time of a 78-rpm record was about four and a half minutes). In the late 1930s, Alex Steinweiss (1917–2011) was a young designer at Columbia Records tasked with creating promotional material. He suggested that he be allowed to design a cover for an upcoming album. For this, Steinweiss arranged for the sign over the entrance to a New York theatre to read 'Smash Song Hits by Rodgers & Hart', and then had it photographed. Steinweiss added the characteristic grooves of a record to the cover design to explain its content. When the album was released in 1940, sales were sensational, and Steinweiss found himself designing record

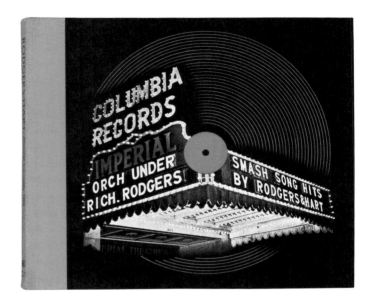

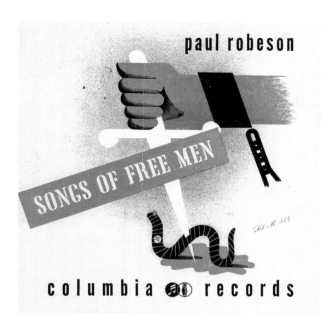

Alex Steinweiss
Songs of Free Men
Paul Robeson
Columbia Records
1943

Album cover.

covers full-time. After war service, Steinweiss was on a retainer with Columbia when, in 1948, it developed the first long-playing (LP) records. Steinweiss designed the prototype of the cardboard jacket. When he left Columbia in 1954, he continued working on a freelance basis for recording companies in the US and UK, creating almost 2500 covers.

Columbia felt a particular need to keep up with the cover art of Blue Note Records, an American jazz record label, established in 1939, that grew to become one of the most prolific, influential and respected jazz labels of the mid-twentieth century. Francis Wolff was an executive, record producer and talented photographer. The photographs he took during session rehearsals were initially used for publicity material; then, around the mid-1950s, when Blue Note began producing 12-inch LPs,[6] Reid Miles (1927–1993) was employed to design its covers and happily utilized Wolff's photographs. Miles designed

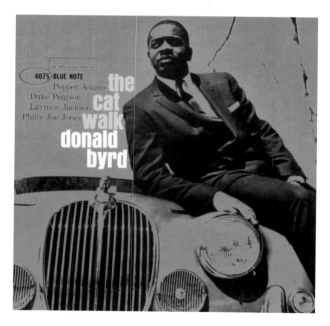

Reid Miles
The Cat Walk
Donald Byrd
Blue Note Records
1962

LP cover.

Reid Miles
The Rumproller
Lee Morgan
Blue Note Records
1965

LP cover.

more than 500 covers for Blue Note, often limiting himself to two or three colours to create tightly composed compositions in which his type and Wolff's images were intimately connected. However, Miles's later covers became increasingly typographic, using words and colour alone to suggest accent and tempo.

By the early 1960s, record covers, even more than book jackets before them, had become an important means of cultural expression, and were integrally linked to the music contained within. Portraits on covers were accompanied or replaced by inventive typography, popular cultural references and personal artefacts – all of which were employed in Peter Blake's design in 1967 for *Sgt. Pepper's Lonely Hearts Club Band* by The Beatles, an LP that included a cut-outs insert, printed lyrics and a gatefold cover, despite holding only a single disc.

The rapidly expanding cultural influence of pop music in the early 1960s led to the organization of music festivals before the end of the decade. However, festivals for other music genres, such as jazz, folk and blues, had been established since the 1950s and some classical music festivals considerably longer.

One example is the Aldeburgh Festival, founded in 1948 by the composer Benjamin Britten and singer Peter Pears. Originally intended to be a modest affair with small-scale concerts given by friends, the concept grew to include readings of poetry and literature, drama, lectures and exhibitions. The typographer John Lewis was commissioned to design a programme to present the growing number of events. Lewis's cover designs, from the mid-1950s to 1960, mark his move away from the romance of pre-war British Arcadia and his tentative step towards European modernism.

Michel + Kieser was founded in Offenbach in 1953 by college friends Günther Kieser (1930–2023) and Hans Michel. Although all the work emanating from their studio

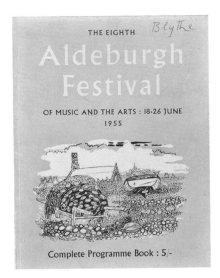

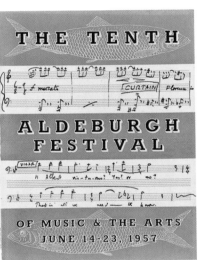

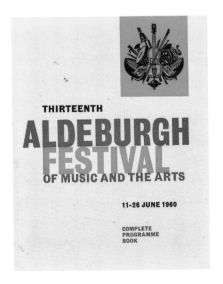

John Lewis
Aldeburgh Festival of Music and the Arts
1955, 1957, 1960

Programme covers.

Rudolph de Harak
*Nothing But
Percussion*
Byron Parker and His
Percussion Ensemble
Westminster Records
1961

LP cover.

Rudolph de Harak
*Shostakovitch Piano
Concerto No. 1
Opus 35 & No. 2
Opus 102*
Eugene List
Westminster Records
1961

LP cover.

**Michel + Kieser
and Holger
Matthies**
Jazz 1966
1966

*Front cover of
record catalogue.*

was credited jointly, they generally worked independently. Much of their graphic work was for cultural and communications organizations such as Hessischer Rundfunk (the public broadcasting corporation in Hesse) and Deutsche Bundespost, independent theatres, music festivals such as the annual Deutsches Jazzfestival in Frankfurt, art galleries and film companies; it included posters, programmes, brochures, books and record covers. The Jazzfestival was organized by the concert promoters Horst Lippmann and Fritz Rau, and through them Kieser found himself designing poster campaigns for the likes of Dizzy Gillespie and Count Basie. Lippmann and Rau are best remembered for introducing their groundbreaking American Folk Blues Festival (AFBF) tours to a European audience during the 1960s. They also recorded the AFBF artists in the studio and in concert, which led to a treasure trove of albums. When Kieser and Michel ended their partnership after a decade, Kieser continued working for Lippmann and Rau. He became renowned in Europe for his album covers and posters, and was a major influence on the psychedelic-poster movement and on publishers of underground newspapers in Britain and the United States.

By the early 1970s, the hippy underground press was becoming predictable, even cosy, and its demise was sudden. Distinctly less cosy was the left-wing quarterly magazine *Tricontinental*, published by the Organization of Solidarity with the People of Asia, Africa and Latin America (OSPAAAL) between 1967 and 2019. Influential as the multilingual, Havana-based magazine undoubtedly was, it was the folded posters contained in almost every issue – with strong, often simple but brightly coloured images, and text printed in English, French, Spanish and Arabic – that carried the message most effectively. At its height, *Tricontinental* reputedly had 100,000 subscribers, mainly

Günther Kieser
Berliner Jazz Tage
1965

Poster for jazz festival.

Günther Kieser
American Folk Blues Festival '65
1965

Poster.

Günther Kieser
Spiritual + Gospel Festival '65
1965

Poster.

Michel + Kieser
*Internationale
Polizeiausstellung*
1956

*Stamp for Deutsche
Bundespost to
commemorate the
International Police
Exhibition in Essen.*

Michel + Kieser
*50 Jahre
Luftpostbeförderung*
1962

*Stamp for Deutsche
Bundespost to
commemorate
50 years of airmail.*

students, and its posters were a common sight in student digs around the world.

The collapse of the underground press coincided with the rise of the zine. A rough-and-ready DIY approach had been important in the initial success of the underground press, but zines were quite different. Their creators were almost always one person acting as author, editor, designer and production manager, with no ambition other than to get the latest issue into a local bookshop. Production relied on felt-tip pens, a typewriter, the photocopier in the nearest library and a stapler. Makers of home-made zines during the 1960s were most likely to be fans of a particular TV, film or literary genre such as science fiction, of fashion or of a style of music ('zine' is a contraction of 'fanzine'). Their main purpose was simply to network with like-minded individuals – but also they made zines for the pleasure of writing and the joy of creating without restriction. In the following decade, the rise of punk culture would be fuelled by the raw immediacy of hundreds of home-made zines. Everyone could now be a typographer.

Designer unknown
Brno 1969
1969

*Originally created
as matchbox covers
promoting the
Track Cycling World
Championships in
Brno, Czechoslovakia,
these designs have
since been scanned,
enlarged, framed and
sold as decorative art.*

Atelier Populaire
Halte à l'expulsion!
1968

Silk-screen printed poster.

Lazaro Abreu
Solidarity with the African American People
OSPAAAL
1968

Poster incorporating an image created by Emory Douglas, official artist and Minister of Culture for the Black Panther Party.

Mark Perry
Sniffin' Glue 5
November 1976

Front cover of the first UK monthly punk zine.

M

K

entrée :

15 NF

étud. :

10 NF

EN

62

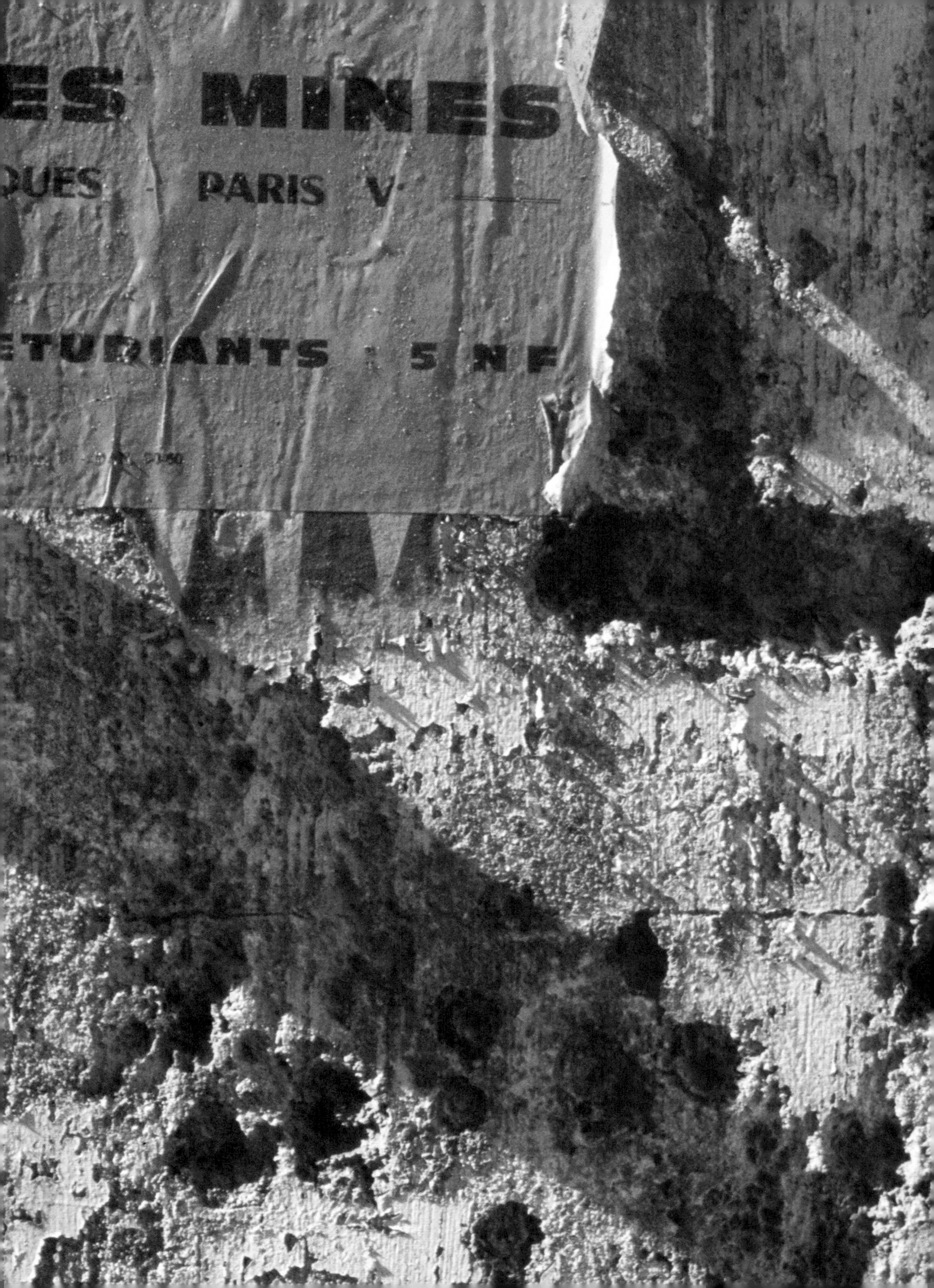
ES MINES
QUES - PARIS V
ETUDIANTS : 5 NF

NOTES

INTRODUCTION

1 Warde's lecture was given to the British Typographers' Guild (later renamed the International Society of Typographic Designers) at the St Bride Institute, London, on 7 October 1930. It was published several times thereafter, most famously in a collection of essays: Beatrice Warde, *The Crystal Goblet: Sixteen Essays on Typography*, London (Sylvan Press) 1955.

2 From Morison's final Lyell Lecture at Oxford University, 1957, republished in Stanley Morison, *Politics and Script: Aspects of Authority and Freedom in the Development of Graeco-Latin Script from the Sixth Century B.C. to the Twentieth Century A.D.*, ed. Nicolas Barker, Oxford (Clarendon Press) 1972, p. 339.

3 Beatrice Warde, 'Typography in Art Education', in *Crystal Goblet*, p. 90.

4 W.A. Dwiggins, *Layout in Advertising* [1928], rev. edn, New York (Harper and Brothers) 1948, p. 193.

5 Herbert Spencer, from his introduction to *Typographica*, no. 1, 1949, p. 1.

6 For a comprehensive account of the necessary skills and tools of the predigital typographer, see Ruari McLean, *The Thames and Hudson Manual of Typography*, London (Thames & Hudson) 1980. The paperback edition, essentially unchanged, was published in 1988.

TYPE DESIGN

1 The Lumitype (or Lumitype-Photon) combined the technologies of a keyboard-entry system, a telephone relay system and a photographic unit. Letters were keyed in by an operator and simultaneously stored in a computer memory bank. On command, each stored letter would call up its correct position on a glass disc that contained the outlines of 1400 characters of a typeface in different sizes, weights and styles. Once the disc was positioned correctly, a strobe light exposed the required letter on to paper. Each exposure took microseconds, enabling approximately eight characters to be transferred to paper per second.

2 Heidrun Osterer and Philipp Stamm, *Adrian Frutiger – Typefaces: The Complete Works*, 2nd edn, Basle (Birkhäuser) 2014, p. 80.

3 Emil Ruder, 'Univers, a New Sans-Serif Type by Adrian Frutiger', *Neue Grafik*, no. 2, July 1959; Emil Ruder, 'Die Univers in der Typographie', *Typographische Monatsblätter*, vol. 80, no. 1, January 1961.

4 Karl Gerstner, *Designing Programmes: Four Essays and an Introduction*, trans. D.Q. Stephenson, Teufen (Arthur Niggli) 1964, p. 22.

5 Adrian Frutiger, 'Typography on the Move', single-sheet flyer published by Conways, a London phototypesetting bureau, *c.* 1980. The flyer is reproduced in Osterer and Stamm, *Adrian Frutiger – Typefaces*, p. 250.

6 Sandra Chamaret, Julien Gineste and Sébastien Morlighem, *Roger Excoffon et la Fonderie Olive*, Paris (Ypsilon) 2010, p. 37.

7 John Dreyfus, 'The Speed and Grace of Roger Excoffon', undated press release for the International Typeface Corporation, http://luc.devroye.org/JohnDreyfus--TheSpeedandGraceofRogerExcoffon.pdf.

8 Alessandro Colizzi, 'Aldo Novarese and Alessandro Butti: A Story to Be Rewritten', lecture presented at ATypI conference, 24 September 2018, https://www.youtube.com/watch?v=TdSOmu30vkM.

9 Alexander Lawson, *Anatomy of a Typeface*, London (Hamish Hamilton) 1990, p. 125.

10 *Ibid*. The American type designer William A. Dwiggins was particularly vocal on this matter.

TYPOGRAPHIC JOURNALS

1 Rick Poynor, 'Motif Magazine: The World Made Visible', Design Observer, 3 February 2012, https://designobserver.com/feature/motif-magazine-the-world-made-visible/32978.

2 For example, James Mosley described the lack of unity as a 'shambles': 'I didn't like it much really. I don't think Ruari's design was his strong point. He was better as an editor.' Herbert Spencer said of *Motif*, 'There is some very good material. But it's not presented in a very stimulating way.' Quoted *ibid*. Other quotations in this paragraph are from the same source.

3 Ken Garland, interview with Anne Odling-Smee, 'Reputations: Ken

Garland', *Eye*, no. 66, Winter 2007, https://www.eyemagazine.com/feature/article/reputations-ken-garland.

4 Hostettler was an excellent editor, making his publications an open forum. As editor of *SGM*, he skilfully moderated the heated debate between Max Bill and Jan Tschichold that began in the April 1946 issue of the journal.

5 Emil Ruder, *Typographie: Ein Gestaltungslehrbuch/Typography: A Manual of Design*, Teufen (Arthur Niggli) 1967, p. 6.

6 Helmut Schmid interview, *TM Research Archive*, http://www.tm-research-archive.ch/interviews/helmut-schmid%e2%80%8a/.

POSTERS

1 Georgine Oeri, 'Tendenzen in Schweizer Plakatstil' [Trends in Swiss poster design], *Werk*, July 1946, p. 237.

2 Josef Müller-Brockmann, *Mein Leben: Spielerischer Ernst und ernsthaftes Spiel* [My life: playful seriousness and serious play], Zurich (Lars Müller) 1994.

3 Josef Müller-Brockmann, interview with Yvonne Schwemer-Scheddin, 'Reputations: Josef Müller-Brockmann', *Eye*, no. 19, Winter 1995, https://www.eyemagazine.com/feature/article/reputations-josef-muller-brockmann.

CORPORATE IDENTITY

1 Henrion's major commission for the Festival of Britain was the design of the exhibitions in two pavilions, Country and Agriculture.

2 Henrion quoted in Ruth Artmonsky and Brian Webb, *FHK Henrion: Design*, Woodbridge (Antique Collectors' Club) 2011, p. 21.

3 Frido Ogier, 'A Strong and Lasting Logo', KLM Blog, 7 December 2014, https://blog.klm.com/a-strong-and-lasting-logo/.

4 Danziger quoted in Steven Heller, 'Thoughts on Rand', *Print*, vol. LI, no. 3, May/June 1997, online at https://www.paulrand.design/life/books-articles/articles/print/1993-print-magazine.html.

5 See Romek Marber, *No Return: Journeys in the Holocaust*, Nottingham (Richard Hollis) 2010, online at https://romekmarber.com/portfolio/no-return-journeys-in-the-holocaust/?portfolioCats=21.

6 Ken Garland, interview with Anne Odling-Smee, 'Reputations: Ken Garland', *Eye*, no. 66, Winter 2007, https://www.eyemagazine.com/feature/article/reputations-ken-garland.

7 Garland's manifesto was 'updated' and republished by new authors in 2000 and 2014. 'First Things First Manifesto 2000' was published in its entirety in *Adbusters*, Canada; in *Emigre* and the *AIGA Journal of Graphic Design* in the USA; and in *Eye* and *Blueprint* in the UK. 'First Things First 2014', rewritten by others, is online at https://firstthingsfirst2014.net/.

ADVERTISING

1 Rand quoted in Steven Heller, *Paul Rand*, London (Phaidon) 1999, p. 38.

2 Rand wrote an essay, 'The Trademark as an Illustrative Device', for the book *Seven Designers Look at Trademark Design*, edited by Egbert Jacobson and published in Chicago by Paul Theobald in 1952. The other contributors were Jacobson, Herbert Bayer, Will Burtin, H. Creston Doner, Alvin Lustig and Bernard Rudofsky.

3 Andrew Cracknell, *The Real Mad Men: The Renegades of Madison Avenue and the Golden Age of Advertising*, Philadelphia (Running Press) 2011, p. 56.

4 The J. Walter Thompson London office served primarily as a sales bureau for European businesses hoping to trade and advertise goods in North America.

5 See Maurizio Scudiero and David Leiber (eds.), *Depero Futurista & New York: Il futurismo e l'arte pubblicitaria/Futurism and the Art of Advertising*, Rovereto (Longo) 1986. Depero's manifesto was originally published in 1931 in his book *Numero unico futurista Campari*, a collection of his design work for the beverage company.

6 Introductory essay in *Advertising and the Artist: Ashley Havinden*, exhib. cat. by Michael Havinden *et al.*, Dean Gallery, Edinburgh, 15 October 2003–18 January 2004, n.p.

7 Simona De Iulio and Carlo Vinti, 'The Americanization of Italian Advertising During the 1950s and the 1960s', *Journal of Historical Research in Marketing*, vol. 1, no. 2, July 2009, p. 272.

8 For example, in France, a significant impediment was presented by the indemnity system, whereby if a foreign advertising agency based in France gained a new client, the client's former French agency was entitled to one year's advertising commission from the foreign agency.

9 See Simona Tobia, *Advertising America: The United States Information Service in Italy (1945–1956)*, Milan (LED) 2008.

10 See Inger L. Stole, 'Advertising America: Official Propaganda and the U.S. Promotional Industries, 1946–1950', *Journalism & Communication Monographs*, vol. 23, no. 1, 2021, pp. 4–63.

11 E.S. Turner, *The Shocking History of Advertising* [1952], rev. edn, Harmondsworth (Penguin Books) 1965, p. 288.

12 Sandra Karl, 'An Interview with Helmut Krone', *Think Magazine*, 17 November 1997, from an interview in *DDB News*, September 1968, https://www.think.cz/english/people/an-interview-with-helmut-krone.

MAGAZINES

1 Steven Heller, *Merz to Emigré and Beyond: Avant-Garde Magazine Design of the Twentieth Century*, London (Phaidon) 2003, pp. 134–35.

2 Thomas W. Ennis, 'Helen Valentine', obituary, *New York Times*, 15 November 1986.

3 Pineles quoted in Martha Scotford, 'Cipe Pineles', AIGA, 1998, https://web.archive.org/web/20110617232009/http://www.aiga.org/medalist-cipepineles/.

4 Mary Banham and Bevis Hillier (eds.), *A Tonic to the Nation: The Festival of Britain 1951*, London (Thames & Hudson) 1976, p. 190.

5 Nicholas Olsberg, 'Herbert Matter', Drawing Matter, 27 November, 2017, https://drawingmatter.org/herbert-matter/.

6 Nikolaus Pevsner, *The Englishness of English Art: An Expanded and Annotated Version of the Reith Lectures Broadcast in October and November 1955*, London (Architectural Press) 1956, p. 168.

7 Wolsey quoted in Anne Braybon, 'Town Shaped the Sixties', *Eye*, no. 96, Spring 2018, https://www.eyemagazine.com/feature/article/town-shaped-the-sixties.

8 Usborne quoted *ibid*.

9 In 1963 Ginzburg was convicted of violating federal obscenity laws. He eventually served eight months in prison in 1972.

BOOKS

1 'In time, typographical things, in my eyes, took on a very different aspect, and to my astonishment I detected most shocking parallels between the teachings of *Die neue Typographie* and National Socialism and Fascism. Obvious similarities consist in the ruthless restriction of typefaces, a parallel to Goebbels' infamous Gleichschaltung, and more or less militaristic arrangements of lines.' Jan Tschichold, 'Lecture to the Typography USA Seminar Sponsored by the Type Directors Club, New York on 18 April 1959', *Print*, vol. XVIII, no. 1, January/February 1964, p. 16.

2 *Ibid*.

3 Rick Poynor, 'The Shape of a Pocket', *Eye*, no. 81, Autumn 2011, https://www.eyemagazine.com/feature/article/the-shape-of-a-pocket.

4 Joseph Connolly, *Faber and Faber: Eighty Years of Book Cover Design*, London (Faber & Faber) 2009, p. xviii.

5 See Russell Ferguson, editor at the Museum of Contemporary Art in Los Angeles, quoted in Anne Burdick *et al*., 'The Portable Art Space', *Eye*, no. 22, Autumn 1996, https://www.eyemagazine.com/feature/article/the-portable-art-space.

TRANSPORT

1 In East Germany, the use of DIN 1451 was reviewed in the 1970s. Tests were organized using other typefaces: Gill Sans was found to perform better, and the government resolved to adopt it as the new standard typeface for road signage. After the reunification of Germany in 1990, the signs in Gill Sans were replaced once more with DIN 1451.

2 In 1923 Stempel produced a printing type whose design followed an early DIN standard, DIN 16, which had been released in 1919 for oblique lettering on technical drawings. In 1929 the Berthold type foundry released a similar typeface. In the mid-1980s, Linotype adopted the DIN typefaces, redrawn by Adolf Gropp, for digital photocomposition. Together with Adobe, Linotype released them as DIN Mittelschrift (medium) and DIN Engschrift (condensed) in 1990.

3 For example, Highway Gothic was used for many years in The Netherlands, but in 1997 was replaced by letters designed by Gerard Unger. Spain uses Autopista, derived from Highway Gothic, for its motorway signs.

4 Anderson to Kinneir, 26 June 1958, quoted in Margaret Calvert, 'Battle of the Serif', in *AGI: Graphic Design Since 1950*, ed. Ben and Elly Bos, London (Thames & Hudson) 2007, online at http://www.newtransport.co.uk/.

5 *Ibid*.

6 An orchestrated effort was made in support of Kindersley and to attack Kinneir and Calvert's work. Letters and articles appeared in publications as diverse as *The New Scientist*, *Design*, *The Daily Telegraph* and *The Observer*, as well as *The Times*. The opening salvo was a letter sent to the editor of *The Times* by Brooke Crutchley, printer to the University of Cambridge, published 17 March 1959, p. 11. See Ole Lund, 'The Public Debate on Jock Kinneir's Road Sign Alphabet', *Typography Papers*, no. 5, 2003, pp. 105–106.

7 Jock Kinneir, *Words and Buildings: The Art and Practice of Public Lettering*, London (Architectural Press) 1980, p. 8.

8 An account of the evolutionary history of the New York City Subway system is provided in Paul Shaw, *Helvetica and the New York City Subway System: The True (Maybe) Story*, rev. edn, Cambridge, Mass., and London (The MIT Press) 2011.

9 In 1957 George Salomon, a

typographic designer at Appleton, Parsons & Co. in Manhattan, sent an unsolicited proposal to the New York City Transit Authority titled 'Out of the Labyrinth: A Plea and a Plan for Improved Passenger Information in the New York Subways'.

10 William Lansing Plumb, 'Telling People Where to Go: Subway Graphics', *Print*, vol. XIX, no. 5, September/October 1965, p. 15.

11 A competition was set up in 1964 to design a map of the New York subway. It drew just nine entries and none was chosen. Goldstein was then commissioned to design a map that specifically solved the problem of colour-coding the different lines.

12 Vignelli quoted in Shaw, *Helvetica and the New York City Subway System*, p. 31.

13 *Ibid.*, p. 67.

FILM & TELEVISION

1 Jacques Rancière, 'Godard, Hitchcock and the Cinematographic Image', in *For Ever Godard*, ed. Michael Temple, James S. Williams and Michael Witt, London (Black Dog) 2004, p. 214.

2 Pam Cook and Mieke Bernink (eds.), *The Cinema Book*, 2nd edn, London (BFI Publishing) 1999, p. 273.

3 Godard quoted in 'Jean-Luc Godard, RIP', British Film Institute, 13 September 2022, https://www.bfi.org.uk/news/jean-luc-godard-rip.

4 In early televisions, a cathode ray fired horizontal lines on to the inner face of the television tube twenty-four times a second. There were 405 lines that covered the whole screen. Even when larger screens became available (up to 14 inches, measured diagonally), the image was no clearer; instead, the blank spaces between the lines became wider. In the UK, TV sets improved from around 1964, when BBC2 was launched as a 625-line service, but they were still far inferior to the quality of televisions today.

5 Anthony Hayward, 'Norman Taylor: Creator of the "Howl-Around" Visual in the Original "Dr Who" Title Sequence', obituary, *The Independent*, 10 March 2011, https://www.independent.co.uk/news/obituaries/norman-taylor-creator-of-the-howlaround-visual-in-the-original-dr-who-title-sequence-2237431.html.

EPHEMERA

1 This is the working definition of ephemera used by the UK's Ephemera Society, founded in 1975. See Maurice Rickards, *Collecting Printed Ephemera*, Oxford (Phaidon) 1988, p. 18.

2 For an extensive list of what constitutes printed ephemera, see the contents page in Maurice Rickards, *The Encyclopedia of Ephemera: A Guide to the Fragmentary Documents of Everyday Life for the Collector, Curator, and Historian*, ed. Michael Twyman, London (British Library) 2000.

3 Gilbert G. Germain, *Spirits in the Material World: The Challenge of Technology*, Lanham, Md. (Lexington Books) 2009, p. 92.

4 Major collections of ephemera can be found at the Bodleian Library, Oxford; the Centre for Ephemera Studies at the University of Reading; and the New York Public Library.

5 Brian Grimbly, 'Data for Stationery Design', in *TypoGraphic Writing*, ed. David Jury, Stroud (International Society of Typographic Designers) 2001, p. 30.

6 Until this point, Blue Note had been releasing long-playing recordings on 10-inch discs.

BOOKS

Deborah Allison, *Film Title Sequences: A Critical Anthology*, London (Pilea Publications) 2021

Phil Baines and Catherine Dixon, *Signs: Lettering in the Environment*, London (Laurence King) 2003

Joseph Blumenthal, *The Printed Book in America*, London (Scolar Press) 1977

David Consuegra, *American Type: Design and Designers*, New York (Allworth Press) 2004

Kenneth Day, *The Typography of Press Advertisement: A Practical Summary of Principles and Their Application*, London (Ernest Benn) 1956

Peter Dormer, *The Meanings of Modern Design: Towards the Twenty-First Century*, London (Thames & Hudson) 1990

W.A. Dwiggins, *Layout in Advertising* [1928], rev. edn, New York (Harper and Brothers) 1948

Max Gallo, *Posters in History*, London (Bracken Books) 1989

Steven Heller, *Paul Rand*, London (Phaidon) 1999

David Jury, *Reinventing Print: Technology and Craft in Typography*, London (Bloomsbury) 2018

Robin Kinross, *Modern Typography: An Essay in Critical History*, London (Hyphen Press) 1992

Mac McGrew, *American Metal Typefaces of the Twentieth Century*, rev. edn, New Castle, Del. (Oak Knoll Books) 1993

The Penrose Annual: published from 1949 to 1962 (nos. 43–56) and then from 1964 to 1976 (nos. 57–69); printed and published by Lund Humphries

David Reed, *The Popular Magazine in Britain and the United States, 1880–1960*, London (British Library) 1997

R. Roger Remington with Lisa Bodenstedt, *American Modernism: Graphic Design, 1920 to 1960*, London (Laurence King) 2003

Maurice Rickards, *The Encyclopedia of Ephemera: A Guide to the Fragmentary Documents of Everyday Life for the Collector, Curator, and Historian*, ed. Michael Twyman, London (British Library) 2000

Paul Shaw, *Helvetica and the New York City Subway System: The True (Maybe) Story*, rev. edn, Cambridge, Mass., and London (The MIT Press) 2011

Juliann Sivulka, *Soap, Sex, and Cigarettes: A Cultural History of American Advertising*, Belmont, Calif. (Wadsworth) 1998

Paul Stiff (ed.), *Modern Typography in Britain: Graphic Design, Politics, and Society*, Typography Papers 8, London (Hyphen Press) 2009

E.S. Turner, *The Shocking History of Advertising*, London (Michael Joseph) 1952

WEBSITES: GENERAL & TYPE DESIGN

alexanderslawsonarchive.com
The Alexander S. Lawson Archive: Professor Lawson, of the Rochester Institute of Technology, New York, wrote on the history of typography; includes a listing of his 'Composing Room' columns for The Inland Printer, *the trade journal of the US printing industry, written 1954–66.*

artofthetitle.com
Art of the Title: dedicated to film and TV title-sequence design.

designreviewed.com
Design Reviewed: large digital collection of printed matter from the last century, and other research on the history of graphic design.

eyemagazine.com
Eye: *magazine about graphic design and visual culture, published since 1990, with an extensive archive of online features.*

letterformarchive.org
Letterform Archive: museum and special collections library in San Francisco dedicated to collecting materials on the history of lettering, typography, printing and graphic design; searchable online database.

modernism101.com
Modernism 101: online seller of books and periodicals on design from the modernist period.

paulshawletterdesign.com/category/blue-pencil/
Blue Pencil: 'slog', or 'slow blog', by the design historian and lettering artist Paul Shaw.

sbf.org.uk
St Bride Foundation, based in London, is home to the world's largest print and publishing library; with a searchable online catalogue and digital collections.

studiotype.com/originals
Jeremy Tankard Typography: Ongoing research into the history of designing and making type.

typefoundry.blogspot.com
Typefoundry: blog by James Mosley, former librarian at St Bride, on the history of type and letterforms.

WEBSITES: GRAPHIC DESIGNERS

abramgames.com
Abram Games

alanfletcherarchive.com
Alan Fletcher Archive

alvinlustig.com
Alvin Lustig

elainelustigcohen.com
Elaine Lustig Cohen

herbertmatter.org
Herbert Matter

jockkinneirlibrary.org
Jock Kinneir Library

lubalin100.com
Herb Lubalin Study Center

paulrand.design
Paul Rand

pushpininc.com
Push Pin Studios

romekmarber.com
Romek Marber

With thanks to Nicola Bailey, Margaret Calvert, Sebastian Carter, Claire Chandler, Phil Cleaver, Orna Dawson, Richard Doust, Steven Heller, Will Hill, Hugh Merrell, Paul Shaw, Sarah Smithies, Erik Spiekermann and Jeremy Tankard.

PICTURE CREDITS

t = top, b= bottom, l = left, r = right, c = centre

4: Robert E. Smith/Letterform Archive; 6: © Estate of Abram Games/Victoria and Albert Museum, London; 7: Festival of Britain symbol © Estate of Abram Games/Victoria and Albert Museum, London; 8: New York, Frederick A. Stokes Company; 9t: Beatrice Warde/Monotype Corporation; 9bl: Stanley Morison/Cambridge University Press; 9br: Montoype Corporation; 10: W.A. Dwiggins/Harper and Brothers; 11: Paul Rand/Chronicle Books LLC; 12l, 12r: Rudolf Hostettler/SGM Books; 13: Berthold Ludwig Wolpe/Image supplied by Phil Cleaver; 14l: Norfolk Record Office; 14r: Letraset; 15: Studio International; 16–17: RIBA Collections; 18: Roger Excoffon/Fonderie Olive/Letterform Archive; 19: Intertype Corporation; 20t: Cornerstone; 20c: Mergenthaler Linotype Company; 20b: Harris-Intertype; 21tl, 21tr, 21bl: Adrian Frutiger/Letterform Archive; 21br: Song_about_summer/Shutterstock; 22t, 22b: Walter Baum, Konrad Bauer/Bauersche Gießerei; 23t: Max Miedinger, Eduard Hoffmann/AF Fotografie; 23b: Hans Neuburg, Nelly Rudin/Haas'sche Schriftgießerei/Nick Sherman; 24t: Robert Hunter Middleton/Ludlow Typograph Company; 24b: Morris Fuller Benton/American Type Founders; 25: Herb Lubalin Study Center; 26t, 26b: Berthold Ludwig Wolpe/Monotype Corporation; 27t: Will Carter/Lanston Monotype Company/Image supplied by Sebastian Carter; 27b: Will Carter/Dartmouth College/Image supplied by Sebastian Carter; 28t: Geoffrey Lee/Stephenson Blake Foundry; 28c: Fred Lambert/Letraset/Peter Owen Ltd; 28b: Colin Brignall/Letraset; 29t: A.M. Cassandre/Deberny et Peignot; 29b: Roger Excoffon/Fonderie Olive/Letterform Archive; 30l: François Ganeau/Fonderie Olive/Letterform Archive; 30r: Roger Excoffon/François Ganeau/Fonderie Olive/Letterform Archive; 31, 32l: Roger Excoffon/Fonderie Olive/Letterform Archive; 32r: Aldo Novarese/Società Fonderia Nebiolo/Letterform Archive; 33: Roger Excoffon/Fonderie Olive/Letterform Archive; 34: Alessandro Butti, Aldo Novarese/Società Fonderia Nebiolo/Letterform Archive; 35t: Società Fonderia Nebiolo/Letterform Archive; 35b: Alessandro Butti, Aldo Novarese/Società Fonderia Nebiolo/Letterform Archive; 36: Aldo Novarese/Società Fonderia Nebiolo/Letterform Archive; 37l: Alessandro Butti, Aldo Novarese/Società Fonderia Nebiolo/Letterform Archive; 37r: Giulio Da Milano, Alessandro Butti/Società Fonderia Nebiolo/Letterform Archive; 38, 39t, 39b: Hermann Zapf/D. Stempel AG/Herzog August Bibliothek Wolfenbüttel; 40tr, 40br: Jan Tschichold/Linotype, Monotype and Stempel Foundries/Chris Wakeling; 42–43: Dennis Bailey Archive, courtesy of Nicola Bailey; 44: Herbert Spencer/Lund Humphries; 45t: Oliver Simon/*Signature*; 45b: Beatrice Warde/Monotype Corporation; 46t: Robert Harling/Shenval Press; 46b, 47tl, 47tr, 47b: Robert Harling/Art & Technics,

London; 48t, 48b, 49l, 49r: Ruari McLean/Shenval Press; 50t, 50b: Theo Crosby/Whitefriars Press; 51t, 51b, 52tl, 52tr, 52b, 53l, 53r: Herbert Spencer/Lund Humphries; 54t, 54b: Ken Garland/Council of Industrial Design; 55t, 55c, 55b: Ken Garland/Council of Industrial Design/Archive of Matt Lamont of Out of Place Studio; 57tl, 57tr, 57br: Schweizerischer Typographenbund, Bern, CH/Archive of Matt Lamont of Out of Place Studio; 57bl: Zürcher Hochschule der Künste/Museum für Gestaltung Zürich/Grafiksammlung; 58t, 58b: Josef Müller-Brockmann/Verlag Otto Walter, Olten, Switzerland/Archive of Matt Lamont of Out of Place Studio; 59t: Leo Lionni/Edmund Dulac (Artist)/Print Magazine Archive; 59b: Robert Harling/Stephenson Blake Foundry; 60t, 60b: Eberhard Hölscher/Bruckmann Verlag/Archive of Matt Lamont of Out of Place Studio; 61: Design by Alan Fletcher © The Estate of Alan Fletcher/Image supplied by Alan Fletcher Archive; 62–63: Dennis Bailey Archive, courtesy of Nicola Bailey; 64: Josef Müller-Brockmann/Kunstgewerbemuseum Zürich; 65: Estate of Abram Games; 66t: Edward McKnight Kauffer/Digital image, The Museum of Modern Art, New York/Scala, Florence; 66c: Tom Eckersley Estate/University of the Arts London/Tom Eckersley Collection/Royal Society for the Prevention of Accidents; 66b: Hans Schleger (Zéró) estate/Ben Uri Gallery and Museum; 67t: Design by Alan Fletcher © The Estate of Alan Fletcher/Digital image, The Museum of Modern Art, New York/Scala, Florence; 67c: Dennis Bailey Archive, courtesy of Nicola Bailey/Arts Council Gallery, London; 67b: Design by Romek Marber © The Estate of Romek Marber/Image supplied by John and Orna Designs/London Planetarium; 68l: Walter Allner/Zollikofer/Archive of Matt Lamont of Out of Place Studio; 68r: David Jury Collection; 69t: Otto Baumberger/Plakat, Marque PKZ/Museum für Gestaltung Zürich/ZHdK; 69bl: Peter Birkhäuser/BATA Schuhe; 69br: Herbert Leupin/Bell; 70: Herbert Matter/Digital image, The Museum of Modern Art, New York/Scala, Florence; 71t: Emil Ruder/Gewerbemuseum Basel; 71c: Armin Hofmann/Gewerbemuseum Basel; 71b: Joseph Müller-Brockmann/Zurich Tonhalle; 72: Max Bill/Kunstgewerbemuseum Zürich; 73: © DACS 2023/Ezio Bonini, Max Huber/Zürcher Hochschule der Künste/Museum für Gestaltung Zürich/Plakatsammlung; 74: Hans Neuburg/Kunstgewerbemuseum Zürich; 75: © DACS 2023/Bridgeman Images; 76: Henryk Tomaszewski/© Christie's Images/Bridgeman Images; 77t: Henryk Tomaszewski; 77c: Waldemar Świerzy; 77b: Jan Młodożeniec; 78t: Franciszek Starowieyski; 78c, 78b: © ADAGP, Paris and DACS, London 2023/Roman Cieślewicz; 79t: © Marc Riboud/Fonds Marc Riboud au MNAAG/Magnum Photos; 79b: RMN-Grand Palais/Dist. Photo SCALA, Florence; 80: Saul Bass/Paramount Pictures/Christie's Images, London/Scala, Florence; 81t: Fototeca Gilardi/Bridgeman Images;

81b: Milton Glaser/Digital image, The Museum of Modern Art, New York/Scala, Florence; 82–83: Dennis Bailey Archive, courtesy of Nicola Bailey; 84: Paul Rand/Westinghouse/Letterform Archive; 85, 86tl, 86tr: F.H.K. Henrion/University of Brighton Design Archives; 86bl, 86br: F.H.K. Henrion/Blue Circle Cement; 87tl, 87tc, 87tr: F.H.K. Henrion/KLM; 87 (all other images): F.H.K. Henrion/University of Brighton Design Archives; 88t: Roger Excoffon/Air France/IMEC Images/Tous droits réservés à IMEC Images; 88b: Roger Excoffon/Air France/Swann Galleries; 89t: Roger Excoffon/Jean Fortin (Illustration/Design)/Air France/Archive of Matt Lamont of Out of Place Studio; 89c: Roger Excoffon/Guy Georget (Illustration/Design)/Air France/Archive of Matt Lamont of Out of Place Studio; 89b: Roger Excoffon/Air France/IMEC Images/Tous droits réservés à IMEC Images; 90: Paul Rand/IBM/Letterform Archive; 91t: Paul Rand/UPS; 91c: Paul Rand/ABC; 91b: Paul Rand/Cummins; 92: Dennis Bailey Archive, courtesy of Nicola Bailey; 93t, 93b: Ben Bos/Nederlands Archief Grafisch Ontwerpers; 94t, 94b, 95: Total Design/Reflex; 96t: Alan Fletcher, Colin Forbes, Bob Gill/Studio Books London; 96c: Design by Alan Fletcher, Colin Forbes, Bob Gill/D&AD; 96b: Design by Alan Fletcher, Colin Forbes, Bob Gill/International Die Casting Conference; 97tl, 97tr, 97c: Design by Alan Fletcher, Colin Forbes, Bob Gill/Reuters; 97bl, 97br: Wolf Olins/BOC/LogoArchive; 98tl, 98tr, 98c, 98b, 99tl, 99tr, 99c, 99bl, 99br: Design by Romek Marber © The Estate of Romek Marber/Image supplied by John and Orna Designs; 100t, 100b: Ken Garland/Galt Toys/Unit Editions; 101t, 101b: Ken Garland/Unit Editions; 102–103: Dennis Bailey Archive, courtesy of Nicola Bailey; 104: Costantino Nivola/© Olivetti SpA/Letterform Archive; 105l: Staybrite; 105r: Ault & Wiborg; 106t: © Dumbarton Arts, LLC/VAGA at ARS, NY and DACS, London 2023/Lester Beall/Digital image, The Museum of Modern Art, New York/Scala, Florence; 106b: Alvin Lustig/Knoll/Letterform Archive; 107t: Paul Rand/William H. Weintraub/Dubonnet/Letterform Archive; 107bl: Paul Rand/William H. Weintraub/El Producto/Letterform Archive; 107br: Paul Rand/William H. Weintraub/Coronet Brandy/Letterform Archive; 108t: Numa Rick/Maurice Collet/*Publicité*/Archive of Matt Lamont of Out of Place Studio; 108b: Pierre Monnerat/Maurice Collet/*Publicité*/Archive of Matt Lamont of Out of Place Studio; 109tl, 109tr, 109bl, 109br: Paul Rand/Orbach's; 110t: David Ogilvy/Rolls Royce/Retro AdArchives/Alamy Stock Photo; 110b: J. Walter Thompson/Ford; 111l: Max Huber/Olivetti SpA/Musee National d'Art Moderne – Centre Pompidou, Paris/RMN-Grand Palais/Dist. Photo SCALA, Florence; 111r: Giovanni Pintori/Olivetti SpA/Letterform Archive; 112: Ashley Havinden/Liberty, London/V&A Images; 113t: Ashley Havinden/DAKS/Mike Ashworth Collection; 113b: Ashley Havinden/

Wolsey Ltd/Record Office for Leicestershire, Leicester & Rutland; 114l: Charles Loupot/Atelier St Raphaël; 114r: Roger Excoffon/International Olympic Committee; 115: Eberhard Moes/CBW/Alamy Stock Photo; 116t: Doyle Dane Bernbach/Polaroid; 116bl, 116br: Doyle Dane Bernbach/Levy's Jewish Rye; 117t, 117b: Doyle Dane Bernbach/Volkswagen; 118t, 118b: © Estate of George Lois; 119t: Coca-Cola/D'Arcy Advertising/The John & Charlotte Yarbrough Coca-Cola Collection; 119bl: Coca-Cola Bottling Co.; 119bc: Coca-Cola Bottling Co./Interfoto Scans/AGE Fotostock; 119br: Herbert Leupin/Coca-Cola Bottling Co.; 120t: John Donegan/News UK/News Licensing; 120b: Design by Romek Marber © The Estate of Romek Marber/Image supplied by John and Orna Designs/The Observer; 121tl: Collett Dickenson Pearce/Hovis/The Advertising Archives; 121tr: Collett Dickenson Pearce/Olympus/The Advertising Archives; 121b: Collett Dickenson Pearce/Heineken/The Advertising Archives; 122–23: Dennis Bailey Archive, courtesy of Nicola Bailey; 124: Henry Wolf/Photo © The Richard Avedon Foundation/Paper Pursuits Fashion & Design Print Collectibles/Harper's Bazaar (Hearst); 125: A.B. Imrie/Shelf Appeal/Image supplied by Alan Powers; 126t: Estate of Abram Games/Graphis Press/Archive of Matt Lamont of Out of Place Studio; 126b: Charles Peignot/AMG, Paris; 127l, 127r: Alexey Brodovitch/Zebra Press; 128: Mehemed Fehmy Agha/Eduardo Garcia Benito (Illustration)/Condé Nast/Shutterstock; 129t: Cipe Pineles/Hearst Communications, Inc./Rochester Institute of Technology; 129c: Cipe Pineles/Constantin Joffé (Photo)/Condé Nast/Shutterstock; 129b: Cipe Pineles/Hearst Communications, Inc./Rochester Institute of Technology; 130l, 130r: © Dumbarton Arts, LLC/VAGA at ARS, NY and DACS, London 2023/Lester Beall/National Library of Medicine; 131t: Arnold Saks/Whitney Publications, Inc./Archive of Matt Lamont of Out of Place Studio; 131bl: Alvin Lustig/Whitney Publications, Inc./Rochester Institute of Technology; 131br: Alvin Lustig/Digital Image Museum Associates/LACMA/Art Resource NY/Scala, Florence; 132: Alvin Lustig/Curwen Press; 133t, 133cl: Herbert Matter (Cover)/Julius Shulman (Photo)/Arts & Architecture; 133cr: Alvin Lustig/Digital Image Museum Associates/LACMA/Art Resource NY/Scala, Florence; 133b: Herbert Matter (Cover)/Arts & Architecture; 135t, 135cl: © The Architectural Review/Image supplied by Alan Powers; 135cr, 135b: © The Architectural Review; 136t, 136c: Metron/Editrice Sandron; 136b: Albe Steiner/Stile industria/Herb Lubalin Study Center; 137tl, 137tr: Editoriale Domus Spa; 137bl, 137br: Gruppo Mondadori; 138l: New Statesman Ltd; 138c: New Scientist Ltd; 138r: The Spectator Ltd; 139l: Design by Romek Marber © The Estate of Romek Marber/Image supplied by John and Orna Designs/The Economist Newspaper Limited; 139c: Dennis Bailey Archive, courtesy of Nicola Bailey/The Economist Newspaper Limited; 139r: Design by Romek Marber © The Estate of Romek Marber/Image supplied by John and Orna Designs/New Society; 140t: Dennis Bailey Archive, courtesy of Nicola Bailey; 140b: Maurice Rickards/Retro AdArchives/Alamy Stock Photo; 141t, 141br: Tom Wolsey/About Town/Christopher Gregory Collection/Eye magazine; 141bl: Tom Wolsey/Town/Christopher Gregory Collection/Eye magazine; 142t: Dennis Bailey Archive, courtesy of Nicola Bailey/Town; 142b: Willy Fleckhaus/Horst Baumann (Photo)/Aufwärts; 143t, 143b: Willy Fleckhaus/Past Print; 144t: Willi Landers/Queen/Hearst; 144b: Derek Birdsall/Nova; 145: Design by Romek Marber © The Estate of Romek Marber/Image supplied by John and Orna Designs/The Observer; 146t, 146b: Herb Lubalin Study Center; 147t: International Type Corporation; 147b: Herb Lubalin Study Center; 148t, 148b: International Times/Underground Press

Syndicate; 148c: Richard Neville/OZ Publications Ink Limited/University of Wollongong Archives; 149t, 149b: Gabe Katz/San Francisco Oracle; 150–51: Susan Wood/Getty Images; 152: Herbert Spencer/Sylvan Press; 153: Jan Tschichold/Lund Humphries; 154l: Jan Tschichold (Cover)/Birkhäuser; 154r: Jan Tschichold/D. Stempel; 155t: Jan Tschichold/Penguin Random House UK; 155b: Jan Tschichold (Cover)/Penguin Random House UK; 156t: Hans Schmoller (Cover)/Penguin Random House UK; 156b: Edward Wright/Whitechapel Gallery; 157tl, 157tr, 157bl, 157br: Design by Romek Marber © The Estate of Romek Marber/Image supplied by John and Orna Designs/Penguin Random House UK; 158l: Harry Ford (Cover)/Vintage/Penguin Random House UK; 158c: Walter Baumhofer (Illustration)/Pocket Books/Simon & Schuster; 158r: Robert Brownjohn (Cover)/New Directions; 159t: Elaine Lustig (Cover)/Meridian Books/Letterform Archive; 159bl: Alvin Lustig (Cover)/Meridian Books/Letterform Archive; 159bc, 159br: Elaine Lustig (Cover)/Meridian Books; 160t: Edward Verbeke (Cover)/© Éditions Gallimard; 160bl, 160br: Robert Massin (Cover)/© Éditions Gallimard; 161l, 161r: Robert Massin (Cover/Design)/Studio Vista; 162l, 162c, 162r: Pierre Faucheux (Cover/Design)/Club Français du Livre/Maquettes de Jacques Darche; 163t, 163b: Pierre Faucheux (Design)/Jean-Jacques Pauvert; 164tl, 164tr, 164bl, 164br: © Estate of Berthold Wolpe/Image supplied by Phil Cleaver; 165t: Lund Humphries and Zwemmer; 165b: Walter Neurath (Design)/King Penguin Books; 166t, 166b: Thames & Hudson; 167t, 167b: Willem Sandberg/Stedelijk Museum Amsterdam; 168t: Wim Crouwel/Stedelijk Museum Amsterdam; 168b: Wim Crouwel/Museum Fodor; 169t: Leo Lionni/The Museum of Modern Art, New York; 169c: Digital image, The Museum of Modern Art, New York/Scala, Florence; 169b: Ivan Chermayeff/The Museum of Modern Art, New York; 170t: Richard Guyatt (Cover)/Routledge & Kegan Paul; 170b: Hans Neuburg, Walter Bangerter (Design)/ABC Verlag; 171tl, 171tr: Josef Müller-Brockmann/Niggli Verlag; 171bl, 171br: Cal Swann/Lund Humphries; 171–72: Dennis Bailey Archive, courtesy of Nicola Bailey; 174: George Daulby/Council of Industrial Design; 175: David Jury; 176t, 176c: Ludwig Goller; 176b: Süddeutsche Zeitung Photo/Alamy Stock Photo; 177t, 177c: FHWA Series 177b: American Association of State Highway Officials; 178tl: David Jury; Pryke & Palmer; 178b: Ward/Fox Photos/Getty Images; 179t, 179b: Anthony Froshaug/Council of Industrial Design; 180t, 180b, 181t: Mike Ashworth Collection; 181b: PA Images/Alamy Stock Photo; 182t: Jock Kinneir, Margaret Calvert/Margaret Calvert Collection; 182b: Daily Mail/Shutterstock; 183 (all), 184t, 184b, 185, 186t, 186b: Jock Kinneir, Margaret Calvert/Margaret Calvert Collection; 187t, 187b: Bob Noorda/Milan Metro; 188t, 188b, 189t, 189b: Bob Noorda, Massimo Vignelli/Unimark International/Metropolitan Transportation Authority; 190–91: Lowell Georgia/The Denver Post/Getty Images; 192: Macario Gómez Quibus/Paramount/BFA; 193: Tony Palladino (Design)/Simon & Schuster/AF Fotografie; 194t, 194b: Saul Bass (Design)/© Shamley Productions/TCD/Prod.DB/Alamy Stock Photo; 195l, 195r: Twentieth Century Fox Film Corporation; 196l: Saul Bass (Design)/Otto Preminger Films; 196r, 197l: Saul Bass/Otto Preminger Films; 197r: Saul Bass (Design)/Otto Preminger Films; 198t: Clément Hurel/Les Films Impéria/BFA; 198b: Les Films Impéria; 199l: H. Poussy/Columbia Films/BFA; 199r: Columbia Films; 200l: Compagnie Française de Distribution Cinématographique (CFDC); 200r: René Ferracci/Compagnie Française de Distribution Cinématographique (CFDC)/BFA; 201t: Maurice Binder (Design)/Eon Productions; 201b: Robert Brownjohn (Design)/Eon Productions; 202l: Pablo

Ferro (Design)/© Hawk Films; 202tr, 202br: © Hawk Films/TCD/Prod.DB/Alamy Stock Photo; 203t: Television Age magazine; 203b: Harold Adler (Lettering)/Crown International Pictures; 204t: Geoff M. Sadler/Impact/Buland Publishing/Mike Ashworth Collection; 204cl: ZIV Television Programs; 204cr: National Broadcasting Company (NBC); 204bl: Apex Film Corp; 204br: Roy Rogers Productions/NBC/CBS; 205, 206l, 206r: Bernard Lodge (Design)/BBC; 207: Design by Romek Marber © The Estate of Romek Marber/Images supplied by John and Orna Designs/BBC; 208–209: Dennis Bailey Archive, courtesy of Nicola Bailey; 210: Design by Alan Fletcher © The Estate of Alan Fletcher/Graphic Design: London; 211: Tom Eckersley, Eric Lombers/Curwen Press; 212t: Ladislav Sutnar/Artist's Estate/Scovill Manufacturing Company/Letterform Archive; 212b: Olle Eksell/Efficiency-Groep/Archive of Matt Lamont of Out of Place Studio; 213t: Design by Romek Marber © The Estate of Romek Marber/Image supplied by John and Orna Designs/Heal's; 213b: Schriftguss AG; 214t: Dennis Bailey Archive, courtesy of Nicola Bailey; 214bl: Design by Romek Marber © The Estate of Romek Marber/Image supplied by John and Orna Designs/The Observer; 214br: Design by Romek Marber © The Estate of Romek Marber/Image supplied by John and Orna Designs; 215t: Klingspor Museum/Letterform Archive; 215cl, 215cr: Giovanni Pintori/Olivetti SpA/Letterform Archive; 215bl: W.A. Dwiggins/The Society of Printers/Letterform Archive; 215br: Paul Rand/Portfolio; 216t: Ernest Thesiger/The Studio; 216b: Dennis Bailey Archive, courtesy of Nicola Bailey/Jonathan Cape/Penguin Random House; 217tl: Roger Excoffon/Air France/David Jury Collection; 217tr: KLM/David Jury Collection; 217c: Prince Hotel/David Jury Collection; 217bl: The Milwaukee Electric Railway and Transport Co./Letterform Archive; 217br: Gado Images/Alamy Stock Photo; 218t: Strike-Rite Matches Ltd/Maryland Match/Match Corp. of America/The Diamond Match Co./Letterform Archive; 218c: Rolf Christianson/David Jury Collection; 218b: Yusaku Kamekura/International Olympic Committee/David Jury Collection; 219t, 219b, 220t: Alex Steinweiss (Design)/Columbia Records/David Jury Collection; 220bl, 220br: Reid Miles (Design)/Blue Note Records/David Jury Collection; 221t, 221c, 221b: John Lewis (Design)/Aldeburgh Festival of Music and the Arts; 222t, 222c: Rudolph de Harak (Design)/Westminster Records/Archive of Matt Lamont of Out of Place Studio; 222b: Michel + Kieser, Holger Matthies/Verve, Brunswick, Coral, MGM, United Artists/Archive of Matt Lamont of Out of Place Studio; 223t: Günther Kieser/Berliner Jazz Tage; 223c: Günther Kieser/American Folk Blues Festival; 223b: Günther Kieser/Spiritual + Gospel Festival; 224t, 224c: Michel + Kieser/Deutsche Bundespost; 224b: Solo Lipnik; 225t: Atelier Populaire; 225c: Lazaro Abreu (Design)/Emory Douglas (Artist)/OSPAAAL; 225b: Mark Perry

The publisher has made every effort to trace and contact copyright holders of the illustrations reproduced in this book; it will be happy to correct in subsequent editions any errors or omissions that are brought to its attention.

Page numbers in *italic* refer to the illustrations.

First published 2023 by Merrell Publishers,
London and New York

Merrell Publishers Limited
70 Cowcross Street
London EC1M 6EJ

merrellpublishers.com

British Library Cataloguing in Publication
Data. A catalogue record for this book is
available from the British Library.

ISBN 978-1-8589-4707-5

Produced by Merrell Publishers Limited
Designed by Nicola Bailey
Project-managed by Claire Chandler
Picture research by Sarah Smithies
Proofread by Henry Russell
Indexed by Hilary Bird

Printed and bound in China

Page 4
Monotype specimen sheet for Brush Script
by Robert E. Smith, 1942.

Pages 16–17
Sport Pavilion, designed by Gordon and
Ursula Bowyer, Festival of Britain, London,
1951.

Pages 42–43
Dennis Bailey, *Cool Inside, Rawlings,
Maryland*, 1961.

Pages 62–63
Dennis Bailey, *Torn Posters, Paris*, 1964.

Pages 82–83
Dennis Bailey, *Contre le régime, Paris*, 1964.

Pages 102–103
Dennis Bailey, *Grocery Store, USA*, 1961.

Pages 122–23
Dennis Bailey, *Bon jour! Primior, Paris*, 1961.

Pages 150–51
A news vendor looks through the first issue
of *Sports Illustrated* magazine in his stand,
New York, 16 August 1954. Photograph by
Susan Wood.

Pages 172–73
Dennis Bailey, *Chock full o' Nuts, New York*,
1961.

Pages 190–91
Lowell Georgia, *Just Follow Your Nose;
It's easy to find your way through the
intersection*, from *The Denver Post*,
25 September 1964.

Pages 208–209
Dennis Bailey, *Posters, Farringdon
Underground Station, London*, 1962.

Pages 226–27
Dennis Bailey, *K 62, Paris*, 1964.

DAVID JURY is an award-winning
typographer and graphic designer who
lectures on typographic enquiry at the
Cambridge School of Art, Anglia Ruskin
University. His previous books include
What Is Typography? (2006), *Graphic Design
Before Graphic Designers: The Printer as
Designer and Craftsman, 1700–1914* (2012)
and *Reinventing Print: Technology and Craft
in Typography* (2018). He was formerly
editor of *TypoGraphic*, the journal of
the International Society of Typographic
Designers, and is currently editor of
Parenthesis, the journal of the Fine Press
Book Association.

davidjury.com

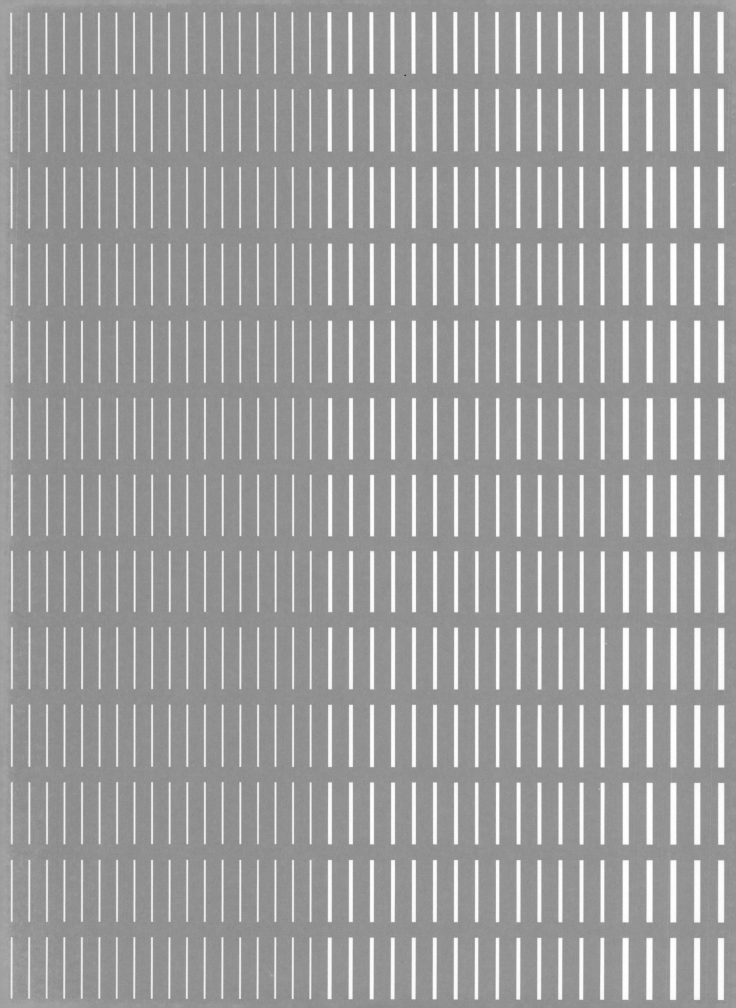